CLIVE WILKINSON trained as a religious studies teacher and taught at a mission school in Rhodesia (now Zimbabwe) before returning to the UK, where he read geography at Newcastle University and undertook doctoral research on human immigration in Lesotho. He spent nearly twenty years training geography teachers and environmental studies specialists.

After retirement he undertook part-time work researching youth homelessness, young people on the edge of society and rural development in Northumberland. The results were published under the title *The Drop-Out Society* and made front-page national news.

When he finally decided to retire properly, he indulged his love of slow travel, crossing continents by train and oceans by container ship – no flying allowed – as well as attempting to drive around England by electric car. His account of freighter travel in the modern age, written in similar vein to *Charging Around*, was published as *Reflections from the Monkey Deck*.

CHARGING
ARUND

EXPLORING THE
EDGES OF ENGLAND
IN AN ELECTRIC CAR

CLIVE WILKINSON

MAPS BY CHRISSIE BUCKLEY

EYE BOOKS

Published by Eye Books
29A Barrow Street
Much Wenlock
Shropshire
TF13 6EN

www.eye-books.com

First edition 2023
Copyright © Clive Wilkinson 2023

Cover design by Ifan Bates
Maps by Chrissie Buckley

Typeset in Minion Pro.

British Library Cataloguing in Publication Data
A catalogue record for this book is available from the British Library

ISBN 9781785633454
Printed and bound by CPI Group (UK) Ltd, Croydon, CR0 4YY

CONTENTS

MAPS

PROLOGUE

I WAS NEVER REALLY a great fan of motoring holidays. I did try it once. It was a camping trip to the south of France. It wasn't a success. The idea that you can relax by staring at a strip of tarmac for several hundred miles, on the wrong side of the road, while at the same time trying to work out whether to go clockwise or anticlockwise at an approaching roundabout, struck me as delusional.

As if this were not enough, there were the *priorité à droite* signs to contend with. You could be chugging along on a busy road when, at any moment, one of those Deux Chevaux cars, with the canvas sunroof fully rolled back and loaded up with agricultural produce, might jump out a few yards ahead without any warning. I was in a perpetual state of alarm, fully expecting to collide with a ton of garlic or asparagus. My reaction to this absurd rule of the road was to crawl along at 30kph, as a result of which a long line of angry drivers built up behind me, unable to overtake because of oncoming traffic, but who, when they finally managed to pass, did so with fists waving and horns blaring.

Add to this the fact that your non-driving partner keeps up a perpetual eulogy about the wonderful landscape that you want to see but cannot, because you're trying to keep both of you alive, and you have a recipe for disaster. It was not a good way to impress a new partner. You could argue a case that this was a perfect opportunity to demonstrate coolness under extreme duress, but I failed the test comprehensively. The whole idea of a driving holiday, I concluded, was a contradiction in terms.

This explains why I've tended to turn to less conventional forms of transport when thinking about a holiday. So, when my brother invited me to visit him in the US, I booked a berth on a cargo ship bound for Chester, Delaware. It took eight days to get there, and was as tranquil and relaxing a journey as any I can remember. And a couple of years later, when Joan and I went to Hong Kong, we decided not to fly but to get on a train at Morpeth in Northumberland and get off ten days later at Kowloon.

We were regaling a group of friends with the details of these journeys while sitting round a dinner table after a particularly strenuous ceilidh dance, when Rob, who was opposite us and getting increasingly agitated, leaned across and said, 'Clive, for heaven's sake, why can't you just be normal?'

'Oh, normal is boring,' I said. 'It's much more interesting living on the edge.'

Which is why, several decades later, when there was a commotion from England's edges, I sat up and took notice. The prime minister of the day reckoned he had his ear to the ground and knew exactly which way the political wind was blowing. He was having to deal with an upstart from the far fringes of the right who was stirring up the people, making them feel disgruntled and blaming it all on our European friends. So Dave called a referendum about whether we wanted to stay friends or split up and go our separate ways. 'It's all right,' he assured his parliamentary colleagues, 'they know on which side their bread is buttered and would never dare to leave. Trust me, I know the people.' He didn't, and we did. As we all know.

His mistake was that he had failed to take note of what was going on, on our edges. The people who lived there were seething with rage because they had been ignored. 'Forgotten,' they said. So when man-of-the-people Dave asked them to support him in sticking with our friends across the Channel, they gave him a kick up the backside and sent him on his way. And when the new government came in, it promised it would look after all those people living on the edge. To prove it, they pronounced a sentence of death on the internal combustion engine. 'We're going electric,' our new man of the people told us.

The unlikely juxtaposition of the referendum and the announcement that we all had to start buying electric cars prompted me to revise my ideas about motoring holidays. Electric cars seemed to me – and, I might add, my long-suffering wife – just what we had been looking for. The previous year, we'd had solar panels put on the roof and part of the deal was a free charge point for the electric car we didn't have but would like to have.

'So,' we said, 'we've got the Pod Point, we might as well have the car.' And that was when we bought the Nissan Leaf. When the Government's bluff was called over the Brexit vote, and most of the 'No' votes seemed to come from England's edges, we were presented with a perfect opportunity to put the Leaf through its paces and find out what was going on around England's coasts.

England's edges seemed to be dying, yet for most of our history, they had been alive with activity. Economically, socially, politically, culturally, our edges had always mattered. Ports and harbours played a key role in the development of our national life. They were the hub through which all our comings and goings of goods, armies, traders, smugglers, priests, missionaries and ideas passed.

The edges of our country that were closest to someone else's edges saw the briskest trade, but also experienced the greatest vulnerability. That is why, throughout our history, the coast of England's south-east corner, just 21 miles from the European mainland, has seen the greatest comings and goings and the greatest change. Pretty much everything came to us through Dover or Sandwich, or other nearby harbours.

Unpredictable as they were, the waters surrounding us were the highways along which everything entered and left these islands. The North Sea was, in the words of Michael Pye, a 'web of connections' that 'made the modern world possible'.[1] We would not be the country we are today without

1 Michael Pye, *The Edge of the World: How the North Sea Made Us Who We Are*, Penguin Books, 2015, pp1-9.

those toings and froings across the North Sea. And that is why our edges mattered: you couldn't to and fro without passing through our edges.

Another twist to the unfolding story of our edges was when people with money to spare turned them into playgrounds. When health-giving spa waters were discovered in Scarborough in the seventeenth century, the moneyed classes started 'taking the waters', and it soon became quite the fashionable thing to do. As did bathing, provided it was done modestly.

This necessitated the invention of the bathing machine. These beach huts on wheels made it possible for women to exchange their fabulous day clothes for equally fabulous body-disguising bathing costumes and to step fully-clothed into the water without exposing a single square inch of flesh. Men, apparently, had no such qualms. Further along the beach and, allegedly, out of sight of the sensitivities of the ladies, they stripped off everything and jumped in the sea in the altogether.

All these fun and games added up to the very first English seaside resort, at Scarborough. It was the beginning of a trend. George IV gave added impetus to this fashion for healthy, but modest, seaside fun with his frequent visits to Brighton, where the therapeutic properties of the sea – and a, no doubt, equally health-improving affair – prompted him to set up home there by the building of the grandiose house we all know today as the Royal Brighton Pavilion.

This idea of the seaside as a place of fun and relaxation was, for a time, limited to the moneyed classes, out of reach of the working masses. But the onward march of technology ensured they didn't have it all to themselves for long. The railway revolution of the nineteenth century brought rapid economic development to what had been inconsequential areas. Folkestone, Middlesbrough and Grimsby, for example, owe their explosive growth to the railway.

But what was truly astonishing was the way in which railways created coastal holiday resorts. Many hitherto insignificant fishing villages, such as Bournemouth and Blackpool, Cleethorpes and Clacton, boomed into life and exploded with fun-seeking visitors. Even isolated Aberystwyth on Cardigan Bay turned itself into Birmingham's favourite holiday resort. Railways made it possible for working people to get away from their factories once a year and enjoy a holiday by the sea. Suddenly, our coastal fringes took on a new significance. Going to the seaside became part of our culture.

> *Oh! I do like to be beside the seaside!*
> *I do like to be beside the sea!*
> *Oh, I do like to stroll along the Prom, Prom, Prom!*
> *Where the brass bands play,*
> *Tiddley-om-pom-pom!*

Much to the discombobulation of the posh segment of society, who failed to understand why they couldn't have these playgrounds all to themselves, everyone could now join in the fun, even the hoi polloi. These developments were given a huge boost with the arrival of the affordable family motorcar. Millions could now take themselves to Britain's coasts for annual holidays, daytrips and weekend breaks, bringing prosperity to places such as Morecambe, Scarborough, Filey, Brighton, Margate and Whitley Bay. The hospitality and entertainment sectors had never had it so good. England's edges prospered.

But the seaside boom didn't last long. A tidal wave of technological change swept over our coasts. The development of telecommunications and air transport meant that, for the first time in our history, we were no longer dependent on the sea for travel and communications, and this meant that our edges could be bypassed; electronically or aeronautically, we were able to jump over them. Package holidays whisked holiday makers to the Costa del Sol, which boomed while our coastal resorts became redundant.

Add to this the post-war decline of the great centres of heavy industry, and it is no wonder that our once-booming edge towns are now in a sorry state, variously described as 'left behind', 'forgotten', 'disenfranchised', and suffering from 'multiple deprivation'. Our edges, it seems, no longer matter.

Now, another revolution is under way. In 1920, when there were only half a million cars on our roads, Britain's very first petrol station opened near Aldermaston village, 46 miles west of London.[2] Thirty years later, there were six million cars; today, there are more than 30 million cars and more than 8,000 petrol stations. A century after that first petrol station, in December 2020, the UK's first all-electric car-charging forecourt opened at Braintree, in Essex, with not a petrol pump in sight. And there are plans for 100 similar

2   Nicholas Crane, *The Making of the British Landscape*, Weidenfeld & Nicolson, paperback edition, 2017, p466; also https://www.britainbycar. co.uk/aldermaston/408-britain-s-first-petrol-station

forecourts to be built over the next five years.

Tomorrow, it seems, belongs to electricity. Or perhaps to hydrogen. As early adopters of this new EV technology, in a car with a disconcertingly limited range, we set out to see what our edges were really like.

SCOTTISH BORDER

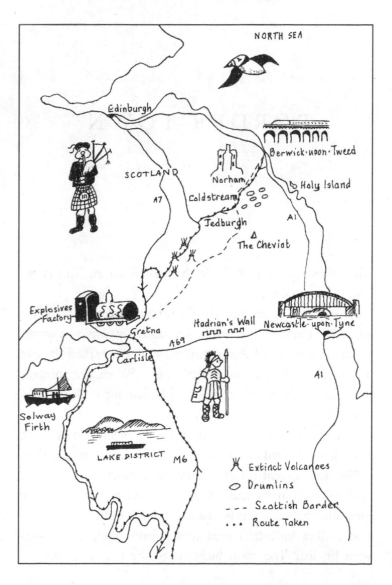

1

BORDER TOWN

'THERE'S NOTHING HERE,' said the forklift driver. 'This is the land that time forgot.'

It was a cold, misty day when we arrived in Berwick. A fret had drifted in from the North Sea, instantly turning a warm summer's day into a dull autumnal day. We parked the car in Tweedmouth, checked the two rapid EV charge points – they were both out of order – and began our walk into old Berwick.

Tweedmouth doesn't look or feel as if it belongs to Berwick at all. It was tacked on for administrative convenience in the 1970s. The ancient military town of Berwick-upon-Tweed, confined within its medieval walls, has spent its history oscillating between Scotland and England. But Tweedmouth, a sprawling industrial area and a mini-port, has always been English. The main business of the port is to service

Northumberland's agricultural industry. Although endowed with a good natural harbour, it has to contend with strong easterly winds and a difficult entrance.

We'd caught it on a quiet day. A lone ship, the *Hesta St John's*, was moored alongside the almost deserted quay. There were no signs of activity. The whole place was wrapped in a chilly stillness. At the far end of a line of warehouses, we'd spotted a light from a half-open door. The forklift driver was organising some bags of barley.

'It's a bulk carrier,' he said, in answer to my query, 'with a cargo of bagged fertiliser from Rouen. The only one in today.'

The medieval Old Bridge links modern, industrial Tweedmouth with the ancient walled town. Built of red sandstone, with fifteen arches and a series of pedestrian refuges, it provides a delightful walkway over the estuary. It's too narrow to accommodate today's traffic, most of which crosses the river by the less elegant but more functional and much higher Royal Tweed Bridge. On Old Bridge, we were almost at sea level; from that low angle we watched a colony of mute swans, most of them sleeping with wings wrapped over their heads, bobbing on the ripples thrown up by a solitary fishing boat. At the far end of the bridge, a sharp left and a steep climb up Bank Hill brought us to the top of the Elizabethan ramparts. From here we had a panoramic view of the walled and tightly-clustered old Berwick and, beyond, the sprawling mass of industry and housing on the south bank.

Berwick-upon-Tweed is on the edge of Northumberland, on the edge of England, on the edge of the North Sea. It is the only English town north of the Tweed. London is 350 miles away, Land's End 550, John O'Groats 330. Berwick is poised uneasily between two historically antagonistic nations, its marginal position making it militarily vulnerable. Throughout its turbulent history, this well-defended town changed hands between England and Scotland fourteen times before finding itself – at least for the time being – in England. That's why Pevsner describes Berwick as 'one of the most exciting towns in England, a real town, with the strongest sense of enclosure.'[3]

All this turbulence resulted in the town becoming separated from its county, which used to be Berwickshire but is now the Scottish Borders. At one time, Berwickshire had the reputation of being the most English county in Scotland; now, Berwick-upon-Tweed is still considered to be the most Scottish town in England. The response of the local people to this troublesome past is that they regard themselves as neither English nor Scottish, but as independent Berwickers. For this reason, the Crimean War[4] was declared in the name of 'Great Britain, Ireland and Berwick-upon-Tweed'; when the peace treaty was signed after the war, Berwick's name was omitted, so Berwick officially remained at war with Russia until 1966. The Mayor of Berwick then decided that enough was enough, signed a new peace treaty and put everything right. But at least the point had been made; Berwickers are their own people.

Berwick's military history explains why the town has such an enclosed feel about it. It grew up with everyone huddling

---

3   N Pevsner (Ed), *The Buildings of England: Northumberland*, Penguin Books, 1992.

4   The first Crimean War (1853 to 1856).

together, always looking over their shoulders wondering where the next raid would come from. It also explains why there is such a conspicuous lack of open spaces. We commented on this to Councillor Catherine Seymour, whom we met when she was doing her stint at the information desk inside the Main Guard Museum on Palace Green.

'Well yes,' she said. 'We were all too busy protecting ourselves and cramming as many people as possible inside our town walls for protection to bother with such luxuries as parkland and gardens. So, are you on holiday, or just here for the day?'

'Just for the day. Heading for Carlisle tomorrow, on the lookout for EV charge points.'

'Ah, if it's charge points you're after, you've come to the right person,' Councillor Seymour said. 'I can tell you, there's one at the Infirmary and another one at the Garden Centre.'

'Problem is,' Joan said, 'they're both slow chargers. We need rapid ones. The Infirmary one is out of service. And the garden centre's closed. Can you imagine – six hours hanging around there with nothing to do, not even a cup of coffee?'

'There're two at Tweedmouth you might try,' the councillor said.

'Both rapid chargers,' I said, 'and both out of order. That's three out of four of Berwick's charge points not working.'

'Why can't you carry a spare battery with you?' asked the councillor.

'Are you serious! They're as big as a couple of railway sleepers and weigh 300 kilograms!'

The councillor took out a notebook. 'You'd better tell me more. I had no idea there were slow and rapid chargers. How d'you know where the charge points are and whether they're working?'

I showed her the Zap-Map screen on my phone showing all of the out-of-commission charge points in Berwick.

'Can I photograph this? I'll bring this up at the next council meeting.'

Holy Trinity Parish Church is a rarity, one of only a few built during the period when England and Wales briefly became a republic. It has Cromwell's austere outlook on life stamped all over it. While it was being built, he called at Berwick on his way to Dunbar to fight one of his righteous battles; he made it clear to the people of Berwick that the church was to have no sinful frills or ornamentation of any kind. Religion for him was a serious business and is why the Parish Church has no tower and is entirely without beauty.

Two hundred years later, the Scottish Presbyterians decided to put this right by building their own church. It was to have all the fripperies that Cromwell had forbidden Holy Trinity. St Andrew's Church would not only have a tower, it would have a spire on top of the tower, and not just one spire, but five. 'It is,' as Pevsner puts it, 'a somewhat arrogant design.' Furthermore, a site was chosen for this new church just a few yards in front of Holy Trinity, making the Parish Church almost invisible from the main road.

That explains why it took us so long to find the Parish Church and, with it, the Parish Centre. We'd planned to attend a talk there about Northumberland's geology. After crossing an empty square known as The Parade, we eventually found the Cromwellian church, where a group of smokers huddled in the doorway. They seemed all of a piece – the grey sky, the drizzle, the dismal building, the hunched shoulders under dreary hoods, and the hacking coughs.

'Do you know where the Parish Centre is?' we asked them.

'Don't know. That place over there is where we do our activities. Don't know what its name is, though.'

They slouched across a courtyard and entered a smart building tacked onto the east end of the arrogant church. We followed them, and inside was a young man at a reception desk.

'Is this the Parish Centre?'

'Don't know what it's called, mate. Sorry, I'm only here from four to five. All kinds of things go on here.'

We poked around until we found a group of elderly people, and immediately felt at home.

'Yes, this is it,' one of them told us. 'Welcome.'

The speaker took a 'shepherd's crown' from his pocket, a piece of flint that had formed inside an almost perfectly spherical sea urchin 100 million years ago. I was surprised at this, because such a fossil is normally associated with chalk, and there is none of that in Northumberland; limestone, yes, but not chalk. It was, nevertheless, a nice little opening. As our lecturer had just found this fossil in the Sussex Downs, I pricked up my ears; we had the Downs as one of our objectives, charge points permitting.

The gist of the lecture was that most of the economic history of the county – at least, in the south-east of Northumberland – was predicated on coal, which was formed 300 million years ago during the Carboniferous Period. Towards the end of this period, subterranean cracks appeared between the layers of limestone, sandstone and shale that lie below much of Northumberland, and into this was squeezed molten rock from deep within the earth's bowels at temperatures in excess of 1,000°C, solidifying to form what we know today as the Whin Sill. It is made of an extremely hard, dark rock known as dolerite or, to give it its local name, whinstone. After millions of years of erosion of the softer rocks, the Whin Sill has become exposed at the surface, creating much of the scenery that is so characteristic of the north-east of England and which forms the basis of Northumberland's tourism industry. Hadrian's Wall is built on the Whin Sill, as are Dunstanburgh and Bamburgh Castles. Without the Whin Sill, there would be no Farne Islands.

'So, where are you heading now?' asked one of the geologists.

'Carlisle, via Coldstream and Gretna.'

'Sounds complicated. Wouldn't the A69 be easier, following Hadrian's Wall?'

'We want to keep close to the border, the geological edge, where the great collision was.'

2

SUBJUGATION

'THEY CALL ME A WHITE SETTLER,' said the man with the dog.

'White settler! Last time I heard those words was in Southern Africa,' I said. 'Been here long?'

'Fifteen years. Anyone who moves here gets called that, even if only from a couple of miles away. We like it that way, like to keep ourselves to ourselves. We've got Tesco's in Berwick, just four miles away. It's nice and quiet here. Lots of clubs and activities. We don't need to go outside for anything else.'

Horncliffe is England's most northerly village. We reached it at the end of a narrow unclassified lane, tucked inside a meander of the River Tweed. With a population of just over 400, wrapped around on three sides by the river and on the fourth by agricultural land, it is off the beaten track and easily missable. But its isolation seems to be a source of pride to locals. It's even too isolated and too small to qualify for a church. An English Presbyterian Church was founded there in the mid-nineteenth century, but it morphed into a United Reform Church in the twentieth century, before closing in 1995 for lack of customers.

'And then,' said the man with the dog, 'it became the rather fine house and B&B you can see behind you. Church services moved next door to that tiny church hall, numbers continued to dwindle, the village hall took over, and now the nearest church is at Norham or Berwick.'

Norham (population 600) is just three miles further on and, like Horncliffe, inside a meander. Both villages are on England's northern margin, but 800 years ago, Norham's physical setting was what made it more important than Horncliffe was ever destined to be. The Normans chose its prominent knoll on which to build one of their castles. The cliff-like river banks on three sides meant that only a short stretch of moat to the south had to be dug out manually. It was a superb defensive site, giving the castle a commanding position over the village that subsequently developed to its west. Militarily brilliant, in a later age this elevated riverine location was considered to be aesthetically charming.

Sir Walter Scott, in his epic poem *Marmion: A Tale of Flodden Field*, celebrated the castle's setting:

> *Day set on Norham's castled steep*
> *And Tweed's fair river, broad and deep,*
> *…the flanking walls that round it sweep,*
> *In yellow lustre shone.*

JMW Turner celebrated it with oil and water colour, dramatically capturing the weather, atmosphere and light of the castle in multiple sketches, paintings and prints that depicted its striking setting and varied moods, nearly always at dawn and against the background of the rising sun.

Romantic as the setting is, however, this should not blind us to the fact that Norham Castle was a symbol of subjugation. England had been invaded, and the Normans immediately set about remaking it in their image. We were no longer to be Celtic or even Anglo-Saxon, but Norman-French. A first step was the building of defensive castles along the frontier with Scotland.

The twelfth-century motte-and-bailey castle at Norham was built by Bishop Ranulph Flambard during the reign of Henry I, the fourth son of William the Conqueror, but was quickly replaced by the almost impregnable stone castle, which has become the 'romantic' ruin we see today. Standing between the castles of Berwick to the east and Wark to the west, Norham was part of a line of castles to be seen all along the Scottish border. This was frontier country, on the margins of civilisation.

But the Normans colonised our souls as well as our land. They inveigled themselves into our hearts by steering our Celtic and Anglo-Saxon forms of Christianity towards Norman-French ways of doing religion. Their religious practices were more closely tied to Roman orthodoxy, and were therefore less likely to lead to independent modes of thinking. Our conquerors wanted to encourage conformity and the suppression of attitudes that might question the new arrangements. To make sure we toed the line, we were inundated with missionaries. From the other side of the Channel, monks from a newly-formed order, the Cistercians, were sent to England to set up monasteries here. Sixty-four of them, all in the twelfth century, swamped us with Norman-French proselytisers. It was a mass colonisation of our souls as well as our physical territory.

The Cistercian order represented a more regulated form of Christianity than the home-grown Celtic approach to religion. In keeping with the new spirit of control, Bishop Hugh de Puiset commissioned a new Norman church on the west side of Norham to replace the former one. Although substantial parts of it were modified during the nineteenth century, it still retains its essentially Norman appearance. When we first came across it, it seemed to us more like a fortress than a church, a kind of mini-Durham Cathedral: solid, powerful, fortress-like, controlling.

This part of Northumberland, known as Norhamshire, used to be an exclave of the Palatinate of Durham, the land of the Prince Bishops, who ruled the northern edge of the country as kings. Prince Bishops had the power to raise armies and taxes; they minted their own coins and owned all the mines in the area, making these clerics some of the richest and most pompous and ruthless men in the country. Here was a classic case of a blurring of the boundaries between the sacred and the secular, the spiritual and the temporal; in the process, the Prince Bishops lost sight of the teaching of their Founder that 'Ye cannot serve God and mammon'.[5] They unashamedly served both. This gravy train lasted until the nineteenth century, when Norhamshire became part of

5   Matthew 6:24

Northumberland with the great Reform Act of 1832.

The geography of power can be seen in the way in which the village of Norham is structured: the castle at the east end, the church at the west, the market-place and the ordinary folk caught firmly between them. The two great organs of power, ecclesiastical and military, church and state, held the people in their grip, which is why you so often find in medieval English settlements the castle at one end and the church at the other.

Before the Normans arrived, this northern region of England was wide open to ideas from Ireland and the monastic island of Iona. Norham began life as Ubbanford, and it was here that Aidan famously forded the River Tweed on his way from Iona to Lindisfarne in 635 CE, bringing with him his kindly Celtic tradition of Christianity. King Oswy founded a monastery on Lindisfarne in 655; Ecfrid, Bishop of Lindisfarne, built a stone church in Norham between 830 and 845; and, in 875 CE, when the monks on Holy Island were fleeing the devastation caused by the Vikings, they rested St Cuthbert's relics at Ubbanford, where they stayed for many years before another generation of monks took them to the saint's final resting place in Durham.[6] If anyone is in doubt about Norham's real origins, look no further than the name: *ham* is a classic Anglo-Saxon suffix, meaning settlement.

However much conquerors try to obliterate the history and culture of a conquered people, they never quite succeed; it always finds a way of poking through. In fact, these events – the clash of the Celtic vis-à-vis the Roman tradition of

---

6   https://www.findagrave.com/cemetery/2130458/st.-cuthbert's-churchyard

Christianity in this part of the country – created a colossal ecclesiastical upheaval that shook the foundations of the Church. It was not until 30 years later, in 664, that the Synod of Whitby resolved the problem.

Just along the road, we passed through the strange settlement of Donaldson's Lodge, famous on the far-flung edges of extreme revivalist Methodism as one of the UK spots where God is alleged to have moved in a particularly dramatic way, visiting this place in the 1870s with a 'glory cloudburst over the thirsty land in the Marmion country'.[7] According to WM Patterson, in his book, *Northern Primitive Methodism*, there was a 'spiritual awakening' here, in which

Joseph Hawkins led the hosts of Israel into the enemy's camp on the Scottish side, and did exploits in the name of the Lord of Hosts... Two young women fell prone upon the floor, cried for mercy, and obtained pardon... Night after night, souls were saved, and it scarcely abated for three years.

[The place became] a centre of spiritual power, from whence mission bands went to all the country round, and grace abounded to the chief of sinners.[8]

It was a totally unregulated, charismatic form of religion: the exact opposite of what the Normans had hoped to achieve with their reforms.

---

7   A reference to Sir Walter Scott's *Marmion: A Tale of Flodden Field*.
8   *Northern Primitive Methodism*, W M Patterson, 1909, https://ukwells. org/wells/donaldsons-lodge

At Cornhill, a five-arched stone bridge took us over the river, out of England and into Scotland. At the Scottish end, on the curve of the road stood the old grey-stone Toll House, also known as the Old Marriage House. Here, as in Gretna Green at the other end of the border, eloping lovers took advantage of the more lenient Scottish laws to make hasty marriages, no doubt to regret them at leisure.

A sharp turn west, and we were following the river on its north side through a short stretch of agreeable woodland, before entering Coldstream. As we entered this border town, a reassuring sign pointed us to the rapid charge point we were looking for, at the far end of a small car park.

The car park had room for about twenty cars, with – in the far corner – a bay reserved for one electric car. The car park was full, including a large black car in the EV parking bay. Not a spare place anywhere. I got out of the car to see how far through the charging cycle it was. But it wasn't charging; it wasn't even an EV. A diesel BMW occupied a space that was clearly marked, on an upright sign and in the parking bay itself, for EV drivers only. It was our first experience of being ICEd – blocked by an Internal Combustion Engine.

There was nothing to do but wait. I took the first watch while Joan walked along the street to get a paper. Fifteen minutes later she returned, and I went to the large car park on the other side of town where there was a loo, plenty of parking, but no charge point. On the way back I, too, bought a paper and we waited and read and nurtured our fury. Eventually, a smart thirty-something woman breezed into the car park with a look of satisfaction suggesting that her business meeting had gone well, a wodge of documents in one hand, keys jingling contentedly in the other, ready for a quick getaway.

'So sorry,' she said cheerfully. 'Hope you don't mind.'

'We certainly do. You've kept us waiting an hour,' Joan said.

'Sorry, there was no other place to park. What was I to've done?'

'You could've gone to the car park at the other end of town?' I suggested. 'Plenty of spaces there.'

'But I'd've had to walk all the way back.'

'So, to save yourself five minutes, you decided it was OK to keep us waiting for sixty.'

'Well, there're plenty of charge points all over the place, aren't there?'

'Wrong. This is the only charge point between here and Gretna. Look, it's the same as going over the road to that garage, parking your car at the only petrol pump and leaving it there while you go to your meeting.'

'That would be ridiculous.'

'But don't you see? That's exactly what you've done to us.'

She blushed, fumbled for her keys and dumped her documents on the passenger seat. Then, turning round, she said, 'Look, I'm very sorry. I didn't think. I've never seen anyone using this before. I didn't realise it was such a big deal. I'm really sorry I've inconvenienced you.'

'It's OK. We're feeling a bit nervy. We've a long journey ahead of us today and we need to charge here. We really don't have any choice.'

After she'd gone, we hooked up to the charger and walked along High Street, where we found the Mad Hatter's Tea Room and had a magical hot chocolate. It took an hour to fill us up. The main street ran the full length of the town, from east to west, and it looked dreary and uninviting. Coldstream did not feel like a place to linger.

But you'd be wrong to judge Coldstream by its high street. It keeps its true genius neatly hidden from view. It was only when we left the high street and poked around to see what was behind its self-effacing frontage that we discovered its real gems: the small Market Square, quirkily behind the high street; Abbey House Hotel, on the site of a twelfth-century priory; and Penitents Walk and Nuns Walk, along the delightful riverside walk.

To be fair, the dreary high street had nothing to do with the spirit of hospitality, or lack of it, on the part of the good people of Coldstream. It was due entirely to its geography. Situated at the lowest fording place on the River Tweed, Coldstream, from its earliest days, was a strategically important crossing point, making it a natural place for Scottish and English armies to pursue each other in the centuries-long conflict between our two countries. Coldstream just happened to be caught in the middle. Armies came and passed through, and then, when their business was done, they came and passed through the other way, leaving behind a trail of destruction and a feeling of transience on the part of Coldstream's inhabitants.

It was all this intense military activity that created the Coldstream Guards. They made a name for themselves in 1660 when they marched to London and helped to put Charles II on the throne after we'd ingloriously chopped his father's head off, and then regretted it. As a sign of our repentance, we made his son the king; this Restoration was the closest England ever got to sticking a beheaded king's head back onto his shoulders. Since then, we've never really been in favour of revolutions.

We, too, merely passed through Coldstream, for the border plunges south here. Leaving the Tweed, it zig-zags through a loose network of unclassified roads and a swarm of drumlins. These are egg-shaped hills, left behind by retreating glaciers, forming a landscape known as 'basket of eggs topography'. It makes for an impressive terrain of long low parallel hills, oriented south-west to north-east, the direction in which the ice retreated. Up to a kilometre long and 50 metres high, they gave excellent cover for the military men of 500 years ago. This left the area between the Rivers Tweed and Bowmont vulnerable to military raids and difficult to defend; given the uneasy relationship between Scotland and England, the area became a war zone.

On the north-east edge of this drumlin field, near the village of Branxton, lies Flodden Field, where the greatest battle of the border conflict took place on 9 September 1513. It was here that the English soldiers used their 'bills' with such deadly effect to cut through the Scottish pikes like matchsticks. It was the last great medieval battle on British soil. Scotland lost a king that day, when James IV was the last king of Scotland, and of any part of Britain, to be killed in battle. A few months earlier, this same king had captured Norham Castle. Nevertheless he did, perhaps, achieve some good in his short but brutish life by marrying Margaret Tudor ten years earlier, thus paving the way for the union of the

Scottish and English crowns, which we've been squabbling about ever since.

Another effect of the retreating ice was to cause Scotland to go up in the world, literally. If we think of Britain as a kind of giant see-saw floating on a sea of molten material deep down under the earth's shell, we can imagine what a huge pile of ice might do to the see-saw if it's all at one end. Most of the ice was in the northern part of Britain, while the extreme south of the country was mostly free of it. The ice covering Scotland was 30 metres (or 100 feet) thick. That's a lot of ice and a lot of weight, heavy enough to push the Scottish end of the see-saw down. When the ice melted, our see-saw island began to readjust itself, and the whole of northern Britain, particularly Scotland, started slowly rising back up. As it did so, the sea level fell by 10 metres, but rose in the south, where the country, to this day, is slowly sinking. Scotland has been rising and the south of England sinking ever since. This is how Scotland started going up in the world and England started going down. It makes the English nervous and the Scots cock-a-hoop.

3

CRUMPLED EDGES

IN BUYING THE LEAF, we had launched ourselves onto a steep learning curve that involved signing up to a host of charge point providers throughout the country, each with its own territory, all requiring separate membership, all with apps or RFID cards or both. The Electric Highway, Charge Your Car, Polar Instant, Pod Point, Genie Point – we had to sign up to each of them if we wanted to use their charge points, which were all dispersed in the different parts of the country that we intended to drive through. We'd also have to know which connectors to use – CHAdeMO, 50kW, CCS, AC or DC. And to keep track of all the charge points throughout the country, we'd need to download Zap-Map. We carried three different connecting cables with us, each with different plugs to go into different types of charge-point sockets. No standardisation whatsoever.

It was like the glorious muddle that accompanied the railway mania of the nineteenth century, when George Stephenson's 4ft 8½in gauge fought for supremacy with GWR's 7ft ¼in, and dozens of individual rail franchises operated on a proliferation of timetables and an array of fares that were complex enough to perplex the savviest of the rail-travelling public. Thank goodness that's one lesson of history from which we've all learned.

To make it all a bit more human, Joan suggested we give the car a name.

'I used to read about the antics of Lettice Leefe in the *Girl* magazine, when I was a bit younger,' she said.

'My sister Eileen took that comic. Wasn't she known as the greenest girl in school?'

'Couldn't be more appropriate then, could it?'

So Lettie she became.

Bowmont Water wraps itself round the north-eastern rump of the Cheviots like a moat. Rising at Black Hog, 801 metres (2,627 feet) above sea level, it drops rapidly south, then west, then north, passing between the twin settlements of Kirk Yetholm and Town Yetholm in the historic county of Roxburghshire. It then crosses the border into England and turns east, thus completing its encirclement of this part of the Cheviots, before joining the College Burn and morphing into the River Glen. It leaves the Cheviots via a narrow defile, through which our route took us. There are roads on either side of this defile, tucking themselves into the angles where the hills hit the valley floor, as far away from the flood plain as the steeply-rising terrain permits.

On the English side of the border, some of the most beautiful and isolated valleys in Northumberland radiate outwards from this part of the Cheviots – Happy valley, Harthope valley, College valley, Breamish valley – with moorland interfluves of desolate beauty, where you can hear the frantic singing of a skylark, the mellow call of a curlew and the lone keh-leek of a kestrel. On the Scottish side, between the Tweed and the Lammermuir Hills, lies the agricultural lowland area known as the Merse, including Blackadder Water and Whiteadder Water, both tributaries of the Tweed. So fertile is the land here that, as far back as the first century CE, the natives of the area, the Votadini, were producing enough surplus corn to sell to the Romans, who were busy securing the northern borders of their newly extended empire.[9] They did this by building Hadrian's Wall, which was to the south of our position, and a north-south road network comprising Dere Street (the equivalent of today's A68) and the Devil's Causeway (roughly equivalent to today's A1 and A697). All these routes run north-south. We were going east-west.

These were the foothills of the Cheviots. Towering conical hills, 600 to 700 feet high, loomed over us. Lorries carrying agricultural supplies, tractors pulling straw bales, the lumbering bulk of the Northumberland mobile library vans – all came at us, forcing us to seek hasty refuge in one of the many passing places cut into the hedgerows of the excruciatingly narrow roads. Somewhere along the way, we crossed the border back into Scotland and found ourselves at

9   Alistair Moffat, *The Wall: Rome's Greatest Frontier*, Birlinn, 2009, p74.

the northern end of the Pennine Way, at Kirk Yetholm. It was tortuous nerve-wracking driving, but delightful.

This was wild country, raw and rumbustious, marking England's northern edge. It was slow going, through deep wooded valleys, up energy-exhausting hills, over deserted interfluves and through miniscule hamlets – isolated settlements with deep histories, dependent on precarious roads and uncertain public transport. As well as going against the grain of the road network, we were also going against the grain of the country, up hill and down dale, from one valley to the next, from the River Glen at Town Yetholm, up and over to Morebattle in the Kale valley, and then down into Teviotdale at Jedburgh followed by the Jed Water valley, and up and down again into the Rule valley. And so it was, all day: twisty-turny driving, anticipating approaching vehicles round every bend, always on the lookout for a passing place to dart into.

The Scottish border follows the physical geography here, along the watershed separating the rivers that flow north into the Tweed and Teviot catchments from those that flow south into Northumberland. You can feel Scotland and England intermingling and pushing up against each other; it's not quite English, but then not quite Scotland, either. But what is now a line on the map used to be a coastline. At the beginning of things, Scotland and England were on opposite sides of the world; what is now a very hilly and beautiful border region was then a raw continental edge. Six hundred million years ago, Scotland was part of Canada, while England and Wales were in the Antarctic as an appendage of the ancient continent of Gondwanaland. These two pieces of what is today Great Britain were 4,000 miles apart on different shores of the Iapetus Ocean, the predecessor of what is today the Atlantic Ocean.

For the next one hundred million years, Scotland and England slowly drifted towards each other at the giddy pace of 4.5 centimetres a year until, about 450 million years ago, they met in a cataclysmic continental car crash. The collision unleashed an earth-shattering paroxysm of energy that threw up the Caledonian Mountains and the Cheviot Hills, set off a cluster of active volcanoes in what is now the Border region, and released a huge mass of molten rock which pushed its way up from the bowels of the earth, eventually solidifying into the huge granite pluton that we know as The Cheviot. The Cheviot Range dominates the northern skyline of Northumberland and the southern horizon of the historic county of Roxburghshire. All along here, the previously tortured landscape has been worn down over the ensuing millennia into the beautifully rounded hills we see today in the Southern Uplands.

That collision of the land masses caused the northern edge of England to be pushed under the southern edge of Scotland, a process known as subduction. This meant that Scotland, geologically speaking, came out on top – another reason why Scotland is going up in the world and England going down. The English don't like not being top dog, and we've been at loggerheads over the matter ever since, so much so that we're still not sure if we want to continue to live with each other. Scotland is thinking of pulling out of the arrangement, with the hope of restoring the old geographical arrangement when they were part of Canada and England was in the Antarctic, well away from Europe.

If you climb the 2,600 feet to the top of The Cheviot, you will be able to survey the scene of this crash and the magnificence of the landscape it created. It's a doddle walking there when you're young, but the going is a bit more challenging when you advance beyond seventy. It's still worth the effort. From the summit, on a clear day, you see a panorama of Scotland.

But perhaps the best view of the remains of those ancient volcanoes can be seen where the A68 crosses the border at Carter Bar. Here, at 1,371 feet (418 metres) above sea level, you are truly on the knife-edge of England. You couldn't find a more dramatic boundary to a country than at this point, nor a more impressive edge. Scotland drops spectacularly away through a landscape of volcanic hills into the Jed Water valley and Teviotdale.

This border country coincides roughly with one of the fundamental geological boundaries in Britain, known as the Iapetus Suture. This suture is the post-operative geological scar tissue, showing where our two countries met in that explosive conjoining. The Iapetus Suture runs diagonally along a line roughly from Berwick to the Solway Firth, separating older from newer rocks, and ancient landscapes in Scotland from more recent ones south of the border. It marks the line where our two countries were crumpled up into the profusion of loveliness and profligate beauty that it is today, which we call the Scottish Borders. It was approximately this line we were following: England's raw geological edge.

The country here, between England and Scotland, is the ancient home of the Otadini, the Celtic people who once occupied the region from the Tyne to the Lammermuir Hills that overlook Edinburgh and the Firth of Forth. Ancient Britons built their homes in safe places atop these old volcanic peaks. There's a strong correlation between volcanic cones and ancient British campsites: Akeld Hill, Yeavering Bell, Woden Law, Castle Law, and so many more conical hills of andesitic lava were chosen by ancient Brits to make their hilltop dwellings within the encircling embankments of earth and stone that are often still clearly visible today.

The most significant of these forts was Yeavering Bell. About 130 roundhouses were built on top of this spectacular 361-metre-high (1,184 feet) conical hill. The people who lived there would have been able to look across to other similar hillforts and to see people working in the fields below them. They saw the Romans come and they saw them go; they survived into the Dark Ages that followed the collapse of the Roman Empire. These ancient Britons left their mark on the landscape here two thousand years or more before the Romans came and before they even had an empire.

There must surely be some special corner of hell reserved for those who make you go the full length of a road before telling you that your intended exit is closed. We had taken the tortuously narrow road linking Jedburgh and Gretna, the B6357. Above the Jed valley, we came upon a landscape of rounded hills and truncated cones, ancient long-dead volcanoes – Dunion Hill, Black Law, Rubers Law – all remnants of the fiery conflagration that had accompanied the conjunction of Scotland and England half a billion years earlier.

The land fell away again as we dropped into the valley of the Rule Water and, at Bonchester Bridge, the road circled round Bonchester Hill – another remnant volcano. Up again we went, and then down and along the valley of the Hyndlee Burn, where we skirted the great coniferous plantations of Wauchope Forest.

Coming off this upland region, we quite thought that we were now done with all that battery-exhausting up-hill and down-dale driving. We were looking forward to a gentle glide down Liddesdale into Eskdale and then Gretna, where we'd find our charge point. That downhill stretch should have lit a few green dots and replenished our battery just a little. But instead, just before Newcastleton, we turned a bend and there, right across the road, was the sign: ROAD CLOSED. We were to be diverted back over Wauchope Forest through the valley of Hermitage Water, almost parallel to the way we had come. It was going to cost us the best part of an extra 20 miles.

There are some places that seem to carry the burden of ancient wrongs, so much so that the feeling of terrible pain is almost tangible. This little valley was one such place. It had a dark and troubled feel about it. It used to be a war zone, and piles of old stone now mark where once there were pele towers and fortified houses. A little way up the valley, beyond Newlands, in a narrow vale at the foot of Lady's Knowe, stands defiantly what is left of the Hermitage Castle. Godfrey Watson, in his book *The Border Reivers*, tells us that it is known as the 'guardhouse of the bloodiest valley in Britain'. He goes on:

Over the wilderness of Liddesdale there still broods the

lowering mass of Hermitage Castle, the scene of all kinds of medieval horror, where Sir Alexander Ramsay was left to starve to death in the dungeon, and the Wicked Lord de Soulis weaved his wizard spells. Here, in this stark and gloomy pile that seems to reflect all the cruelty and horror of Border warfare, dwelt the keepers of Liddesdale, and here it was that Mary Queen of Scots came to visit the wounded Bothwell.[10]

We are accustomed to thinking of borders as tidy lines separating one group of people from another. But this is a modern invention. At one time, they were more often zones of overlap and the intermingling of mutual interests and hostilities, and never was this more so than in the Border Marches. To calm the combatants down, the Border Marches were concocted as a kind of buffer zone, an attempt to keep the warring factions apart. Liddesdale however, where we now were, was once part of the Scottish Middle March, but its inhabitants were too unruly to allow themselves to be administered by anyone but themselves. They therefore detached themselves from the Middle March and devised their own rough system of laws. They became the Debatable Lands.

According to Graham Robb, it was Walter Scott who first declared this road open. Apparently, Scott's 'little gig' was the first wheeled vehicle that had ever been seen in that valley, and the people stared with astonishment at this thing that they'd never set eyes on before.[11] It may well have been the

---

10   Godfrey Watson, *The Border Reivers*, Sandhill Press, 1994, p118.
11   Graham Robb, *The Debatable Land: the Lost World Between Scotland and England*, Picador, p52

first wheeled vehicle, 200 years ago, but so devoid of life did this benighted valley seem to us as we passed through that we could easily have imagined we were the second.

At the Hermitage, we forked left onto a narrow road that led us through a dark corridor with towering moors on either side, clinging to the Hermitage Water for much of its length. Cresting the interfluve, the road, now unfenced, entered the equally deep and brooding valley of the Carewoodrig Burn. This took us onto the A7, into the upper reaches of the Ewes Water valley and out onto the wide floodplain of the River Esk.

Somewhere on the A74(M), just outside Gretna, were the two Ecotricity charge points we were trying to locate. We gave Lettie the details and she promptly dumped us in the middle of what looked like a deserted airfield, with mysteriously empty roads as wide as runways, on the margin of nowhere, a vast area of concrete barrenness, a no-man's-land. It had about it the feel of sudden abandonment, as if a busy town had evacuated without warning.

When reading about this area I'd come across a reference to an abandoned explosives factory that had been built on the edge of Gretna in World War I. Apparently it occupied about 12 square miles; thousands of women worked there, and it had its own transport system. I guess those roads were the remnants of that factory, the redundant geography of wartime Britain, a soulless place for which an alternative use hadn't yet been devised, filled with the ghosts of all those women who kept the country going and fed our war machine.[12] We were lost in a spectre-filled maze, not knowing how to find our way out.

'Let's try and retrace our steps,' said Joan.

'But I've no idea which way we came. I was just following Lettie's instructions.'

'Just do what I tell you. I can get us back to the main road. We'll start again from there.'

With her unerring eye and directional instinct, she got us back on the A74(M) and turned us south until we came to a services sign, which pointed to a location on the other side of the motorway.

'Follow that Shell sign.'

It took us to the inappropriately named Welcome Break service station.

'Look at that,' Joan said. 'Signs for everything – toilets, drinks, giant burgers, the crispest and least fatty chips in the world, nappy-changing rooms, back massage machines, newspapers and magazines, ice creams, slot machines and manicure bars. Massive signs for petrol and diesel pumps. Everything except the one thing we're looking for.'

They were huge, neon-lit affairs, and as we got nearer, there were massive arrows in the road pointing to petrol pumps, but nothing to indicate where the EV charge points were. Eventually, we came across two Ecotricity chargers, lurking on the side of the car park. Alongside them was a suite of Tesla Superchargers, smart, up-market and unavailable to us; our technology was incompatible with theirs.

'That one's been out of commission for three weeks,

---

12   Nicholas Crane, *The Making of the British Landscape*, Weidenfeld & Nicolson, 2016 p465.

mate, and the other for over a month. Come this way every day. No one seems to bother,' said a fellow EV driver, as we approached

Ecotricity got into the charge point business early, right at the beginning, and concentrated on creating a motorway system of charge points – their 'Electric Highway'. This made sense. Motorways serve the central axes of the country, where the busiest traffic is, linking the major centres of population and commerce. As a result, nearly every motorway service area and Ikea store has an Ecotricity charging cabinet. But perhaps they were now paying the penalty for having entered the market too early, with equipment that was beginning to show its age. The success rate we'd experienced with their charge points was not good.

'At least they're doing their bit for the planet, though, so perhaps we shouldn't grumble,' Joan said.[13]

I phoned the helpline and spoke to David.

'I'll see if I can get you going remotely,' he said. 'It's often caused by the previous user not signing out properly. Hold on while I try to restart it.'

Five minutes later he came back.

'Very sorry. That one's refusing to connect. Let's try the other.'

But that, too, refused to come to life.

'Very sorry, but you know, if you run out you can always arrange with Nissan to tow you to the nearest charge point or even take you home. So you'll be OK.'

'Thank you, David, but I really was hoping to avoid that scenario. What's the one down the road like – the one on the

---

13   Ecotricity's electricity comes from renewable sources.

M6 at Todhills?'

'It's looking good. All in working order.'

As I put my phone away, two Teslas pulled up alongside the ultra-posh charge points specially reserved for them. Out of the side of one of these superior beasts, a door slowly swished open and upwards and remade itself into an awning. Two black, patent-leather, stiletto-heeled shoes emerged, followed by a black skirt, a white silk camisole and a head of shoulder-length flaxen hair. It was a woman in her mid-forties. A few seconds later, a much younger carbon copy of this apparition appeared out of the second Tesla and swivelled towards her mother. They smiled in self-congratulatory smugness, inserted hoses into their respective limousines, set the charge points whirring, linked arms and sashayed off to a taxi that had just drawn up to whisk them away to some superior residence, where they wouldn't have to mingle with the hoi polloi while their cars charged.

'Look at that, Joan. You can go to any petrol pump in the country and be certain the nozzle will fit into your petrol tank. We're in the middle of a government-promoted car revolution, but it doesn't seem to have occurred to anyone, least of all the government, to knock heads together to get EV manufacturers to agree on common connector hoses and charging standards. Four chargers in this place, and we can't use any of them.'

We slunk into Welcome Break where, in dire need of a hot drink, and to the raucous jangle of slot machines and someone screeching about undying love, we were handed a cardboard mug of warm water, a teabag, a capsule of milk and a wooden stirring stick. We did our best with these idiotic accessories and the resultant brew tasted like sawdust soup.

Our battery was down to 22 per cent when we arrived at Todhills Travelodge. The charging went smoothly, but it was a bleak business, making unwanted coffee and biscuits last for 50 minutes in a soulless atmosphere.

We spent what was left of the early evening sauntering through Carlisle and the Citadel, with its twin-drum bastions built by Henry VIII as a precaution against reprisals from Europe for his dissolution of the largely French Cistercian monasteries. Trouble with Europe has gone on for a long time. And yet, if the London Road was anything to go by, Carlisle seemed a remarkably cosmopolitan town. Apart from the charity shops, tattoo parlours and the places that were boarded up, there were eateries of every imaginable nationality. A brief count gave us the following: Malaysian (two), Thai (two), Indian (three), Spanish (two), Chinese (two), Italian (three), and one each of Aussie, Brit, Portuguese, Polish, Irish, Vietnamese and Filipino. There were also 12 barbers and hairdressing emporia. We are, it seems, a nation of fashion-conscious cosmopolitan food lovers.

NORTH-WEST COAST

4

EV AFICIONADOS

AFTER THE RAGGED SEVERITY of the border country, we came upon an utterly flat land of brilliant light, wide skies and shimmering water. Here, along the intangible margins of the Solway Firth, the land and sea get confused, merging into each other until they become indistinguishable. Between the road and the water's edge was an in-between world, a wide expanse of totally flat and marshy pasture lands, which regularly alternates between land and sea. Twice a day these lowlands are flooded by salt water and twice a day they are exposed as marsh. At Burgh-by-Sands, a good mile from the coast, frequent signs warned that at high tide the road may be as much as three feet under water. From the estuary of the Esk to Maryport, this is an Area of Outstanding Natural Beauty. Migratory waders and wildfowl overwinter here; dunlin, oyster catchers and plovers abound, as do shelduck, snipe and lapwing. Cattle sauntered across the road, sulkily ignoring us as we nudged our way forward.

The road was narrow, scarcely wide enough for two cars to pass. It was eerily quiet and flat, as if we had come across an undiscovered part of the world uncontaminated by noise and busyness. The air was still, and it had turned cold and clammy, the temperature never above 12 or 13°C. The radio was off, and so was the heating. Keen to save battery, we piled on the layers and put rugs over our knees.

We pulled in against a stone wall that looked as if it had been growing there for a thousand years. Opposite was an opening to a farmyard. Two elderly farm workers leaned against an ancient stone wall, watching my manoeuvring. It seemed as if they, too, had grown out of the land.

'That's not a good place to park,' one of them said as I got out. 'There's a heavy piece of machinery coming in here. We're waiting for it. It'll crush your car to pieces!'

'We can't find anywhere to park.'

'This place wasn't made for cars, let alone for parking,' said the other one.

'Where can we go?'

'You should go along this road,' he said, pointing westwards, 'towards Bowness. You'll learn some history there, all the way along the road. You'll see. Look out for the old railway, the canal, Hadrian's head, the old viaduct.'

And they were right. All along here, we could see history etched into the landscape, yesterday's endeavours discernible in today's geography. It was a palimpsest, traces of each generation's imprint on the land written over by succeeding generations, each layer still clearly visible.

Following the wall, the road was dead straight to Drumburgh, where there was a fortified medieval farmhouse: a bastle. It was built in 1307 using red sandstone from Hadrian's Wall. Bastles are a common feature of England's border country, all part of a series of defensive structures throughout the region, aimed at warding off border reivers and brigands, specialists in cattle theft who lived by launching murderous raids, taking cattle and, if necessary, human lives, then retreating to the refuge of the Debatable Land. A thousand years after the Romans had left, it seemed the problem of brigands had still not been resolved.

That building material, the New Red Sandstone, is typical of the region. It is sometimes referred to as 'desert sandstone' and was laid down when Britain was indeed a desert. In such an environment, the iron compounds in the sediments were easily oxidised, producing their characteristic red colouring, which explains why so many buildings in Cumbria make use of this beautiful pink-red stone.

Port Carlisle, on the edge of the Solway Firth, boasts a thousand residents. Its central feature is the Hope & Anchor, opposite which is the bowls club. A match was just finishing as we arrived, and members were putting their gear into the boots of their cars before crossing the road for lunch.

'Do you realise,' the club secretary said, 'that you're standing on a railway platform?'

It was a neat car park, with a smart gravelled surface, and running along its entire length, dividing the car park in two, was what looked like a line of old, smoothed kerbstones.

'That is the edge of what used to be the platform of the Port Carlisle railway station. The Carlisle railway terminated here, opposite the Hope & Anchor.'

Looking east along that line of stones, we could make out the full extent of where the platform had been, now overgrown with grasses and shrubs. The railway ran parallel to the line of Georgian houses that form the heart of Port Carlisle, which was developed as a port at the beginning of the nineteenth century to carry grain from Liverpool for Carlisle's thriving biscuit industry, 12 miles inland. Initially, a canal was built to carry the grain there, but when that proved to be a financial liability, it was drained and replaced by a railway in 1853. Mainly goods trains ran, although a horse-drawn passenger service was also introduced, pulling coaches known as dandy cars. The old retaining walls of the canal are still clearly visible, though almost totally silted up and overgrown.

Poking around this old canal for a while, we came across Roger, whose ramshackle workshop was tucked out of sight behind the bowling club. Roger Brough made a bit of money as a sign-maker.

'Where've you come from?' he asked.

'Oh, the North Sea. Berwick way.'

'Tell me how far you've come, and I'll make a sign.'

'Since yesterday, we've done 79 miles.'

He made a sign – ELECTRIC CAR 79 – and pointed it east. Below it was another sign, made for a couple from WALLSEND 83 the previous day. From the other direction had come visitors from BOWNESS ON SOLWAY 1, as had USA WALKERS, from too far away to measure. We put some money in the box.

'I come from a no-good family,' Roger said. 'My forebears

were bad'uns and just managed to escape from northern France and the guillotine. Here, in this border country, we were known as sheep stealers and cattle rustlers. Reivers, we were. We had quite a reputation. So we fled to northern Scotland, up near John o'Groats, where there's a place called B-R-O-U-G-H, Brough. It's right up there, the most northerly village on the British mainland. Oh yes, quite a bad lot we were.'

The village of Bowness-on-Solway has fewer than 100 houses, and the wider parish boasts 1,126 souls. It was here that we found Hadrian, another proud man, his head perched on top of a signpost telling us that it was 1,150 miles to Rome, 84 miles to Wallsend to the east, and 26 miles to Maryport, where we were headed. This wasn't a Roger sign, though; it was a local authority sign. It told us that this place was both Bowness-on-Solway and Maia; not only did Hadrian end his wall here, he also built a line of forts, and this one, at Bowness, was called Maia. Even before Roger's forebears entered the fray, this was dodgy country, open and vulnerable to incursion by the uncivilised brutes from the north, whom the Romans tried in vain to keep out. That says something about the Brits.

There's a delightful bust of Hadrian at the centre of the sign. HADRIANVS AVGVSTVS looks particularly pleased with himself. He had reason to be. He'd finished his wall, done a good job, and was now feeling full of the joys of spring. So he called this fort at Bowness, Maia, the Roman goddess of springtime, warmth and increase. Maia gave her name to the month of May. I used to live in the south of England and always experienced May, my birthday month, as a time of warmth and sunshine. In May, it was always summer. Through this gentle heat, Maia breathed out onto the world, causing plants and all living things to grow. I live in the cooler North East now, and miss the gentle warmth of Maia.

The 1,900-year-old boundary dividing 'barbarians' from civilised Romans ends here, at Bowness-on-Solway, 73 miles from where it begins at Wallsend-on-Tyne. We parked the car and walked beside the vallum. I've never understood why this ditch was called a vallum, because it's not a wall, but a ditch, and our English word 'wall' derives from 'vallum'. The puzzle was resolved when I recently read Alistair Moffat's book, *The Wall*. At the time Hadrian was building his wall, vallum meant 'a palisaded rampart', but 'the normally meticulous Bede of Jarrow' applied the word to this defensive ditch. He was wrong, but the label has stuck.[14]

The vallum was intended to restrict access to the frontier area, acting as a control zone, and the chain of Roman forts along the Solway coast was built for added security. But the empire still rotted away, leaving only this physical reminder of past glories. Together, the vallum and the wall now serve a leisure rather than military purpose – a coast-to-coast walk, known as the Hadrian's Wall Trail. Some weary walker had discarded a pair of white size-five trainers, leaving them in the vallum.

Just along the road from Maia, we looked out across the wide expanse of the Solway Firth. At the tip of a bluff jutting out into the firth, we could see the remains of what used to be, until 1921, the Solway Junction Railway. It crossed the

14 Alistair Moffat, *The Wall: Rome's Greatest Frontier*, Birlinn, 2009, p173.

Solway in a magnificent 1,950-yard-long viaduct. This was the age of railways and of iron, and Cumberland, as it was then, grew rich on it. This railway was built in the 1850s to move Cumberland's high-grade iron ores as efficiently as possible to Lanarkshire's iron works on the other side of the Solway Firth by means of the viaduct. We looked at its remnants, a few girders hanging forlornly over the sea with nowhere now to go. It seems that history had tired of trying to keep out the uncivilised brutes from the north and had decided, instead, to look for ways to build connections.

'Time for coffee and cake,' said Joan.

'There's nothing around here, is there?'

'Oh yes there is. I saw a sign back there.'

And that was where we found the Wallsend Guest House.

This Wallsend is a bit smaller than the Wallsend-on-Tyne at the other side of the country, where Hadrian's Wall begins and where, a couple of thousand years later, we built ships bigger than anything Hadrian could possibly have imagined.

'I wonder what Hadrianus Augustus would have thought, if he'd known that the area which he'd been at such pains to fortify would end up as a tea room,' Joan said.

'Perhaps he'd be pleased that he'd finally succeeded in pacifying the natives.'

We were peacefully attacking the coffee-and-walnut cake when Lynn came in.

'Are you the electric car aficionados?' she asked.

'That's us.'

'Are you on a day trip?'

'Bit longer than that,' said Joan. 'We've got this crazy idea of driving round the coasts and borders of England to see how ready we are for electric cars. Not very, we've discovered so far.'

'You're the first electric car we've seen here. We used to have a Renault Twizy and we still have a Pod Point. The idea was to encourage people to take it out for the day to see the area, especially walkers, to enable them to explore the region more fully. But there was no interest. In four years, just three people used it, and two of those were the same person. It just didn't catch on. There's a whole network of chargers along Hadrian's Wall. Best of luck on your project.'

It was lunch time, and a chill mist had crept in from the firth. On the way to Silloth, we passed another magnificent red sandstone building, Holme Cultram Abbey. Founded in 1150 by Cistercian monks, it was yet another sign of the Norman determination to control our religious inclinations. Henry VIII dissolved the abbey, but its heart survived as a lowly parish church, while the rest of the abbey crumbled to almost nothing around it. Such a huge and beautiful place in the midst of an insignificant village seemed oddly out of place. But the monks left their mark on the land in more ways than just this building, for they knew how to turn this marshy area into productive land. They built dykes, drained the land, grew crops and raised sheep. They were also iron workers and tanners. If that's all they did as monks, it would have been an excellent way to worship whatever God there may or may not be.

In the most unlikely places, the most unexpected delights turn up. At down-at-heel Silloth, we looked for a sandwich and happened across the Fairydust Emporium on Eden Street. Its decorated and bunting-clad exterior, with windows containing artwork, fabrics, quirky comments and food, drew us in. It was heaving with merriment; its décor was whimsical and there was a party atmosphere. Several tables had been arranged end to end and covered with a gigantic spread of tiered sandwiches and cakes, platters of rolls and cheeses, and bowls of salads and fruits. In another section, sofas and easy chairs, with colourful throws and cushions, were arranged around a low table. On a charming dresser was a display of soft toys and fabric mushrooms. A tall lamp stood in the corner, with a floral fabric shade with tassels. This was more like the comfortable lounge of a large family home than a restaurant, a fairyland of happiness and comfort. Tucked away in corners were smaller circular tables set for four or six, with brightly coloured tablecloths. Baubles, decorations and tinsel, wall pictures and bunting made of it a cornucopia of delight.

'Is it normally like this?' Joan asked.

'Every day. Today, it's a birthday party at one table, and that one over there is a lunch club. If you're wanting a table, there'll be one in about half an hour.'

'How about some takeaway sandwiches?'

'We can do those for you in about ten minutes.'

In the midst of all that delightfully happy catering, they managed to find the time to fit us up with hefty cheese, salad and prawn sandwiches, which we took with us to the edge of the firth at Beckfoot. We should have been able to look across to the Dumfries coast, but all that was visible was a wall of fog. The coast was littered with caravan parks here, though no one seemed to be at home. We found a rough-hewn lay-by on the edge of a silent sea where a few languid waves wearily slopped onto a black shingly beach.

'Just the place to eat our sandwich and have a snooze,' Joan said. 'This miserable weather won't last long, but I can see a patch of blue sky moving in from the east. It'll be here soon, you'll see, and meanwhile I'd like you to switch the windscreen wipers on so that I can at least see the sea.'

'Would that be wise? I mean, we'd need to have the engine switched on all the time, and we don't know where we're going to charge yet, do we?'

'Sounds a bit obsessive, Clive.'

'Someone's got to think ahead.'

'Oh well, might as well finish this sandwich then, and go into an early afternoon snooze. Where did we put those blankets?'

According to Zap-Map, the nearest charge point was at Workington, at Tesco on New Bridge Road. Following Lettie's instructions, we headed south, through Maryport. It was three o'clock and the uniformed youngsters were coming out of school. They engulfed the streets, held up the traffic, climbed into buses, cars and coaches, and filled the air with their chatter and laughter. For these few moments, the town was gridlocked, but it was worth the delay just to see youngsters happily releasing all the tension of the day's lessons.

The slow-moving line of traffic edged towards Workington, and along the coast we could see the wind farms of Oldside and Siddick waving their arms triumphantly, stirring up local discontent. Along the roadside was an array of posters:

NO TO TURBINES and NO MORE. In the mid-1990s, these two wind farms had been given permission to operate for 25 years, but the decision had been controversial. It was argued that they would spoil the natural beauty of the Cumbrian coast, perhaps even turn tourists away, and in any case, it was doubtful they would produce as much electricity as a single nuclear-powered station. A decade earlier, the then Workington MP, Tony Cunningham, had warned planners about the 'need to balance the cumulative visual intrusion against the electricity they produce'.[15] Now, approaching the lapse of that 25-year agreement, an application had been made for a 10-year extension. This had stirred up those long-buried resentments and the local populace was in a protesting frame of mind once more.

We were now in Genie territory, a charging provider we had not used before. Happily, I had read something about Genie's operations in this neck of the woods and had duly signed up and been issued with an RFID card. In doing so, I had received a letter welcoming me to the GeniePoint Network. This was 'the beginning of a revolution', it boasted. But there was no sign of any charge point anywhere in the Tesco's car park that Zap-Map had indicated to us.

'Sorry. Know nothing about it, mate,' the store manager told us. 'There could be one at Allerdale House, a few hundred yards away. It's where Allerdale Borough Council has its offices. Seems a likely place.'

It was by now raining heavily and we were nearing the end of the day. In the dusky half-light, Joan spotted the familiar white box, in the corner of a small car park, carpeted with

15   *Times & Star*, 26 October 2007.

rain-sodden early autumn leaf-fall. As fixing up the charging was often a long and tedious business, it was clear this was going to be a waterproofs job, the full works – trousers, coat, hat. I was pretty good at getting dressed in confined spaces. I'd acquired the skill when I was a child and needed to get dressed for school under the blankets in a bitterly cold bedroom.

'I'll just wait in the car. There's no point in both of us going through all that, is there?'

I inserted the CHAdeMO hose, swiped the RFID card and waited for the charge to begin. Nothing happened.

'Not working,' I called through the fractionally opened window. 'I'm going to have to call them.'

With the light of my mobile phone, I searched for the helpline number, dialled and spoke to Jo.

'What's the ID of the charger?' she asked.

'GP10315.'

'Can you confirm the number of your RFID card?'

I fumbled to read it in the half-light.

'Ok, I'll try to operate it remotely. Hold on a few moments.'

'Nothing happening here, Jo.'

'Give me your number and I'll phone you back in a few minutes.'

I had a choice of getting back into the car in my dripping wet clothes or going for a short walk. I explored the local environment. It was depressing. Ten minutes later, Jo called, and my heart momentarily lifted at the thought that I might be relieved of my misery.

'Very sorry, but we don't seem able to fix it. I'm afraid you'll have to find another charge point.'

'Ok, Jo. Thank you. We're making for Whitehaven. What's the condition of the charge point there?'

'We know it was working a couple of hours ago. You should be all right.'

What had started out as a magnificent day, dull weatherwise but full of historical interest, was rapidly disappearing into a black hole. My old religious paranoia began to return. I must have done something wrong, must have offended God, or perhaps one of the Roman gods. Can you imagine drivers of conventional cars having to fill their tanks, drop by miserable drop, with an avalanche of water falling on them, and taking the best part of an hour to do it? There'd be a public outcry; demonstrations in the streets; London would be brought to a standstill; questions would be asked in Parliament. They'd probably even blame the EU. Perhaps there was a case to be made for taking up the matter with the European Court of Justice over infringement of human rights. If my MP could take this matter up with Parliament, she'd make a name for herself and probably be awarded a Dameship, or some such thing.

'The stupid thing is,' I said to Joan, as I tried to get my wet things off in the car without doing too much damage to the upholstery, 'our hotel is just a couple of miles away from that charge point, and we're going to have to kill time in Whitehaven while we refuel because no one's got the nous to think about putting one at the hotel.'

We got to Senhouse Street car park in Whitehaven without any bother, and the equipment worked perfectly, though it would still take an hour to fill us up.

'How're we going to spend this time, Joanie?'

'We need tea. Proper afternoon tea. You know – sandwiches and cake.'

'D'you think we'll find it here? It seems so impoverished.'

Whitehaven grew rich during the Industrial Revolution, mainly on account of its coal. It was also a port, at one time the second busiest after London, with important trading links with the American colonies. Those trans-Atlantic links gave the port its notorious connections with the slave trade, by which many people became very rich. Many fine buildings were put up in the Georgian period in the heyday of its prosperity, often using the prolific New Red Sandstone. So many things of great beauty often come from shadowy backgrounds. Since then, in common with many other coastal towns and with the decline of coal and heavy industry, the town has struggled to survive, and finds itself lagging behind the rest of the UK economically.

We took a walk along Millennium Promenade to the harbour area, the coastguard centre and the lighthouse. The only place that seemed mildly welcoming was the Waterfront pub, but at least it would be indoors and possibly warm. We weren't expecting much. Apart from the barmaid, there was just one punter in the huge public bar area.

'Any chance of a cup of tea?'

'How about some freshly baked scones with strawberry jam and a selection of cakes as well?'

'Perfect,' Joan said.

'Just go through to the dining room and I'll bring it along.'

There were about a dozen tables, but we were the only customers. Within five minutes, a large pot of steaming hot tea was on the table. Twenty minutes later, two huge scones, fresh out of the oven, were put before us, with a dollop of butter, a dish of jam and a generous selection of cakes. The gods were on our side after all.

It was just over two miles to our hotel. The manager happened to be at reception and greeted us.

'Had a good journey?' he enquired.

'It's not been without its problems, but an excellent afternoon tea at the Waterfront pub put it all right.'

'We could have done that for you,' he said.

'Not unless you have a charge point for an electric car. You don't, do you?'

''Fraid not.'

'Well, there you are then. That's why we couldn't have tea with you. That's an opportunity cost you're incurring. Nothing would have pleased us more than to have been able to come here and have tea and cakes while our car was charging. Best Western is beginning to do it. Why not you?'

'Oh yeah, I'd never thought of that. I'll definitely put it on the agenda for the management meeting next month.'

5

I'LL STICK TO MY DIESEL

ON EGREMONT'S MAIN STREET was a sculpture of a haematite worker. Bent low, almost horizontal, he pushes a railway wagon loaded with ore, the bulging muscles of his lean body taut and as hard as the steel they are destined to produce. Haematite is the name of the rich iron ores found along the Cumbrian coast, and this and similar sculptures are a striking commemoration of the muscle, ingenuity and endurance that made Cumbria rich during the Industrial Revolution. They were created by Colin Telfer using iron dust and resin. He had worked at the pit tops as a winder and engine man; when he was made redundant, he went to Carlisle College of Art and soon began producing these magnificent works that adorn so many streets in Cumbria and Northern Ireland.

Egremont lies a little inland from St Bees. As well as haematite, geography also endowed the region with the

Cumberland coalfield. It was this juxtaposition of iron ore and coal that made the Cumbrian coastal region, as far south as Barrow-in-Furness, one of the erstwhile powerhouses of the British economy.

Our route was along the A595, a road that separates two different worlds. To the east is the Lake District, much of it prosperous and thriving. It earns its living through farming and tourism, heaving with visitors for much of the year, especially in the summer months. The western coastal strip, however, bears the scars of a brief wave of prosperity that quickly came and – just as quickly – went. Millom, on the Duddon estuary, was created around iron ore. It was a tiny hamlet until the 1860s, when the railway came, iron works and furnaces were opened, and Millom Newtown was built. There were jobs aplenty, the population grew, the town thrived. In 1967, the population was 11,000, but the following year the mines and the ironworks closed and within a year the population had fallen to 7,000. The story of Millom is the story of the Cumbrian coast. A wave of prosperity comes and moves on, leaving wounds in the social fabric that take decades to heal.

We decided to be extravagant, put the heating up to 17.5°C and look for a sandwich. That's how we found Broughton-in-Furness, a few miles up the River Duddon. If there had been a blazing sun, we might have imagined the shady square where we parked to be in the south of France, but the effect was spoiled by the stair-rodding rain. It was a small, tightly-packed cobbled square, with a large central horse chestnut tree, ideal for sitting under on a sweltering day.

The square was Georgian, designed by John Gilpin Sawrey.

We happened to pull up in front of a set of stocks, behind which an obelisk commemorated the jubilee of George III. The Tourist Information Centre occupied a small corner of what used to be the Town Hall, and inside was another Roger, of no relation to the signpost Roger of Port Carlisle. 'Dapper' was the word Joan used to describe him. He was sporting a red tie with diagonal black stripes, a burgundy jacket, brown corduroy trousers and matching cap, and military-brown polished brogues. Not a hair was out of place, and he spoke with a crisp Home Counties accent.

'Busy today?'

'No, you're my first visitors. No one's been.'

Joan told him about our mission and about the wonderful morning we'd had on Solway the previous day.

'Now that's the kind of place that has history,' Roger said. 'But no one wants to go there. Everyone wants to go to Windermere and Keswick. They forget all the history in places like Millom next door, and now it's all been side-lined; forgotten. All that history has just gone.'

'Quite agree. But right now, we're wondering if you can tell us where the nearest charge point is for electric cars.'

'Ah, now you've put me on the spot.'

'Well, the government's on the spot too,' I said. 'They've come out with this policy of getting us all to drive electric cars by 2040, but don't seem to have given a thought to the provision of charge points.'[16]

'I'll stick to my trusty diesel,' Roger said.

'Ah, but wait 'til 2040, when you'll have no choice.'

'This octogenarian isn't going there,' he said. 'If you're

---

16   Later, the deadline was moved to 2030.

going to write about your exploits, you should call it the elusive charge. The trouble with these people in London is that they don't know we exist. They haven't got a clue. They're very tall and go round with their heads in the clouds. They just don't know how we live here.'

'On another, more pressing subject,' Joan asked, 'Is there by any chance a café attached to this delightful T.I.C.?'

'We have two, but they're not attached. Detached.'

'We don't mind detached.'

'Right,' said Roger. 'The first one is across the square. What I would call a proper English tearoom. No table has legs of the same length and no chair is the same as another. The other one is…'

And here he just gestured by pushing his nose up with his index finger.

'We'll take the proper English tearoom.'

'It's called The Square. Just on the corner, over there. Say hello to Jane.'

Joan ran across, head bowed, hood up. I retrieved my notebook from the car, pushed it inside my raincoat and scurried across to The Square. The door opened onto bare boards, a row of coat hooks on the wall bearing a heavy burden of sopping coats, an umbrella stand and a collection of wellies and walking boots. Jane was crossing from one room to the other.

'Are you Jane?'

'Yes, I am.'

'Roger says hello.'

'Stand-by-your-bed Roger?'

'Stand by your bed?'

'Yes. Roger is a retired colonel. Very proper, very correct. Does everything by the book.'

The Square lived up to Roger's description. Wooden floor in one room, tiles in the other. The tables all looked as if they had come from the kind of kitchen we had at home in the 1950s – wooden, scrubbed, drawers under the surface with metal handles, each one different from all the others. I sat down next to Joan and immediately found myself three inches lower. Joan, who is small, towered above me.

Entering Barrow-in-Furness, we turned into a giant industrial estate; a huge range of businesses filled every space – engineering, timber, furniture, carpets, kitchen showrooms, BAE systems engineering, Asda, Argos, Poundstretcher. Haematite had been worked in Furness since prehistoric times and up to the 1940s. Here, it was known as 'red earth', and almost overnight, it made Barrow's fortune. Red earth, the railway mania, and the fever of speculation that gripped the country in the nineteenth century, combined to create a powerful magnet, drawing workers in from far and wide.

Barrow was one of the fastest growing towns in the country in the nineteenth century. In 1851, its population was a mere 450. Ten years later, it had multiplied six times. Another 10 years, and the population stood at 19,000. By 1881, it was 47,000, more than one hundred times its level of 30 years earlier. There was tremendous overcrowding, with an average of seven people for every dwelling. The town became a building site. That era in Britain's economic history saw one of the biggest mass migrations of all time, a great shaking loose of migrants from the countryside, a huge movement of people from the land to the emerging industrial towns and cities. So rapidly did Barrow expand that it outgrew its infrastructure, with insufficient hospitals and churches and no administrative base in the form of local government or a police force.

The special quality about the iron ore here on the Cumberland coast was its purity. Most of Britain's ores were useless for steel-making because of their phosphorous content, so the Cumbrian coast, with its haematite, had a competitive edge over other iron ore regions. Towards the end of the nineteenth century, however, a way was found of removing the phosphorus, so that the cheaper phosphoric ores on the other side of the country could be used for steel making. This was one of the factors that caused Barrow to lose its geographical advantage. One region's fortune is another's misfortune. Barrow fell, Teesside rose.

When the decline came, it came quickly. Furnaces were turned off and, for one-industry towns like Barrow, the consequences were grave and immediate. The social dislocation that resulted provided the stimulus for a new migration stream, this time to the New Worlds of the United States, South Africa and Australasia. Migration has always been with us; there's nothing new about it.

Barrow's population peaked at about 83,000 in 1921; a decade later, it had fallen by 10,000. According to the Office for National Statistics, the population of Barrow-in-Furness is in long-term decline, largely because of out-migration. Today, the biggest employer in town is BAE, but a bright star on the horizon is the 'Green Revolution' and the offshore

Walney Wind Farms. It is the new industries associated with sustainable energy on which many coastal areas are pinning their hopes.

We were making for Hampsfell House Hotel, in Grange-over-Sands. Joan knew this area. She and her family used to have holidays there, and her dad went to live in a local preachers' retirement home on the other side of the town. She wanted to see the place again. Grange could have been in a completely different world from Barrow, a universe away from the down-troddenness of the general run of coastal communities.

In a secluded location tucked away at the head of Morecambe Bay, Grange is wealthy and up-market. With a population of just over 4,000, it has the air of a community that is well satisfied with itself. It is also part of the Duchy of Lancaster, and no doubt that helps to boost its self-perception of specialness. Posters along the way declared NO PYLONS.

'I bet they want their electricity, though,' Joan said.

There's something endearing about large English houses that have been sensitively converted into hotels with modern facilities, and Hampsfell House was no exception. What was once a substantial room had had a corner taken away to accommodate a shower. A cosy armchair that once would have spread elegantly in a spacious environment was now squeezed comfortably into the bay window, which itself had been divided into two, the other half appearing in the new en suite. Old picture rails 18 inches from the ceiling now served a different decorative purpose, separating two different pastel shades of wall.

The whole house was full of intriguing twists and turns,

alcoves filled with elegant furniture from a distant age, ancient sideboards, rickety wardrobes, jardinières supporting vases filled with flowers from the garden. There were twisty staircases with shiny, well-used banisters. Landings were provided with stools or cosy chairs, or small cupboards with plants on them. Brass hooks had been thoughtfully screwed to the backs of doors to provide much-needed hanging space in the bedroom and there were proper, well-placed bedside lamps. Breakfast prunes had been stoned, the marmalade was offered in little dishes, each with a spoon, tea was in a teapot with a cosy.

All this ensured that, despite all the necessary modernisations, Hampsfell House retained its atmosphere as a grand family house and home, contrasting delightfully with the bold, brash uniformity of the modern purpose-built hotel. The test of real comfort is to be able to forget that you are in a hotel. The manicured orderliness of the modern hotel all too often puts appearance and style above practicality and comfort.

At dinner that evening, Rose, the proprietress asked, 'Are you just touring around, then?'

'Kind of,' I said. 'We're doing it by electric car.'

'Where do you charge up?'

'Nearest place with a rapid charger is Ulverston. We had to spend an hour in a pub just before we came here, snacking stuff we didn't want, just to kill time. Tomorrow, we're going to a hotel in Lytham that we know has a charger.'

'What hotel?'

'Best Western. I have a list of all their hotels that have charge points. That's why we're going there.'

'Is it a rapid one?'

'No, not necessary. We're staying overnight, so it can be a slow one. We'll be able to top the battery up while we sleep. Perfect.'

'Can you just plug into an ordinary socket?'

'Yes, but it's not advisable if the wiring is old. Because of the high current demands of EVs and the long time spent charging, it puts a strain on the system and could blow it. It's best to have a dedicated charging unit. I can't tell you how much we appreciate it when there's a charge point at a hotel. Killing time somewhere else, when we could be having afternoon tea in a place like this, is ghastly.'

'Oh, I'm going to get one,' she said. 'Then I'll put on our website, "Drivers of EVs welcome." Thank you, thank you.'

Brian, her husband, came across and joined in.

'I can easily do that. I've already got outside wiring. It was intended for a motor home. Yep, I'll put a Pod Point in. Easy.'

Over breakfast the next morning, Joan pointed out two old muskets on the wall.

'I wonder,' she said, 'if one of those was used to kill Humphrey.'

'Who was Humphrey?'

'The last wolf in England. He's believed to have been killed on Humphrey Head.'

'Not possible,' Brian said. 'Muskets weren't invented 'til the sixteenth century and Humphrey was killed 200 years before that. They're shotguns, by the way.'

'Oh dear. We've got the detail wrong, haven't we? But it makes a good story.'

Humphrey Head Point juts into Morecambe Bay and for

the most part is surrounded by water, so poor Humphrey was cornered and didn't stand a chance. We walked down there and spent a pleasant morning moseying along the promenade. Across the bay and 10 miles away, we could see the square outline of the Heysham I nuclear power station. A couple in their sixties came along on their electric bikes. They had cycled all the way from Inverness, used to live in Berwick, and were on their way to see relatives in Oxfordshire.

'How far can you go on a full battery?' I asked them.

'Seventy miles,' the man said. 'That's enough for a day. Then we unclip the battery, take it with us into our B&B and charge it overnight.'

I drooled with envy over those bikes. What superb machines! What a magnificent way to travel!

'What about you?' the woman asked. 'How far can you go?'

'Yesterday,' I said, 'we did 74 miles on two-thirds of the battery.'

'So where are you off to now?'

'Down there,' I said, pointing across the wide expanse of the bay. 'Morecambe, Blackpool and then Lytham St Annes, where we're staying the night, before moving on to Liverpool the next day.'

6

RAILWAYS FOR THE MILLIONS

'WE MUST HAVE RAILWAYS for the millions', proclaimed Thomas Cook in 1841.

Even then, this iconic gentleman could see which way the wind was blowing. By the middle of the nineteenth century, railway lines had begun to redraw Britain's geography. When the Lancashire cotton mills closed once a year to allow the machinery to be serviced, railways made it possible for streams of workers to make for the fast-developing seaside resorts. Pleasures that were once the province of the wealthy became available to everyone. Quaint seaside villages were transformed into thriving seaside resorts open to the masses, and places like Morecambe, Blackpool, Scarborough, Skegness and Brighton mushroomed.

A major attraction at Morecambe was the vast waters of its famous bay. From the promenade at Morecambe, you can look across Morecambe Bay to the Lake District, hovering on the horizon. Morecambe Bay is blessed with long stretches of open shore and vast reaches of sand, but this is a mixed blessing; those sands, and the waters that wash over them twice a day, are fraught with danger. The same ice that left a swarm of drumlins on the edge of the Cheviot Hills also dumped an eighty-metre-thick layer of soft sediments into what is now Morecambe Bay. The vast mass of water released into the oceans by the melting ice caused sea levels to rise. The Bay was flooded and the estuaries of the five rivers that drain into it were drowned, giving rise to huge tidal estuaries that coalesced to form the largest expanse of inter-tidal mud flats and sand in the country. If you wanted to paddle in the sea when the tide is out, you'd have to walk several miles to get to it. As for incoming tides, the funnel shape of the bay turns these surging waters into tidal bores, with speeds of up to nine knots. This is more than 10mph, and is faster than most people can jog.

The vicious currents that carve out deep channels and hollows also fill them with lethal quicksands, making Morecambe Bay exceptionally dangerous. This was demonstrated in February 2004 when a team of cockle pickers, unlawfully brought into the country by criminal gangs and put to work at night – the best time for picking cockles – was caught by an incoming tide. Twenty-one of them were drowned. The dangers have long been understood, and it is for this reason that, for those wishing to walk across the sands, royal guides have been appointed since about the sixteenth century. Cedric Robinson, the Queen's Guide to the Sands since 1963, reckoned that the tide comes in faster than a horse can gallop.

When the railway arrived in Morecambe in the middle of the nineteenth century, it marked the beginning of a whole new era for the town, bringing visitors in their thousands. The two piers were built in the nineteenth century to be the main entertainment hubs of the fledgling resort, and some of the country's best-known shows and entertainers with huge national appeal gravitated there. Eric Morecambe, the town's most famous son, and its equally famous daughter, Thora Hird, who began her acting career at the Royalty Theatre, symbolised the entertainment spirit of Morecambe in its heyday.

But almost as quickly as all this came, it went. Several changes brought the town down: both piers were lost, through fire and storm; our domestic textile industry gave way to foreign competition; package holidays whisked all those holidaymakers away to the sunshine belt of Southern Europe; and the cold open-air swimming pool became redundant because no one had ever really enjoyed swimming in bitterly cold water, even though we Brits are good at pretending we love such torments.

We arrived in Morecambe on a sunny and cheerful September day and walked from the car park at the new railway station through gloomy streets of tired terraced houses. It seemed to be a rather sad and down-trodden town. The once-bustling terraces with thriving B&Bs and 'No vacancies' signs had become shabby, with peeling paint and boarded-up windows. Brave attempts had been made on the promenade and Marine Road to maintain a sense of jollity, with the usual cheap and cheerful facade of souvenirs, candyfloss, amusement arcades and ice cream parlours. But it was a lukewarm, weary jollity. Morecambe had the air of a has-been town.

Morecambe Bay Coastal Community Team was trying to turn the appeal of the town's tourism base around by promoting holidays focusing on coastal walks, ecology, birdlife and heritage trails. On Marine Road, near the stone jetty and opposite the Midland Hotel, we found a hub of optimism. We'd been looking for lunch and found ourselves in what used to be the Morecambe promenade railway station, which opened in 1907. This magnificent stone building was the terminus of the former North Western Railway. Now, it was a bustle of bright and purposeful activity. Sally, who came from South Shields and had recently graduated with a degree in tourism, had just landed a job as the manager of the Platform arts centre, a cluster of tourism and entertainment facilities within the station building, including an Information Centre and the excellent pub-cum-restaurant where we dined. As well as providing good food, it also had a fully-booked schedule of live entertainment for the year ahead.

It was time to move on to our next charge point, which was at the Nissan dealership, just to the south of Blackpool. We could be relaxed about charging at Nissan. Nothing, surely, could possibly go wrong there. It would be an opportunity, too, to enjoy a stroll along the promenade in the warmth of a perfect autumn day.

The main difference between Morecambe and Blackpool

is that of size. With a population of 139,000, Blackpool is four times the size of Morecambe. In the 1990s, Morecambe cancelled its seafront illuminations because it couldn't compete with Blackpool's. Like Morecambe, Blackpool too grew rapidly, and once again, it was the railway that did it. From 1851 to 1881, its population multiplied by more than five times to 14,000. Two decades later, it had more than tripled again to 47,000 and by 1951 it had tripled again, making Blackpool the holiday mecca of the country and what is today Lancashire's largest town.

It wasn't just the railway that did it. It was the first municipality in the world to have electric street lighting. In 1879, about 100,000 people travelled to Blackpool from all over the country to witness the turning on of this 'artificial sunshine', and in 1912, 10,000 light bulbs were switched on to celebrate the visit of Princess Louise. And that was the beginning of the Blackpool Illuminations. Blackpool also had its piers – the only resort in the country to have three – and, of course, its tower. By the 1950s, it was pulling in 17 million pleasure seekers a year.

But Blackpool's bonanza couldn't last. It went the way of so many of our coastal communities, destroyed by the tsunami of technological and industrial change: the textile industry nose-dived as competition from overseas increased; package holidays were invented; the motor car and a greatly improved road network made us all more mobile. Why stay at Blackpool for a week and shiver, when you can just as easily sunbathe on the Côte d'Azure? Blackpool's fall was catastrophic. On Thursday 1 March 2018, when BBC television's *Question Time* visited Blackpool, the chairman, David Dimbleby, introduced the show by announcing that Blackpool was the fourth most deprived local authority in the country and that, in the recent referendum about whether the UK should leave or remain in the European Union, 67.5 per cent had voted to leave. The statistics for the municipality for 2017 were sobering: the fourth highest rate of antidepressant prescriptions in the country, the highest proportion of the working-age population who were too sick to work, the highest rates of obesity, smoking and alcoholic liver disease and, in one council ward (Broomfield), the lowest male life expectancy in the whole of England and Wales.

At the Nissan charge point, a couple were charging their car. We checked with the manager to see if it was OK for us to charge there.

'Go ahead. It's on us. By the way,' he said, 'we're now bringing out the new Leaf. It's got a range of 220 miles. Soon they'll be doing more than 300 miles. You won't need a charge point then. We'll all just be charging at home. Make yourselves comfortable over there. Help yourselves to hot drinks.'

We settled to read some magazines, sip hot chocolates and wait for our turn with the charge point.

'So, d'you think we'd better upgrade?' I said to Joan.

'No. Don't even think about it.'

After thirty minutes, the call came. 'We're full up. It's all yours.'

So we plugged in and had some more hot chocolate while it charged.

'What an excellent day this is turning out to be, Joanie.'

Forty minutes later, we finished our third hot chocolate, said an amiable goodbye to the manager, and got into the car. I slipped it into reverse.

There's a kind of unthinking devil-may-care insouciance that can overtake you when you think everything is fine with your world. You feel invincible, that nothing can touch you, and you slip into a calm indifference to the manifold dangers that lurk round every corner. I recently heard Jared Diamond say on *Desert Island Discs* that, now that he had become elderly, he had developed an attitude of mind that he described as 'creative paranoia'. The environment out there is dangerous, he said, and it's out to get you, so think about everything that can go wrong and prepare yourself for it. He reckoned that the main danger for those who have reached a certain age is falling and breaking one of their bones, so they need to make sure that they hold the banister when going down the stairs, are aware of unevenness in the pavement, watch out for obstacles and take avoiding action. I did none of those, and was brought down to earth by Joan's shout.

'What?'

'You've hit something.'

'But I can't have done. It was perfectly clear behind us when we came into this bay.'

'That was an hour and a half ago.'

A cold sweat ran off me. I knew I'd been a complete prat.

I had reversed straight into a beautifully refurbished red car, just arrived on the forecourt and put up for sale right behind us. There was a scratch on its nearside wing panel, and similar damage to our offside rear panel. If I drove away quickly now, no one would notice. But just at that inconvenient moment when I desperately needed to disappear, a little voice inside reminded me that that may not be quite the right thing to do.

'I'm convinced that camera has a blind spot.'

'Yes, dear. It must have. There can be no other explanation.'

'I'm going to have to go and confess, aren't I?'

''Fraid so.'

'I don't suppose...'

'Don't even think of it. There are many things I'd do for you, and I love you dearly, but this time you are on your own.'

In the nineteenth and early twentieth centuries, the good people of the delightful town of St Annes, a few miles to the south, made it their business to encourage an altogether better class of visitors than the working-class hoi polloi who went to Blackpool. They wanted an up-market town, definitely not the cheap and cheerful kind of resort that characterised their northern neighbour. They wanted to discourage those oiks from visiting their hallowed precincts and bringing nasty habits to their exclusive paradise. This was achieved by charging higher prices and by providing more in the way of refined entertainment, which they assumed those ruffians wouldn't understand, let alone enjoy. The pier was designed for sedate promenading, and the powers-that-be had ensured that the only places where alcohol could be purchased were the bars of the 10 licensed hotels. It was assumed that no common people would dare to enter these.

However, what the town lacked in pubs, it made up for

with its abundant supply of churches. This was a definite deviation from the norm. In most towns and cities, and even in most villages, it's the other way round, with more pubs than churches. The reason for this is simple: the British trust alcohol more than they do theology, because it's more reliable![17] And so it was that the Moorish-styled pavilion on St Annes pier hosted concerts, operas and vaudeville acts, attracting such famous performers as George Formby, Gracie Fields and Russ Conway. It wasn't until the 1950s that standards were allowed to slip and an amusement arcade was built on the pier, followed, in the 1970s, by crazy golf.

Although today it belongs to the southern end of Greater Blackpool, Lytham St Annes has managed to retain something of its air of exclusivity. It helps that it is the home of one of the premier golf courses in the world – the Royal Lytham & St Annes Golf Club – and with its clutch of additional golf courses, its well-tended gardens, pretty parks, boating lake and lovingly restored windmill, set in the midst of manicured lawns, it well-deserves the soubriquet of 'garden town by the sea'.

An elderly woman was sitting on the grass, close to the statue of Les Dawson and next to the entrance to St Annes pier. The lawned area rose away from the pavement and she had stepped up to it to avoid a large puddle. There was a pained look on her face.

'That woman doesn't look happy. The grass'll be soaking. It's been raining all night,' Joan said.

'Are you alright?' I asked as we drew level.

---

17   Penny Mordaunt and Chris Lewis, *Greater: Britain After the Storm*, Biteback Publishing, 2021, p22.

'I can't stand up,' she said.

'I think I know you,' Joan said. 'You were in the hotel, weren't you?'

'Yes, I was. We've just come here for a bit of a stroll to look at the pier.'

'Do you want help?'

'My husband's gone to get help. But he's so embarrassed by it all. That's him coming now.'

He was a tall thin man, carrying a brown paper bag. When he saw us from several yards away, he stopped dead in his tracks.

'It's awful,' said the woman. 'He's so embarrassed. I think he's got the beginnings of dementia. He can't bring himself to tell anyone that he needs help.'

He came slowly towards us, looking appalled.

'Hello,' we said.

But there was no response.

To the woman I said, 'Do you want help to stand up?'

'Yes.'

'Will you be all right if we get you standing?'

'Yes.'

'Will you be able to walk?'

'Yes, I just need getting on my feet.'

So we took an arm each and lifted her, while her husband turned away in embarrassment.

7

GIANTS AND SLAVES

LIVERPOOL BURST UPON the British public in the 1960s and '70s with the *Liver Birds*, Ken Dodd, Cilla Black and the Beatles. But at the same time, quietly beavering away and with less razzamatazz, Bessie Braddock was also making her mark on British life as a Liverpool MP. We'd called at Lime Street railway station to admire her life-size statue, alongside that of Ken Dodd. Bessie had one hand raised to greet the comedian, with the other holding an egg; Ken was flourishing his tickling stick. A steaming mug of coffee sat on Bessie's shoulder and a tall, lean man in a smart Italian coat was consulting his phone.

'Like my table?' he asked, as we approached.

'Ah, so it's *your* coffee. Thought someone must have been in a rush and left it.'

'Do you know what she's holding in her hand?'

'Well, it's an egg of course.'

'Yes, but can you see what's on it?'

We peered.

'It's a lion.'

Bessie Braddock, he reminded us, was MP for Liverpool Exchange from 1945 to 1970, and she campaigned on social issues, especially housing and public health. She was also responsible for getting the lion mark on British eggs, a safety scheme introduced by the British Egg Marketing Board to reduce cases of salmonella poisoning caused by eggs from unreliable sources. Nevertheless, in 1988 Edwina Currie threw the cat among the pigeons by announcing in Parliament that most UK egg production was affected by salmonella, for which she was sacked. Although Ms Currie had probably exaggerated the problem, there was undoubtedly some truth in her comments. The real breakthrough came only in 1998, when vaccination of hens at farms using the new British Lion mark became routine.[18] Now, we are assured that our eggs are not only safe, they are also healthy; we can all 'go to work on an egg', as the advertising slogan had it, with complete peace of mind.

'I've just come back from Geneva,' our new friend said. 'I'm writing a book – a serious one – about refugees.'

'We met a Polish man on our way here,' I said. 'It was in Southport and he was living on the pavement. He was a handsome, well-spoken man in his thirties. Been there for thirteen years. He came here with his father. Had a good, steady job, but his life fell apart when his father died. Became ill, couldn't work, couldn't pay the rent and lost his home.

---

18   *The Independent*, 17 November 2006.

He couldn't get any financial help because he didn't have an address, and he couldn't get an address because he didn't have any money. Does he count as a refugee?'

''Fraid not. My name's Dan by the way. Dan Jones. What're you doing here, anyhow?'

Joan explained.

'Ah then you must go to see Danielle. She will be able to tell you all about charge points in Liverpool. You'll find her at the Q-Park, in Liverpool ONE, on the other side of the city. I'm Dan, she's Danielle. No relation.'

'Where's Liverpool ONE?'

'Ask anyone. They'll tell you how to get there. Can't miss it.'

'And what is it?'

'It's a shopping complex, the largest in Liverpool.'

Inside the Shiraz Palace, on the corner of Ranelagh Street, we found a confusion of bubbling happiness. It wasn't until 4 am, we were told, that the night revellers had dispersed. When we dropped in to write up the conversation with Dan, the 20 or so generously proportioned tables were filled by a more sober crowd – mostly fifty-somethings enjoying Saturday morning brunch. Groups of buddies were talking amid a scattering of newspapers; well-married couples studied the news in comfortable silence; one couple consumed their ginormous meal in matrimonial isolation, mutually invisible – their silence uncomfortable.

Most of the sounds of happiness came from one long table of 16 women having a girlie weekend. They were from Wales – mostly Anglesey – plus one from Maidstone in

Kent. They told me they were a friendship group, celebrating just that – friendship. Above us, a sprinkling of red lights the size of bilberries intermingled with a filigree of twigs, supporting a sign urging us all to 'Think Happy'. We obeyed this instruction by ordering two Mediterranean breakfasts at £6 each: lettuce, olives, tomatoes, gherkins, fried egg, superb vegetarian sausages made on the premises, haricot beans, a piccalilli-type chutney and pitta bread.

Along Ranelagh Street near the bottom of Church Street we met two young women, Amy and Martha, both wearing red tops, holding clipboards and heading towards the waterfront.

'We're looking for Q-Park and Liverpool ONE,' Joan said.

'Oh, we're going there. We'll show you.'

'You look very business-like. What're you doing?'

'We're checking the place over for Christmas lights.'

'It's a bit early for that, isn't it?' said Joan.

'It's a big job. We need to do the planning.'

'How d'you get into that kind of job?'

'We both have degrees in marketing. Just take the lift to the basement and you'll find Q-Park there.'

Q-Park is a secure, upmarket car park provider, and Liverpool ONE a massive retail and entertainment mall close to the waterfront area. It was in this car park, in the rather clinical concrete bowels of the earth, that we met Will, a car park attendant.

'Do you know Danielle?' I asked.

'I think she's just gone for her lunch, but I'll have a look. Who's asking?'

'We've come here in our electric car. We've been told she

knows about charge points, and that's what we're interested in. We'd like to pick her brains.'

Will took us down another level and led us to a neon-lit office in the concrete depths of the building, next to a noisy ventilation system. Danielle had just put her coat on and was handing over to Ian for the lunchtime shift.

'You must be Danielle,' Joan said.

Danielle looked slightly bemused and excited, a broad grin on her attractive round face framed by ash blonde hair.

'This is so random,' she squealed with delight. 'Why's anyone coming to ask for me by name? No one's ever done that before.'

'Oh my god,' she continued, with further yelps of delight. 'How did you know? This is so random.'

'We met a man called Dan – Dan Jones – and he told us about you. We're researching EV charge points. Dan said something about small electric vehicles you have here for ferrying customers to and from this car park to the various stores up above.'

'Oh, that was some time ago, but we've discontinued it now. It wasn't worthwhile. Not enough people used it.'

'Do you have any charge points here?'

'I'll show you.'

She led us to a Franklin Energy charge point another floor down. Franklin Energy got ahead of the game by installing the UK's first privately funded charging network and the first publicly accessible charging point, here in this car park, in March 2016.

'This is so random. This is the weirdest day of my life,' Danielle said again, as she kindly led us to the lift before a final non-random farewell.

'Well, you never know,' I said, 'I may even put you in the book I'm going to write about all this.'

'Oh my god,' she whooped with delight. 'What a random day!'

At the top of Liverpool ONE, we had lunch overlooking the sprawling city below us. On our way back to the Adelphi hotel, a homeless man was sitting on the pavement amid the remnants of his possessions.

'Can you spare a coin?' he asked as we drew level.

'Hello,' I said. 'What are you doing here?'

'I'm hoping to get across to Birkenhead for a night's sleep on a friend's sofa.'

'Is that what you need some money for?'

'Yes, look at me. I had a shave yesterday at a friend's home. He let me sleep on his sofa. You should've seen the water when I'd finished with it. It was black. I try to keep clean but it's hard on the streets.'

I squatted, the better to hear him.

'What's your name?'

'Steph, short for Stephen.'

'What happened to you?'

'I had a job and was living with my girlfriend. We had twins, but they died. She had a mental breakdown and I turned to drink. I lost my job. Couldn't pay the rent. Lost the home. She's living in London now. Got married.'

If you want an example of faded splendour, look no further than the Adelphi hotel. A few minutes' walk from Lime

Street railway station, in the heart of old Liverpool, it is an impressive building, one of those magnificent Edwardian-style edifices that reflect the optimism of the time, just before the calamity of World War l. The public rooms on the ground level were magnificent, specialising in conference facilities, but higher up, it all began to deteriorate. Frantically endeavouring to catch up with what a hotel should be in the twenty-first century, its efforts had not yet reached the top floor.

A leak from the toilet got us moved from our first room. In the second room, valiant attempts had been made to install double glazing, but the panes were a foot apart, the outer ones were ajar and could not be closed, and the inner panes were broken. The result was a gale blowing into the room. Corridor radiators were beautifully warm, but ours were stone cold. Rotting woodwork was amateurishly patched with Polyfilla, the wallpaper was peeling, the utilitarian furniture came straight from the austerity days of the immediate post-war years, and the drawer of the bedside cabinet fell to pieces when I opened it. This was enough to get us moved yet again to a third room. But what do you do when you have a magnificent stone building in the heart of this wonderful city, that was built for a different era?

We got up after a disturbed night and ate the first Williams pear of the season, which we'd brought with us from our garden. It was a perfect starter for the breakfast we set off to find. As the lift doors were about to close, two dishevelled young men looking rather the worse for wear squeezed themselves through the narrowing gap and dumped their bags on the floor.

'Whew! Just made it.'

'Where're you chaps from?'

'Sheffield.'

'Good night out?'

'Rough.'

'Celebration?'

'Yes, colleague's leaving do.'

'Going far?'

'New Zealand.'

It was Sunday, and by the entrance to the hotel stood a fragile, wan-looking young woman holding a placard inviting all and sundry to attend Hope City Church. It meets at the Adelphi every Sunday at 10 am. She looked as if hope was the only thing she had in her life, but no one was paying her any attention.

Liverpool began its life as a 'muddy pool', which is what its Anglo-Saxon name *Lieurpul* means. How the city reached its present state of rejuvenating vivacity is a story of glory and shame, of heroic enterprise and cruel exploitation. One of many possible starting points is the arrival of Europeans in the Americas – first the Portuguese and Spanish, later the English, French and Dutch – from which two significant developments followed. The Europeans brought death and destruction on a vast scale to the inhabitants of these newly discovered lands, through indiscriminate and deliberate slaughter, but even more, through common diseases – smallpox, measles, typhus – which annihilated most of the population of indigenous people, who had no resistance. All this death brought about the second change: a huge shortage of labour for the new sugar, cotton, coffee and tobacco plantations that were rapidly established in South America, the Caribbean and what we now know as the United States of America. To fill the gap, the estate owners looked to Africa, and so began the notorious slave trade.

Slave trading began in Liverpool in the mid-eighteenth century, and the port rapidly became the epicentre of the trans-Atlantic trade. It was responsible for transporting 1.5 million Africans into slavery. Profits from the slave trade transformed the economic and industrial landscape of Great Britain and Europe. The vast fortunes that were made helped finance the investments in iron, coal and banking that made Britain's industrial revolution possible and enriched Europe and the Americas.

The legacy of the slave trade is still writ large today in Liverpool's cityscape. Much of the wealth that financed the development of the Liverpool-Manchester Railway derived from slavery; one of the four deputy chairmen of the company, John Moss, owned vast sugar plantations in the West Indies. John Gladstone MP received £90,000 from the Slave Compensation Commission to recompense him for the loss of his 'property' when slavery was abolished in 1833, forcing him to free his slaves. Parr Street, Tarleton Street and Blackburn Place were named after slave traders, while Cropper Street and Roscoe Street were named after civic dignitaries who were active in the abolitionist movement.

Another legacy of the slave trade is England's rotten teeth. In 1598, the German traveller, Paul Hentzner, observed that Queen Elizabeth's blackened teeth were 'a defect ... which the English seem subject to, from their great use of sugar'.[19] Elizabeth I imported her sugar from Morocco, but it was the Portuguese plantations in South America and the Caribbean that fed her subjects' appetite for it. By the middle of the eighteenth century, sugar was more important than grain in European trade; before long, it was Britain's most valuable import, most of it coming from the West Indies, and much of it through Liverpool.[20] Once a luxury, sugar had rapidly become a necessity. It became more important than bread.

But the legacy of the triangular trade lives on in other ways. Many whose wealth derived from slavery invested it in the new industries that were springing up at this time, such as salt manufacture, banking, shipbuilding, rope making and coal mining. And so, from being a muddy pool in Anglo-Saxon times, by the beginning of the eighteenth-century Liverpool was on course to become Britain's most important west coast port.

In 1707, the engineer, Thomas Steers, was commissioned to prepare a hydraulic survey of Liverpool Dock. Based on his research, he planned the port's first wet dock, which occupied nearly nine hectares. It subsequently formed part of a complex of docks with the capacity to dock 100 ships.[21] In the final years of the slave trade, 75 per cent of all slaving voyages passed through Liverpool. Building on this momentum, Liverpool's heyday in the 1920s included more than seven miles of docks, with the accompanying

19   Jerry Brotton, *This Orient Isle: Elizabethan England and the Islamic World*, p2.
20   https://en.wikipedia.org/wiki/History_of_sugar
21   Nicholas Crane, *The Making of the British Landscape*, Weidenfeld & Nicolson, paperback edition, 2017, p387.

warehouses, factories, chandleries, taverns and lodging houses.

It is true that we stand on the shoulders of giants, but we also stand on the backs of slaves.

There is much to celebrate in this modern scintillating city. From the turbulent days of social and political upheaval and the 1981 Toxteth riots, Environment Secretary Michael Heseltine could see the city's huge potential and, taking a radical approach to generate change, organised Britain's first International Garden Festival in 1984. Its objective was to kickstart economic recovery and today Liverpool is a city of entrepreneurial and transformational flair. Especially on a Friday and Saturday evening, the dock area is a conglomeration of joyfulness.

The Royal Albert Dock has been delightfully and thoughtfully transformed into an abundance of retail, leisure and gastronomic delights. Here, you find Tate Liverpool, the International Slavery Museum, the Beatles Experience – with more-than-life-size statues of the Fab Four, the Maritime Museum and restaurants and cafés aplenty. The dockland bustles now with a different and more wholesome international flavour, a fitting and appropriate transformation of an area that carries such grim memories and which thrived on the back of horrific inhumanity.

That evening we went to the Smugglers' Cove in the Albert Dock. We immediately realised that we were old. It was Friday, the night for an endless stream of hen parties of all shapes and sizes; outrageous costumes on inappropriately shaped bodies, so tight-fitting that they revealed morphological irregularities about which the wearers were clearly unconscious. There were glad rags galore and glitz and bling and extraordinary fascinators. During the time it took us to order and eat our meal, tables filled and emptied and filled and emptied again, as these gloriously happy young women ate and strutted their stuff on wobbly heels and staggered on to yet another venue for more frantic fun.

Joan and I shared a mezze selection and took two hours over it. This atmospheric eating hole would not be quiet again until three or four in the morning, and then only for an hour or two before preparations for the next gastronomic day began. At this point Joan received a text: 'Please come to my 70th birthday party.'

'We've got to go,' Joan said.

'But what about the Welsh borders and Devon and Cornwall?'

'Oh, let's do the east coast.'

And so it was decided. Back we'd go, by motorway where possible, do the party, and then head south. We'd spent nine leisurely days driving 412 miles from Berwick to Liverpool. Now we set ourselves the target of doing the more direct 187-mile return journey in a single day.

8

SHAP

POOR LITTLE SHAP HAS ALWAYS had a bit of a reputation. As far back as the middle of the nineteenth century, it was thought of as remote, difficult to get to, and with not very much going for it once you got there. Even today, the long haul up the M6 to Shap is notorious; it rises to over a thousand feet at Shap, where two roads, a railway and a river are squeezed through the narrow defile of the magnificent Lune Gorge, constricted by the harsh geography of the Cumbrian mountains and the Pennines.

It was Anthony Trollope who introduced me to Shap. He saw it as a bleak little market town set high up in what were then known as the Westmoreland fells. In those days, a journey to London was going 'up' and away from London was going 'down'. Never mind that London was at sea level and Shap in the mountains, London was always 'high' and anywhere outside of London, however high, was always 'low'. Today, at least for anyone living north of London, we go 'down' to London because, as everyone knows, south is down and north is up.

In Trollope's novel *Can You Forgive Her?*, George Vavasor, 'went down to Westmoreland; and took himself to a small wayside inn at Shap among the fells...' It's worth reading the full description of Shap as it was a couple of centuries ago.

> *There is a station at Shap, by which the railway company no doubt conceives that it has conferred on that somewhat rough and remote locality all the advantages of a refined civilisation; but I doubt whether the Shappites have been thankful for the favour. The landlord at the inn, for one, is not thankful. Shap had been a place owing all such life as it possessed to coaching and posting. It had been a stage on the high road from Lancaster to Carlisle, and though it lay high and bleak among the fells, and was a cold, windy, thinly populated place, filling all travellers with thankfulness that they had not been made Shappites, nevertheless, it had had its glory in its coaching and posting. I have no doubt that there are men and women who look back with a fond regret to the palmy days of Shap.*[22]

It's the same story today, of course. A new technology comes along and fundamentally changes people's lives - good for

22   Anthony Trollope, *Can You Forgive Her?* Oxford University Press, London, The World's Classics as a double volume 1968, pp. 481-2 (first volume).

some, bad for others. Those weary horse-drawn travellers of Trollope's day urgently needed some refreshment and relaxation after the long haul to Shap, and the hospitality business had thrived. Those were the days when you were up against geography and you couldn't help but be aware of your terrain; it must have taken a lot of horses to pull those coaches up to Shap. Then along came the new-fangled railway and destroyed the coaching and postal services at a blow. It brought with it, however, a railway station and the forward march of civilisation.

Geography can be very inconvenient at times. Most of our transport technology has been designed to eliminate as much of it as possible. It all started with the Romans. In their obsessive drive to extend their empire and thus acquire glory and immortality, they thought nothing of driving straight lines through inconveniently irregular landscapes. Railway engineers had the same mindset.

Bill Hoskins, in his classic volume, *The Making of the English Landscape*, first published in 1955, was despairing of this trend towards obliterating geography. He was particularly scathing about urban bypasses. The M6 – Britain's first motorway, of course – began its life as the Preston bypass; I remember it being opened to much fanfare by the then prime minister, Harold Macmillan, on 5 December 1958. Three years earlier, this is what Hoskins had to say about such bypasses:

> *Great bypass roads, like the East Lancashire bypass, now plunge straight across the country, regardless of contours, using cuttings and embankments to keep as even a*

gradient as possible. They are entirely without beauty. Is there anything uglier in the whole landscape than an arterial bypass road, except an airfield? Old roads have been straightened, and have lost all their character, historic and otherwise.[23]

Continuing the theme 60 years later in his book *The Making of the British Landscape*, Nicholas Crane bemoans the remorseless increase in motor traffic thus:

The most common vehicle in this pungent, racketing metallic armada is the car. There are 30.2 million of them. Road culture has created linear motoring landscapes. Road surfaces and verges are daubed with vehicular instructions and advertising hoardings sized to catch the eye of passers-by in top gear; intersections are punctuated with traffic lights and roundabouts; slip roads and clover-leaves isolate islands of intoxicated grass...[24]

As if to emphasise the bleakness of Shap, an abbey was built there at the end of the twelfth century, in 1199, the last one to be founded in England. Shap Fell rises to 1,397 feet, and if you wanted to be away from it all, this was definitely the place to be. It was set up by an order of canons (not monks or friars) known as the Premonstratensians. When I first came across this name, I thought it must denote some arcane

23   W G Hoskins, *The Making of the English Landscape*, Book Club Associates, London, 1981, p247.
24   Nicholas Crane, *The Making of the British Landscape*, Weidenfeld & Nicholson, paperback edition, 2017, p509.

aspect of Christian theology, but Wikipedia tells me it derives from nothing more sinister than the fact that the order was founded early in the twelfth century at Prémontré, in France.

The Premonstratensians were heavily influenced by the Cistercians, who, in the twelfth century, helped the Normans to consolidate their conquest of England by sending their missionaries to us and founding no fewer than 64 Cistercian abbeys, from Waverley in Surrey to Newminster in Northumberland. The Premonstratensians seem to have been distinguished by the white habits of the canons, which is why they are sometimes known as the *White Canons*, and by a ritual solemnity centred on the rule of St Augustine, with particular emphasis on austerity. This was in keeping with the austerity of the landscape around Shap. The quiet, peaceful ruins of the abbey still stand high up on Shap Fell on the eastern edge of the Lake District National Park, overlooking the furiously busy A6, M6 and West Coast Main Line railway, all manically vying for space in the tightly restricted corridor between the Lake District, the Yorkshire Dales National Park and the Pennines.

Beyond Penrith, the landscape opened out as we entered the broad plain of the lower Eden and its tributaries. From here on, driving was low and easy until, on the eastern edges of Carlisle, we turned onto the A69, which would have taken us all the way to Newcastle, had we not decided to take what is known locally as the Military Road (the B6318).

The Military Road is probably one of the most exciting roads in England to drive along. For most of its length, what is left of Hadrian's Wall is just a few metres away, almost within touching distance. Once the Romans left, the wall was plundered by local people for building material, but even so, the remnants are impressive. You can feel the pull of deep history here. The Military Road has the added zing that it is like a switchback, with deep dips and blind summits, and can be extremely dangerous for drivers who don't know it. For all that, however, the Military Road was not built by the Romans. It owes its existence to the Jacobite uprising of 1745 and the need to shift military equipment from Newcastle to Carlisle as quickly as possible, so the Roman Wall was ransacked as a ready source of road-building material.

We turned onto the Military Road at Greenhead and drove along the dead straight, switchback road to Twice Brewed, also known as Once Brewed if you approach it from the east. This tiny hamlet owes its confusing identity to Lady Trevelyan. In 1934, she was invited to open a new youth hostel that had been built a couple of hundred yards from the Twice Brewed pub. Lady Trevelyan was a committed teetotaller, and during the opening ceremony she is reported to have said, 'Of course, there will be no alcohol served in these premises, so I hope the tea and coffee will only be brewed once.' Thereafter, the youth hostel became known as the Once Brewed Hostel.[25]

There's been a youth hostel here ever since 1934, but it has recently been completely rebuilt and incorporated into the spanking new visitor centre known as The Sill, on Hadrian's Wall, and it must now be one of the smartest youth hostels in the country. The Sill has been developed by Northumberland National Park, and this was our first visit since construction

25   *Once Brewed or Twice Brewed – the Story of an English Pub'.* https://h2g2.com (*The Hitchhiker's Guide to the Galaxy*).

began in 2015. It is a 'state-of-the-art landscape discovery centre in a UNESCO World Heritage Site'. We were delighted to discover several EV charge points here, all slow chargers, in anticipation of a long stay for each vehicle. An official of the Northumberland National Park Authority told us about its plans for rolling out an EV charging programme. It was a refreshing change to see the EV revolution being taken so seriously.

Our last sight of Hadrian's Wall had been 40 miles to the west, where it ends at Bowness-on-Solway; much of it had almost disappeared. Here at Twice Brewed, however, the wall was truly impressive. As we were reminded at the lecture in Berwick, the Romans took full advantage of Northumberland's landscape by building several miles of their wall on the Whin Sill. This 1,900-year-old structure, perched along mile after mile of solid cliff, in places almost perpendicular, is a magnificent sight. It is so ancient and weathered that it has become part of the landscape, wall and sill welded together in perfect symbiosis. Vindolanda, Britain's most complete Roman fort, is just a short walk away from the visitor centre, on the south side of the wall. Here, it is possible to get some idea of what it must have been like to live and work on that remote outpost of the Roman Empire.

Hadrian's Wall was built as a border to separate civilised people from barbarians; today's border separating England and Scotland lies 20 to 60 miles north of the wall, and between wall and border is England's largest forest and one of Europe's biggest man-made lakes: Kielder Forest and Kielder Reservoir. This sparsely populated area is home also to the Northumberland International Dark Sky Park.

Winter nights are the best in Northumberland, when clear, unpolluted night skies reveal a miracle of cosmic glory, of breath-taking wonder, a nightly spectacle of unbelievable brilliance. Northumberland is renowned for its low levels of light pollution. We have some of the darkest skies in the country and ours was its first Dark Sky Park. The International Dark Sky Association has awarded the skies over Kielder Gold Tier Dark Sky Park status.

In winter especially, the Milky Way appears as a broad swathe of delicately speckled silken sheen winding its way through the universe, trailing across the heavens like an infinitesimally light pashmina draped over the shoulders of the cosmos. 'Where were you,' God asked Job, 'when the morning stars sang together, and all the heavenly beings shouted for joy?'[26] Northumberland's skies echo that biblical sense of the numinous.

On the very edge of the Dark Sky Park, on the edge of Northumberland and on the edge of England, is Carter Bar, overlooking the Scottish Borders. There, as well as maps of the landscape around you, you will also find maps of the skies above you, a set of different sky maps for all four seasons of the year. This is one of the darkest places in the Dark Sky Park and one of the best vantage points from which to view England's dark skies.

And yet it seems that most people have never seen a truly dark sky. About 85 per cent of us live in towns or cities, and when we look up, we cannot see the stars because of the polluting effects of artificial light. What a price to pay for our urban lifestyle, never to see the stars.

---

26   Job 38:7

With 44 per cent of battery left and 37 miles to go, we reckoned we had a good margin. From Twice Brewed/ Once Brewed, the Military Road took us east, every mile demarcated by Roman turrets and milecastles perched on the edge of that giant slab of dolerite. The road took us north, away from wall and sill, into what the Romans thought of as 'barbarian' country. Here, the low-lying limestone moors are bleak, but it is rich in agriculture, a landscape of isolated farmsteads, fine country houses, slow-moving waterways and scattered coniferous plantations. The narrow roads dogleg their way across country, a tedious sequence of right-angled bends marking the boundaries of ancient land holdings. We arrived home with Lettie warning us that we might not have enough battery to get to our destination. But we made it, 187 miles in just over six hours, including two recharging stops.

Truth to tell, we were glad of the opportunity to get back to Northumberland. The change of plan gave us time to catch up on ourselves. We were surprised by how tiring this business of touring was, especially as we'd set ourselves the task of finding out all we could about the practicalities of touring on battery power, on top of our usual curiosity about each place we visited. This meant a lot of foot-slogging and internet-slogging: reading historical plaques; calling at information centres, museums and libraries; talking with local people; observing the lie of the land; making copious notes; and researching locations of charge points. Those points were always the main issue: where are they? Will they be rapid or slow? Will they be working? And, will we get through to helplines if things go wrong? These issues determined how each day went; they were a constant source of low-level – and sometimes major – anxiety.

As our home is close to the Northumberland coast, our unplanned return meant that we were able to spend the next few days treating ourselves to daily outings, with home as our base. This enabled us to explore the full length of Northumberland's magnificent coast, taking in detail we'd previously missed, and looking out for EV charge points, something we'd never previously had to consider. It was a pleasant change to be free of 'range anxiety', thanks to the luxury of guaranteed charging using our own electricity when we returned to base each evening.

This arrangement also gave us time to prepare for the much longer leg down the rest of England's east coast. The trick was to find hotels and rapid charge points as close together as possible. Armed with a list of Best Western hotels with on-site charge points, we hoped this first choice would simplify the trip. Unfortunately, we discovered that there were not as many as we'd have liked. All part of the trials of being an early adopter and pioneer!

NORTH-EAST COAST

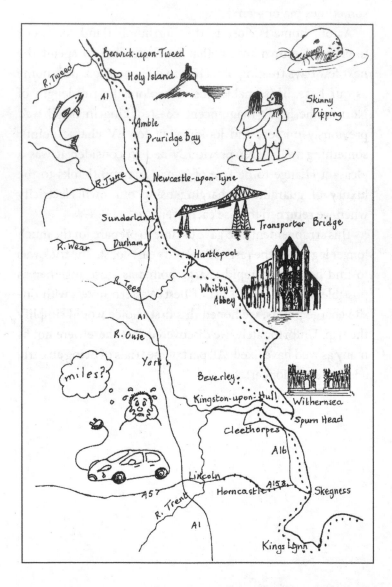

9

THIN PLACE

IN PHILIP PULLMAN'S *His Dark Materials* trilogy, his protagonist, Will, stepped through a window of air by the side of an Oxford road and found himself in a different dimension, a parallel universe. Quite by chance, Will had discovered a 'Thin Place', an opening into another world.

Lindisfarne, Holy Island, just off the edge of north Northumberland, has also been described as a 'thin place', where only a thin veil of perception separates the spiritual realm from the physical. The ancient Celts used this expression to describe places like the island of Iona in the Inner Hebrides or Glastonbury in Somerset. For centuries, Glastonbury has been a key focal point for both Christian and pre-Christian spiritualities, and tenacious myths about Joseph of Arimathea, Jesus, King Arthur and the Holy Grail have become deeply embedded there. When you are in a thin place, you can unexpectedly find yourself slipping from one way of understanding reality to a different kind of reality.

On Lindisfarne, you can sense the thinness of the place the moment you enter the Parish Church of St Mary the Virgin, a few yards from where the priory was founded 1,300 years ago. Here, in this beautiful little church, you can feel history and deep reverence wrapping themselves round you. As you go through the heavy door, just to your right you will meet the beautiful wooden carving by Fenwick Lawson known as the *Journey*. As tall as a man, it is a representation of six strong and utterly devoted monks, bearing on their shoulders the coffin of St Cuthbert as they take him on his final journey to Durham Cathedral. Cuthbert was buried on Lindisfarne in 687, but more than a hundred years later, in 793, Vikings raided this peaceful monastic community, looted the holy relics and murdered many of the monks. A few perceptive monks could see what was coming; fearful that Cuthbert's body would be desecrated, they exhumed it and carried it with them as they fled for their own safety. For more than a hundred years, succeeding generations of monks carried Cuthbert's body on their shoulders around the north of England, looking for a safe place to rest their beloved teacher. They eventually found such a place at Durham Cathedral, where it lies to this day.

You cannot be on Lindisfarne without feeling that you are in the presence of profound history, into which has been concentrated centuries of intense spiritual and religious endeavour. If you step through the window, you will be transported to this other realm. Visitors come from all over the country to visit this 'thin place' and to take in its history and mystique. In fact, Holy Island (Lindisfarne) is one of the most popular tourist attractions on the northeast coast. Fewer than 200 people live on the island, but each year it receives 650,000 visitors from all over the country. This means that, on an average day, its population increases by a factor of roughly 10; in the summer, numbers rise by much more than this.

To cope, there is an abundance of teahouses, cafés, restaurants, pubs, hotels and B&Bs. The island's economy is built on tourism, and there is a large car park which, on the day we were there, was full. Twice daily, the incoming tide makes the island inaccessible, and visitors have a six-hour slot to explore before it becomes unsafe to risk returning to the mainland. This would be ample time for EV drivers to plug in, spend the day enjoying the island, collect their car six hours later with a full battery and get safely back over the causeway.

As it happens, we had sufficient charge to get us back home, but we did look for a charge point, and couldn't find one. It's places like Holy Island that are ideal locations for charge points. And they wouldn't need to be the expensive rapid chargers either. People go to these places for the whole day, so the slower, less expensive charging points would be ideal.[27]

Despite the obvious gaps in provision, according to Newcastle's *Evening Chronicle*, Northumberland has the fifth-highest number of charging points of all the UK's local authority areas and is comfortably in the top 20 per cent for

27 Charge points with four connectors have now been installed on Holy Island.

charge point provision.[28] The evidence bore this out. As we worked our way south along the Northumberland coast, we came across charge stations in unexpected places.

As far as seaside towns go, Seahouses, just down the coast from Holy Island, may not be in the Scarborough or Brighton league, but it is, nevertheless, a bustling seaside town where you find ice-cream stalls on every corner, fish-and-chip shops vying with each other to offer the crispiest chips, the chunkiest fish and the mushiest peas. On good days, the usual seaside paraphernalia of buckets and spades, saucy post cards, candyfloss, wind-breakers and kites spills out onto the pavements. More famously, Seahouses is where you board one of Billy Shiels's boats for the three-hour trip around the Farne Islands on the edge of the Whin Sill, to see grey seals and visit the Inner Farne bird sanctuary. And, to cap it all, Seahouses has had the very good sense to install a rapid charge point. Just what we needed.

As we were charging the car, we went for a walk along the shore. An hour later, we returned to find that the hose had been unplugged and inserted into another Leaf. I was just poking around to check that everything was in order, when a large, jovial man came along.

'Ah,' he said, 'wondering what's going on?'

'Well, yes.'

'I saw you were fully charged so undid you and plugged into mine.'

'Didn't know you could do that.'

'It's part of the etiquette. We're pioneers, members of an exclusive club. Had yours long?'

28   *Newcastle Evening Chronicle*, 17 April 2019.

'Just over a year.'

'Had mine three years,' he said. 'Love it. Use it to commute from Gateshead to Morpeth every day. Suits me perfectly. Wouldn't want to go back to petrol.'

Northumberland's coast, from the Scottish border to Druridge Bay, is one of the finest in the world. The sheer delight of walking along the 62-mile (100 kilometres) stretch of the Northumberland Coast Path beats Bondi Beach any day. That Antipodean pocket handkerchief of sand – just over half a mile in length – sees 35,000 visitors a day, and you have to pick your way through thousands of prone bodies whose sole intent is to be toasted to ever deeper shades of bronze. By way of contrast, you can walk for a 100 kilometres along the silver sands of Northumberland's coast and hardly see a soul. The coastal path takes in the broad sweep of Cheswick sands; the Holy Island sands, with the Pilgrim's Way to the island when the tide is out; past Budle Bay and the Farne Islands to Beadnell Bay; Embleton Bay; ending along the top of the silky white dunes of Alnmouth Bay. At the north end of this bay is Alnmouth itself, built around the medieval port that had to be abandoned after the lower course of the River Aln realigned itself in a catastrophic storm in 1806.

A thick fog hung over Alnmouth as we approached. The North Sea defines the weather of eastern Britain. Whenever warm, humid air from the continent flows across the cooler waters of our North Sea coasts, there is always a bank of fog, blanketing our coastal communities with gloom up to five, ten or even twenty miles inland. In Scotland, these fog banks are known as 'haars', over the border in Northumberland they are 'sea-frets', and in Lincolnshire and Yorkshire the term 'sea-roke' or simply 'roke' is used. These are classic advection fogs, and they dampen the spirits of North Sea coastal dwellers with depressing frequency.

At the southern end of Alnmouth Bay is the remarkable village of Warkworth. The approach from the north is described by Pevsner as 'one of the most exciting sequences of views one can have in England'. Warkworth is an excellent example of the geography of power. Like medieval Durham on the River Wear, the whole of Warkworth is on a peninsula formed by a meander of the River Coquet. There's a new bridge over the river now, but you can see the medieval bridge on your right as you cross. Parking in the market square, we walked to St Lawrence's Church.

Pevsner records this church as 'unique in Northumberland in being a large, fairly complete Norman church'.[29] But it was not always so. The information plaque outside the church records that, in 737CE, the settlement of Warkworth, along with its church, was gifted to the abbots and monks of Holy Island further north. Warkworth owes this generosity to the saintly Anglo-Saxon king of Northumbria, Ceolwulf,[30] after whom Ceolwulf Cottage in Ceolwulf Close on the east side of the village are named. Ceolwulf was uncomfortable in the kingly role and had yearnings for the monastic life, so in the same year that he made this endowment, he decided to abdicate in favour of his cousin Eadberht and retire to

---

29   According to Pevsner.
30   Northumbria is not Northumberland. It literally means 'north of the Humber'.

Lindisfarne. So, well before the present Norman church was built, an Anglo-Saxon church had stood on the site of St Lawrence's since at least 737CE, most probably long before that. At that time, Warkworth was known as Wercewode, after the abbess Werce. The 'wode' or 'worthe' part of the name is an Anglo-Saxon term meaning a palisaded enclosure, so Warkworth literally means 'Werce's settlement', or the place where Werce lives. This history, and the lives of women generally, is celebrated by the Morpeth-based women's choir known as Werca's Folk.

The Anglo-Saxon predecessor of St Lawrence's Church is necessarily ignored by Pevsner, since his focus is on buildings as they are today. Yet this 'fairly complete Norman church' is another example – alongside that of Norham on the River Tweed – of the Normans' practice of stamping their authority on England's landscape.

Passing the market cross, we walked up the steep rise of Castle Street, terraces of rather fine eighteenth and nineteenth century houses on either side. These houses have long back gardens – sometimes very long and always exactly the width of the house. They are the remnants of medieval burgage plots – narrow strips of land that were rented from the king or lord by the burgesses, the merchants and craftsmen of the day. The houses served as dwellings, business premises, workshops and retail outlets, and the long strips of land behind them provided subsistence crops and raw materials. The burgesses paid their rent in produce, labour or, later, cash. Poking around in little alleyways, we could see that many of the burgage plots had been built on, some with attractive mews houses. But the basic structure of the medieval village is clear today: land organised in long, narrow strips, along the edges of a transport route, thus providing land for growing subsistence crops and also giving access to transit routes to facilitate commerce.

All of this explains the mental contortions I had to go through at school in the 1940s and '50s to get to grips with sums involving length and area. It all sprang from the fact the basic unit of measurement used to calculate the dimensions of these burgage plots was the 'rod' (confusingly also known as 'pole' or 'perch'), and it is equivalent to 5.5 yards. If you measure the width of the houses along Castle Street, you'll find that they are usually multiples of this basic measure. The smallest house we saw was just over seven and a half of my paces, roughly equivalent to one rod, or 5.5 yards, which is not very big at all. Mind you, the house did go back quite a long way; it was a long thin house. So if, in medieval times, you had a plot that was two rods wide, you had a frontage onto the high street of two times 5.5, which is 11 yards. If you were very wealthy, you could afford to rent a plot four rods wide, giving a frontage of 4 x 5.5 which is 22 yards, or one chain, the length of a cricket pitch.

And so we get the quirky mathematics of my youth:

12 inches = 1 foot

3 feet = 1 yard

5.5 yards = 1 rod (pole or perch)

4 rods = 22 yards

22 yards = 1 chain

10 chains = 1 furlong (the length of a medieval furrow)

8 furlongs (or 1,760 yards) = 1 mile

1 chain x 1 furlong = 1 acre, the area of land that could be

turned over by one man in a day using just one ox to pull his plough.

This medieval system of land allocation dictated the basic structure of most of today's settlements. An interesting relic is that today's allotments are still measured in rods, a typical allotment size being 10 square rods, or 10 x 5.5 x 5.5 square yards.[31] Doing long division and multiplication using numbers like this was, to my boyhood brain, far more complicated than today's easy stuff of merely shifting the decimal point.

From the castle, we looked down onto Castle Street, the terraced houses, the burgage plots, and the Norman church at the far end, all neatly encapsulating the geography of Norman-medieval power politics, all writ large in today's townscape. Until as recently as the 1980s, two rooms in the castle's tower were maintained for occasional use by the Duke and Duchess of Northumberland and their guests – a superb vantage point from which to keep an eye on one's fiefdom.

Following unclassified roads where possible, we made our way slowly round the broad sweep of Druridge Bay. A dedicated band of conservationists has defended this local beauty spot from multiple attempts to turn it into an industrial site. The coastal plain here is littered with the evidence of the now-exhausted southeast Northumberland coalfield: Hauxley, Togston, Chevington, Acklington, Widdrington are all names

---

31   I have used the following websites to refresh my memory about these things: Harrod Horticultural, Ashford Allotment Society, the University of Nottingham (Manuscripts and Special Collections), Wikipedia.

intimately associated with mining and opencast operations. For a century and a half, it fuelled the country's industrial revolution.. That's all gone now. Today, it's in the process of reinventing itself. But I wanted to mosey around Lynemouth, at the southern end of Druridge Bay, because it reminded me of Harold Wilson and Alcan.

'What!'

'Harold Wilson. Did you know he resigned as prime minister on 5 April 1976?'

'I thought you weren't good at trivia.'

'I'm not, and in any case, this isn't trivia. Harold Wilson had quite an impact on the North East's economy. He saw how the heart had been torn out of this community by rapid industrial decline, and he made it his business to put it back.'

Wilson's big idea was the 'white hot technological revolution'. He managed to magic up some figures showing that there were, potentially, abundant supplies of cheap electricity in the region. Alcan took the bait and was hooked. It was a most unlikely location for an aluminium smelter, because the biggest raw material, bauxite, had to come from Africa, South America or Oceania, and that incurred a lot of transport costs. More important than this, however, was the electricity bill.

To produce one tonne of aluminium required as much electricity as would keep an average British family going for 20 years. Wilson's solution was to build a thermal power station at the Lynemouth pithead to deliver electricity direct to the smelter. The bauxite was imported at the deep-sea port of Blyth, half a dozen miles away, there was a good network of railways, and as several local coalmines had been closed, there was a good supply of unemployed men who were used to heavy physical work. Add to this mix a good dose of government financial assistance in an era of strong regional policy, and the fact that under Heath we were now in the EEC and therefore also inside the European aluminium import tariff barrier, and you have a very attractive set of inducements to entice a heavy industry to come to an area that had been suffering for many years from high structural unemployment, and which, under normal market conditions, would never dream of coming to such an unlikely place. It was a good example of politics and geography working together. The Alcan aluminium smelter was opened in 1974 and closed in 2012.

It so happened that I'd taken a group of students to Lynemouth on the very day Harold Wilson chose to resign. We'd been studying the factors influencing industrial location, of which this was an excellent example. Our party was just stepping onto the coach for the return journey when it was announced on the driver's radio.

'Got that everyone? The man who brought aluminium production to the North East has just resigned.'

'Oh, really?'

Love him or loathe his memory, I can't help feeling a smidgeon of sympathy for the man. It was rumoured that he had just been diagnosed with cancer and that early signs of Alzheimer's had been detected. The least that can be said of him is that he had the courage to go when he felt he was no longer up to the job. Now there's a lesson for some of our politicians.

All this was played out at the southern end of Druridge

Bay. The Northumberland Coast Path finishes here, and it is here that two stretches of coast with antagonistic claims meet each other, at this iconic Northumberland beauty spot. To the north is an area prized for its beauty, history and leisure utility, miles of unspoilt beaches and long-distance walks, while to the south is a sweep of coast prized for its industrial potential.

These two sets of demands have, in recent years, turned Druridge Bay into an environmental battle zone. The first serious sign of conflict came in the 1980s, when an application was lodged to build a nuclear power station there. Years of claim and counter claim ensued, but no sooner was this threat seen off than it was followed, in the 1990s, by a proposal for large-scale extraction of sand, and in 2015 further environmental concerns were aroused when an attempt was made to start opencast coal mining in the area. If this had been successful, it would have seriously discombobulated the local skinny-dippers, who have a habit of gathering on the beach to celebrate the autumn equinox by subjecting their polymorphic bodies to the torments of the bitterly cold waters of the North Sea.

I can think of many ways of celebrating the annual retreat of the sun. But if you really want to mark the turn of the year, I can think of no better way of doing so than to gather in some warm, cosy place, like the nearby Woodhorn Museum, slowly wander round the stunning collection of paintings by the Ashington Group of pitmen, and then enjoy a steaming mug of hot chocolate. Skinny-dipping in the North Sea by comparison seems more like torture. It must have something to do with the English penchant for self-flagellation that was brought to these islands by early Christian missionaries. So far, the skinny-dippers have been left to continue dipping, and Druridge Bay retains its charm as a venue for day trippers.

However, things are changing. Wind turbines have replaced old pitheads, the former Alcan complex is now part of a regeneration project known as Lynefield Park, the former power station has been converted into a biomass plant producing electricity for the national grid, and Lynx Precast is there, producing concrete flooring systems. And just down the road, at Newbiggin-by-the-Sea, where the coast juts out into the North Sea, is what the art critic, Jonathan Jones, described as an 'eye-wounding erection'.

It arrived as part of a regeneration project, which included a new playground, half a million tons of new sand to liven up the beach, and a new breakwater to stop the sand being eroded away. Sean Henry's *Couple* stand on this new breakwater, 300 yards out to sea. They stand side by side, looking to Scandinavia. This seems to me to be entirely appropriate, for behind them, on the promenade, is the evidence of Newbiggin's long outward-looking history. Cable House marks the point where the first submarine telegraph cable came ashore in 1868, linking the north-east coast of England with Scandinavia.

Despite the criticism, the people who live there have taken *The Couple* to their hearts and, what's more, it has inspired something of an artistic renaissance in the area. This coast is constantly renewing itself and continuing to look outwards. That's why, in the Victorian era, the people of Newbiggin built a Mechanic's Institute for themselves, where working men could meet to read and learn and discuss the issues of the day. It was all about self-improvement, or what Dan Jackson calls 'auto-didacticism'. You can see the evidence of this push for learning all over the North East: working men's clubs, reading rooms, literary institutes, libraries, technical schools and colleges. The people of the industrial North East had a reputation for learning. They were literary people, self-taught and well-read, so it is no surprise to learn that this used to be the largest centre of publishing outside of the capital. Auto-didacticism was alive and well in the North East.[32]

It was the 'Northumbrian Enlightenment' that gave birth to the Newcastle Literary and Philosophical Society on the Westgate Road, near Newcastle railway station, Britain's largest private members' library outside of London. The Lit and Phil is still the largest independent library outside the metropolis, still thriving as a lending library for members, still a free reference library for the public, and still a flourishing venue for literary, musical and artistic events.

Until Sean Henry placed his *Couple* in the sea, it is doubtful whether anyone had heard of Newbiggin. By all the usual criteria, it is still an insignificant little place, and that's why we were surprised to find a rapid charge point there, in the car park of the new community centre. A top-up here was just what we needed to get us back to base.

---

32   Dan Jackson, *The Northumbrians: North-East England and its People, A New History*, Hurst & Company, London, 2019, p87.

10

BLACK GOLD

ON A DULL NOVEMBER morning in 1965, I got off the bus in Commercial Road, Wallsend, and walked down the hill to Raby Street school, where I was doing a short spell of teaching before leaving for an overseas posting. Ahead of me, the vast bulk of the Sir Winston Churchill oil tanker filled the horizon and loomed over us all through the window of the cosy Victorian classroom. Shipbuilding here was part of the everyday lives of the families whose children I taught at Raby Street. Heavy industry based on coal, iron and steel lined both banks of the River Tyne. It was what the region was all about.

More than half a century later, this same stretch of water has a very different feel about it. Cranes, winches, hoists and chandleries have given way to apartments, chic eating places, boutique theatres and law courts. Coal staithes and slipways have been replaced by walkways and cycle tracks. The Sage Music Centre and Baltic Centre for Contemporary Art, on the Gateshead side of the river – linked with Newcastle by the blinking eye of the Gateshead Millennium Bridge – have transformed Gateshead and Newcastle, with its universities, museums and theatres, into a nationally renowned cultural region.

Over half a century, I have watched the banks of the Tyne emerge from the smoky grime of its industrial past into a new era based on clean, low-carbon industries, with a completely transformed and more pleasing physical environment. Nevertheless, it was the legacy of those heavy, dirty industries that defined the character of much of the northeast coast, as we were to discover as our road trip continued south.

Our day trips now over, it was time to pack our bags once more and set out for the long journey down the east coast, starting at Tynemouth. We had all our EV charge point cards and apps with us, plus Ordnance Survey maps, new notebooks, pens and pencils, and a list of hotel bookings.

The drive along the north and south banks of the Tyne takes you through a kaleidoscopic coalescence of histories: Tynemouth with the remains of the Norman Castle and the eighth-century Priory; Wallsend where the Romans began building their wall; the ultra-modern second Tyne Tunnel to Jarrow and the Anglo-Saxon monastery of St Paul's; the historic industrial towns of Wallsend, Hebburn, Jarrow and South Shields; and the spanking new Quayside on both sides of the river. The sights along our route took us through all of these, epitomising our history and emergence as a nation and signalling that this is a region that is constantly reinterpreting itself.

We parked at Frenchman's Bay, South Shields, in the recreational area known as The Leas. There, we ate our sandwiches looking across the Tyne estuary to the rugged outline of the remains of the Priory and Castle. In cosy cohabitation, these two pillars of the establishment stand tall above the rocks known as the Black Middens. The limestone promontory on which they perch has near-vertical cliffs on three sides, forming a superb natural defensive position. Behind us on the south bank, the land rose in a smooth dome to 84 metres (277 feet) above the North Sea; this little hill is made of the same limestone that we could see across the water.

Known to locals as the Cleadon Hills, this enclave of rural charm sits high between the estuaries of the Tyne and the Wear. They owe their existence to the Zechstein Sea, which inundated the northeast of England about 280 million years ago. The deposits left on the floor of the Zechstein Sea eventually became the unique limestone that we now know as magnesian limestone, or dolomite. Magnesian limestone's real claim to fame, however, is that it solved the problem of how to remove phosphorus from the ironstones to be found in the Cleveland Hills 50 miles to the south and overlooking the Tees estuary. Until this problem was solved, the Cleveland iron ores were useless for steelmaking. This technological breakthrough helped to launch Teesside's steelmaking career, and so lessen Cumberland's competitive edge in steel production.

About 70 million years before the Zechstein inundation, Britain sat astride the equator and was covered with tropical rain forests and swamps. These eventually turned themselves into coal to heat our houses and fire our furnaces. Although we were blissfully unaware of it at the time, that black gold has ever since been remorselessly unleashing a mass of problems of which we are only now beginning to be aware. While the 200-year-old party lasted, however, this subterranean treasure trove proved to be a very good thing indeed for Britain, and especially for the northeast of England. It turned us into the first industrial nation. We had a ball, and in time the rest of the world joined in the jollifications. And now we're all trying to undo the damage we have unwittingly been inflicting on ourselves.

The road from South Shields took us along the top of the limestone cliffs, from where we could see the mouths of the Tyne and the Wear, just half a dozen miles apart. Between them, these two rivers dominated the North's industrial revolution. Past the now defunct Whitburn Colliery and through the coastal village of Whitburn, we found the charge point we were looking for in a car park to the south of the village. It was a Charge Your Car point, for which we had an RFID card. It worked without a hitch and, while waiting for the battery to fill up, we walked back along the cliffs, drawn towards the frantic screams of kittiwakes and gulls and the chatter of cormorants.

When I first visited Sunderland in the 1960s, the banks of the River Wear, on which the city is situated, were unlike anything I had previously seen. I saw a depressing mass of grime and smoke, but soon realised that it was honest dirt, the product of industries based on the region's main resource: coal. The estuary was crowded with coal staithes, ship-building yards, marine engineering workshops, glassmaking factories. Two thirds of the workforce were employed in these heavy industries; today, more than three quarters are employed in service industries.[33] It has been an astonishing turnaround. Sunderland has undergone a massive economic restructuring from manual work to jobs in the service sector, leaving a legacy of endemic unemployment, a feeling of having been left behind by the globalisation process, and a seething anti-government resentment.

When Sunderland, in the early hours of 24 July 2016, announced that 61.3 per cent had voted to leave the EU, the pound plummeted and it became known as 'the city that crashed the pound'.[34] These anti-EU sentiments were not unique to Sunderland. In a broad band down the eastern edge of the country, from Northumberland and South Tyneside to Dover in Kent, 'Leave' votes exceeded 'Remain' votes, often by a considerable margin. Many commentators at the time saw Sunderland's Brexit vote as an act of self-mutilation, an expression, especially among men, of a sentimental yearning for a past that was irretrievably gone.[35] One thing is clear,

33   www.centreforcities.org/competing-with-the-continent/factsheets/sunderland

34   Harry Bromley-Davenport, Julie MacLeavy and David Manley, *Brexit in Sunderland: The production of difference and division in the UK referendum on European Union membership*, Politics and Space, 2019, Vol. 37(5) pp795–812.

35   Dan Jackson, *The Northumbrians: North-East England and Its People, A New History*, Hurst & Company, London, 2019, pp211–212.

however; something was happening along England's edges to provoke this collective anti-establishment sentiment.

We parked at Sunderland Civic Centre, and strolled along the short walk to Wearmouth bridge. From here we looked down on the lower reaches of the River Wear, to Bishopwearmouth on the south bank, Monkwearmouth on the north. These two areas form the historic core of Sunderland, and as we looked down on them I was reminded of an exhibition of street art I had visited 40 years earlier at what used to be the Ceolfrith Arts Centre, not far from where we were standing. It is symbolic of how Wearside has been transformed that this art centre morphed into the Northern Gallery for Contemporary Arts, which is now housed in the University of Sunderland, Monkwearmouth. There is a deep process of continuity here, for Monkwearmouth was an ancient centre of Anglo-Saxon learning. It was here that two men, Ceolfrith and Benedict Biscop, formed an ecclesiastical partnership that was to have profound implications for the development of England's story about itself.

The story began with Benedict Biscop, who founded St Peter's monastery at Monkwearmouth, in 674, near where the St Peter's campus of Sunderland University stands today. A few years later, in 684-5, Biscop founded a second monastery, St Paul's, six miles away at Jarrow near the mouth of the Tyne, of which his friend Ceolfrith was the first abbot. The monastery and church were built with stone taken from Hadrian's Wall. These two monasteries subsequently combined to form the double monastery of Monkwearmouth-Jarrow, and Ceolfrith became the abbot of this double house. About this time, a young boy called

Bede came into Ceolfrith's care; he had been dedicated to the church by his parents at the age of seven, a common practice then. Bede became Ceolfrith's ward.

A short while later, the plague struck the region and wiped out almost all the monks at this double house and also the monks of the monastery on Holy Island, Lindisfarne. It was left to Ceolfrith and the young Bede to rebuild the monastic community at Monkwearmouth-Jarrow virtually from scratch, which they did very successfully. In 716, Ceolfrith, realising that he was nearing the end of his life, had one more thing he wanted to do. He set sail, carrying with him one of the most beautiful books ever made, a copy of Jerome's Vulgate Bible, the Codex Amiatinus. This was the Latin translation of the Bible that became the standard text throughout northern Europe, and which, several centuries later, was formally adopted by the Catholic Church as its official version of the Bible. It was the same version my mother used for her devotions. The text had been copied out and the book assembled in Northumbria, at the monastery of Monkwearmouth-Jarrow, and Ceolfrith carried it with him to present to Pope Gregory II. His timing was just a bit out, however, for he never reached his destination; he died in Burgundy. Although his precious manuscript probably reached Rome, it eventually made its way to the Abbey of the Saviour, Monte Amiata in Tuscany, and now resides in Florence.[36]

Ceolfrith's protégé, Bede, became a prolific writer himself, and his works travelled over the North Sea to Europe, where

---

36   Medieval manuscripts blog, https://blogs.bl.uk/digitisedmanuscripts/2016/09/1300th-anniversary-ceolfrith-leaves.html

they were widely read. Drawing on other people's memories and what written evidence he could find, Bede put together a book which was called the *Ecclesiastical History of the English People*. According to Michael Pye, 'His book was not scientific, and not historical in a modern sense'; it was rather a 'brilliantly considered scrapbook', a 'Saxon account of Saxon triumphs, a Christian treatise.'[37]

Bede's story, as told by Bede, became England's founding myth, written from a Christian point of view. It was the story of how Anglo-Saxon missionaries came to these islands and persuaded us all to convert to the true version of Christianity. But the way we all became 'Christian' wasn't always through the gentle process of a change of heart. Bede believed that both the plague and the disaster that befell the Britons at the hands of the Anglo-Saxons were God's punishments for living unholy lives. Britons were heretics, because they didn't accept the Christian doctrine of Original Sin. This tells us we are full of sin from the moment we are born, but the pagan British had the shameful idea that we are free to act as responsible adults and make our own moral choices.[38] For this grave error, they had to be punished, and if possible, eliminated. So the Anglo-Saxon take-over was seen as God's way of giving us the opportunity to make a new start – a Christian start – in much the same way that the human race was given the chance of a new beginning after God destroyed sinful humanity in Noah's Flood.

Northumbria also produced the Lindisfarne Gospels 1,300

37   Michael Pye, *The Edge of the World: How the North Sea Made Us Who We Are*, Penguin, 2014, p.23.
38   Ibid. pp23-25.

years ago. They are kept in the British Library; many people in the North East feel they should be kept where they were produced, but the British Library is of the opinion that they should stay in London. It did, however, let northeasterners see them at Durham Cathedral for a few weeks in 2013, and has loaned them to the Laing Gallery on a couple of occasions, and this is very kind of them.[39]

This story of who we are, and the way we became who we are, was worked out on the northeast edge of England 1,300 years ago. Although Wearside has recently undergone a painful process of change, it is rightly proud of its deeper history. Sunderland University's presence in Monkwearmouth is a powerful symbol of the continuity of a tradition of learning established by Ceolfrith, Benedict Biscop and Bede on this same site more than a millennium ago.

The tiny port of Seaham, seven miles south of Sunderland, encapsulates the industrial history of the North East. It began life as a farming and fishing community, with the Anglo-Saxon church of St Mary the Virgin at its heart. For centuries, however, the port and its hinterland had been owned and controlled by the Lords of Dalden, Bowes and Collingwood until, in the early nineteenth century, the Londonderry family bought it up, sank the first colliery and built a new harbour to get the coal to southern towns and cities.

The coal was extracted at a heavy cost to human life. Some of the seams being worked were just 18 inches (45 centimetres) thick, big enough only for children to work. Young boys

39   https://laingartgallery.org.uk/lindisfarne-gospels-2022

aged eight to fourteen were employed, and Charles Vane, 3rd Marquess of Londonderry, raged against Parliamentary attempts to forbid the use of such child labour. He argued that if he were to make the underground roads higher to enable fully grown men to work them, he would incur such heavy costs that the mines would become unprofitable. One of the ten richest men in the country at the time, he spent £150,000 on his Irish home, Mount Stewart, and gave £30 to the local committee raising money for famine relief in Ireland.

Men and boys were deformed and killed in the mining of coal, and a succession of disasters in which dozens lost their lives triggered a series of industrial disputes and strikes that marked the beginnings of the North East's history of left-wing politics and militant trade unionism.

With Londonderry family seats at Mount Stewart, Newtownards in County Down; Plas Machynlleth, Montgomeryshire in Powys; and Londonderry House, Park Lane, in London – as well as Seaham Hall in Country Durham, which the family abandoned in the early twentieth century – local miners could be forgiven for feeling that the pit owners were more interested in the maximisation of value and profit than in the health and welfare of their employees. It is easy to see why people all along this industrial coast have become bolshie and seize every opportunity of giving the authorities, in whatever shape or form, a hefty kick on the backside.

Hartlepool, a bit further south, is a good example of this stroppy attitude. Fed up with both Labour and Conservative politicians, in May 2002 they elected a local joker by the name of Stuart Drummond as mayor, under the pseudonym of H'Angus the Monkey, on the promise of free bananas for schoolchildren. He was re-elected in 2005 and again in 2009. And they gave the establishment the ultimate kick in the pants in the 2016 EU referendum with a whopping 69.6 per cent 'Leave' vote.

It's hardly surprising. Hartlepool's economic history had been predicated on iron, coal, shipbuilding and engineering. In rapid succession, they all disappeared. With the local economy crashing, Hartlepool today has the highest unemployment rate in the UK. Places like this, which created the nation's wealth, have seen it being sucked away to the cosmopolitan south, where the vested interests and HQs of powerful industries are located. According to the *New Statesman* in March 2019,[40] levels of child poverty in Hartlepool were among the highest in the country and benefit claimants numbered more than anywhere else; when it was reported that the hospital's emergency unit would be closed, it must have seemed like the final straw.

We walked along Stranton Street, past the splendid modernistic buildings of the Hartlepool campus of Cleveland College of Art and Design on our left. Ahead was the magnificent but abandoned Co-operative Society building. Such buildings were hugely important in these northern industrial towns. Once they began to close, it was a sure sign that the local economy was in trouble. This one dominated the skyline and would not have been out of place on Newcastle's Grey Street or London's Regent Street. It closed three decades ago, and later converted into luxury

40 Anoosh Chakelian, 'There'll be an uprising: Hartlepool on life as a Brexit town with no deal in sight,' *New Statesman*, 4 March 2019.

apartments. Nearby is the Further Education College, which specialised in cookery.

Church Street was in a sorry state of dereliction. The Golden Gate Indian restaurant offered a '5-course special' for £8.95. A group of voluble women in their glad rags after a late night out, tottering on ill-fitting high heels, staggered past the 'Hartlepool Churches Together Foodbank' at number 28. They'd just come out of the Hillcarter Hotel, the only business on Church Street that seemed to have any life left in it, in a street that used to be at the centre of a thriving port.

Over the road, the Dilshead Tandoori restaurant offered the 'Thursday and Sunday Night Special', another five-course meal for £8-95 – 'choose anything off the menu'. On what were once beautiful Victorian dwellings, the stucco was peeling off, gutters were weighed down by sprouting grass and saplings, magnificent bay windows with shabby net curtains attempted to disguise rooms of drear lifelessness.

The once-imposing Athenæum was erected by public subscription in 1851, the year of national optimism when the Great Exhibition was held in the Crystal Palace, London. Now, it was decayed and boarded up. On the opposite corner was the Yorkshire Bank, also boarded up.

The Exchange building on another corner was occupied by a chartered accountancy firm, and on the fourth corner was a decayed and unidentifiable building. A printing firm was housed in what had once been the West Hartlepool Nautical Academy, which had been refurbished in 1985 but was now derelict.

At the end of the road was a brand new building housing

a new campus of the Cleveland College of Art and Design. It was Freshers' Week and one of the tutors was standing outside, welcoming new students. We asked him about the run-down appearance of Church Street.

'Five million pounds from the Lottery Heritage Fund and a similar sum from the local authority is going towards a major refurbishment of Church Street,' he told us. 'It's starting in two weeks, twenty-five years after the development of the Dockland area and the museum.' The aim, apparently, was to turn it into a hub for creative industries and, to kickstart the process, business rates were to be waived.

Church Street abuts onto the recently refurbished dockland area and the spanking new marina, with its smart bars, restaurants and upmarket apartments. Opposite was *HMS Trincomalee*, the oldest Royal Navy warship still afloat in Europe, which is the centrepiece of the National Museum of the Royal Navy. The whole area was interlaced by a network of walkways that took us round the marina and onto pleasing plazas. A young couple with a small boy and girl were walking a few paces in front of us. Reminded of our grandchildren, it didn't take Joan long to establish that the woman, Fran, had been born in Barnsley, Joan's neck of the woods.

'So are you on holiday here or just passing through?' Fran asked.

'We're on a bit of a project,' Joan said. 'Exploring England's east coast. It's by electric car, so half the time we seem to spend being anxious about where the next charge point is.'

'Must be a bit nerve-wracking.'

'There seems to have been a lot of money spent on this

area,' I said, 'but just over there, on Church Street, it looks as if the place is falling apart.'

'Oh,' said Fran. 'They're wanting to put money into that area next. They want to develop it.'

'I've read in the paper that this region has received twice as much EU funding per head as the average for England and that it will be the hardest hit if we stopped trading with the EU. But more than two thirds voted to leave.'

'Yeah, it was difficult to know which way we should go. We thought maybe for the children's future we should stay in, but then maybe there's arguments for coming out, too. It was hard to tell. We'll have to wait and see.'

On the far side of the marina was a block of apartments, red-bricked and red-roofed, in keeping with the rest of the development. From the outside, they looked spacious. They opened onto parking spaces, bollards, block paving, railings and water. They were neat and contained. A young woman was coming out of one of them.

'Those apartments look very smart,' I said, 'and the windows are huge. Must be big rooms.'

'Ah, don't be taken in,' she said. 'Those windows cover two rooms, a bedroom one half and the living room on the other. The wall forms the centre strut of the window. These apartments are actually very small, and they're expensive. I'm moving out, back into town to live with my mum.'

Near the end of a breakwater, a young man was pulling a two-and-a-half-pound cod out of the water.

'The best thing is,' he said, dropping his voice so as not to be overheard by a couple of old chaps behind him, 'those men have been here for hours and have caught nothing. I've actually only been here ten minutes and got this.'

'Are you keeping it?'

'Oh yes.' Then turning to his girlfriend, he said, 'This will do for our dinner tonight, won't it?' She didn't seem particularly enthusiastic about the idea and said nothing.

'She's just learning to fish,' he said.

We passed the two old men on our way to the *Trincomalee* about half an hour later and said hello, but they stared back at us glumly and uttered not a word. They were there the next day, when it was raining heavily. There were four of them this time, and their rods were leaning against the balustrade while they sat in their van watching, hoping to see the twitch that would signal something good for their dinners, too.

Brilliant white mounds of some powdery substance, as bright as freshly fallen snow, overlooked the marina. It was the Hartlepool works of Omya UK, known for its processing of white dolomite to produce white minerals and chemicals used in construction and the manufacture of sheet polymers. This white dolomite is the very same limestone that was able to get rid of the phosphorus in Cleveland's iron ore just down the road and so kick-start the region's steel industry. It was a glimpse of one of the ways in which Hartlepool was trying to make a comeback.

On the other side of this ultra-new industry, however, we suddenly found ourselves back 1,500 years as we entered the original old Hartlepool. It was perched on a promontory known as the Headland and clustered round St Hilda's church. For such a small coastal port, the church was massive and could easily have been mistaken for a cathedral.

'Actually,' said Verity, the rector, 'Hilda came here first, to

Hartlepool, not Whitby, so we claim her and call her by her original name of Hild.'

Hild was appointed Abbess of Hartlepool in 649, and it became the most celebrated religious house in the northeast of England. It was she, as much as Cuthbert on Holy Island, and Bede and Ceolfrith in Monkwearmouth-Jarrow, who put Christianity on the map of England.

'This building came six hundred years later,' Verity said, 'but it's still impressive for a thousand-year-old building, don't you think?'

A few years after she took up residence in Hartlepool, Hild founded the monastery of Whitby. It was a 'double', that is, a unisex monastery, for both monks and nuns, but there was a strict code of practice to cut out any hanky-panky. The reason why Hild, more popularly known as St Hilda, became so famous was because she hosted the Synod of Whitby in 664 to sort out the knotty issue of the date of Easter.

The problem arose because Christianity had come to England by two routes – one from Ireland via Iona and Lindisfarne, and the other from Rome via Kent. This meant we had two difference types of Christianity – Celtic and Roman. The Celtic Christians disagreed with the Roman Christians about the way the date of Easter was calculated. It was all to do with when the Paschal moon appeared, when you reckoned the date of the spring equinox was, whether you trusted the Julian or Gregorian calendar, and whether you wanted to go along with the western Christians or follow the practices of eastern Christians.

Celtic and Roman Christians also disagreed about the correct way to cut their hair: tonsures or no tonsures, long or short, tied up in a bun or worn as a catchy bob. Another bone of contention was the correct style of writing – the 'island script' used by Irish monks or the 'uncial script' practised in the Roman manner. The approach to writing defined which side a monk was on.[41] Hilda got them to stop their bickering and get it sorted, which they did. The Roman view prevailed, whereupon the episcopal centre of Christianity moved from Lindisfarne to York, which meant that from that moment Holy Island in Northumberland became an off-the-beaten-track historical curiosity and York became the flourishing archbishopric it is today.

Whereas in Hild's day, Hartlepool was a thriving community gathered around a prestigious ecclesiastical core, the present-day congregation of St Hilda's Church lives in one of the poorest parts of the country.

'This is an area of high deprivation,' the secretary to the Parochial Church Council told us. 'Since the big industries closed here, there's been no work. We are into the fifth generation of people here who have never worked, never known what it is like to have a paying job. There's nothing here, no work at all.'

'So how do they manage?'

'Many of the locals survive by going to the Hartlepool Foodbank on Church Street.'

The caricature of northeast man as a lazy, chauvinistic, half-drunk slob, always wearing a cloth cap, fag in his mouth, scarf round his neck, owes much to the character invented by local cartoonist, Reg Smythe, and it is an unfortunate one. We

41   Michael Pye, *The Edge of the World: How the North Sea Made Us Who We Are*, Penguin, 2014, p51.

came across a statue of this anti-hero, Andy Capp, on the edge of a small square of grass on Croft Terrace. Predictably, he was lounging against a wall, one hand holding a glass of beer, the other in his pocket, fag in mouth, scarf round his neck and the famous cloth cap over his eyes. Equally predictably, the statue was next to a pub – the Pot House – on the edge of the same Fish Sands where his heroic predecessors would have hauled their cobles onto the beach with the day's catch.

Andy Capp became the epitome of the kind of lassitude into which it is possible to sink when all hope has been lost and getting on your bike in search of a job is a hopeless undertaking, even if you could afford the luxury of a bike. In a half-drunken stupor, he was nonchalantly gazing across Hartlepool Bay to *HMS Trincomalee*, the museum complex and jazzed-up world of the marina. He was looking out to a world that was a million miles away from his own and to which he had long since given up all hope of belonging. Millions of people nationwide have seen the Andy Capp cartoon strip, so it is hardly surprising that this character has helped to shape the perception of the typical northeast man. Unfortunately, stereotypes stick, and it doesn't always play well with northeasterners.

More than a thousand years after the Synod of Whitby, another religious squabble took place just down the road, in Hartlepool proper, at Christ Church. The man traditionally known as the 'founder' of West Hartlepool was the entrepreneur Ralph Ward Jackson. As well as creating a thriving dockland town, he and his company also donated the land for building a church, which was consecrated in 1854, with the Revd John Burges as its first rector. Ward

Jackson encouraged the rector to raise money for a church school; his intention was that it should be for the benefit of the poor of West Hartlepool as a whole. The Revd John Burges, however, believed that only Anglicans should be admitted to the school, while Ward Jackson wanted no such restrictions.

The disagreement became personal. Ward Jackson asked the rector to resign, but he refused. It escalated to the point where Jackson decided that if the new school couldn't be open for the whole town, then neither would the church; he had, after all, given it the land on which it stood. He therefore had the church doors bricked up, and then publicly pronounced that all marriages that had been conducted in the church would be declared invalid. This was no doubt welcome news for some parishioners who saw it as an opportunity to get out of a difficult situation, when a hasty and insincere promise might have been made as part of the seduction process.

The Bishop of Durham, predictably, took the church line and supported the rector's position that the new school should be for Anglicans only. However, the Revd John Burges lost this support when the bishop subsequently retired. His case was weakened and he was forced to resign to take up a living in Birmingham.

Ward Jackson's view prevailed: that the school should be for the poor of West Hartlepool as a whole. The bricks were taken down, the doors of the church were opened and, much to the dismay of the cads who hadn't expected to have to keep their promises, their marriages were declared valid after all.[42]

Christ Church stopped being a church in the 1970s when

---

42   https://northeastbells.co.uk/hartlepool-christ-church/

the population began to decline and there weren't enough churchgoers to put money into the collection plate to support it as a going concern. This lovely Victorian building has been spectacularly refurbished, and today stands proudly in the centre of Church Square, on a traffic island at the west end of Church Street.

At the other end is the already refurbished marina, and in between is the dilapidated Church Street, awaiting renewal. Christ Church is now a rather beautiful and extremely lively art gallery, with an embedded information centre and the delightful Vestry café, situated in the very place where the small-minded Revd Burges would have donned his ecclesiastical robes each Sunday. We found the whole place visually and sensually beautiful. It was freshers' week, and groups of fresh-faced art and design students were being familiarised with both the town and the artistic surroundings that were to be their home for the next three or four years. So it seems that Ward Jackson had won out after all; the former church was there to serve the whole community, not just the parish.

11

THE RIVER THAT
FLOWS THE WRONG WAY

'I'M SHOCKED,' JOAN SAID. 'It's as if the whole area has been used and then dumped.'

To pass through Teesside is to be confronted with a savagely raw industrial landscape, the kind that exacts a heavy human price. This was the crude realism of industrialisation gone mad, all iron and concrete and noise and fumes as far as the eye could see, creating a shocking environment for human habitation. It had a look of devastation about it. If ever there was a community on the edge, it was here, on the physical, economic and social edge. It is no surprise that, in the EU referendum, according to Patrick Cockburn, the highest 'Leave' vote of anywhere in the UK was in the Brambles and Thorntree ward in Middlesbrough. Cockburn reported that it was the less educationally qualified voters in poor, mainly white neighbourhoods who voted to leave the EU. Here, in the heart of Middlesbrough, a record ward-level 'Leave' vote of 82.5 per cent was recorded, ensuring that, although this community had been forgotten by economy and society, this vote at least would be remembered.[43]

The Transporter Bridge is an altogether more satisfying way of crossing the Tees than by the road bridge, which is fast but ugly. The one redeeming feature of the Tees flyover is its speed; apart from this, it is entirely without artistic, aesthetic or imaginative merit. In short, it is ghastly, and the scene viewed from it hideous. The Transporter Bridge, on the other hand, though looking rather like a Meccano model built by a group of talented sixth-formers, is beautifully simple and human in scale. Close up, you realise that this is an engineering wonder. The whole thing is an intricate latticework of blue metal triangles, hundreds and thousands of them. It's a work of art, a creation of metallic lacework, epitomising the proud history of the North East's heritage of heavy engineering. It is, however, slow. You cannot use this way of crossing the Tees if you are in a hurry to get across.

Known affectionately to the locals as the Middlesbrough Transporter Bridge, it is the longest remaining example of its type in the world. The 180-metre-long superstructure spans the River Tees about 50 metres above water level, and from this is suspended a gondola that swings gently as it carries its cargo of cars – maximum load nine vehicles or 600 people. We found it endearing in its functional simplicity and enjoyed the slow, floating stillness of the experience as we

43   Patrick Cockburn, 'On the Brink of Brexit: the Only Thing Most People Outside Westminster Know About Brexit is That It's a Mess,' *CounterPunch*, 22 January 2019.

swayed across to the other side.

Half a century ago, Teesside industries were crying out for water. ICI alone needed 35 million gallons a day, and the steel industry was not far behind. To ensure a steady supply of water, six dams were constructed in Upper Teesdale. The most contentious of these was the Cow Green Reservoir, just a few metres above Cauldron Snout and England's biggest waterfall, High Force. Cow Green Reservoir straddles the border between Cumbria and County Durham and lies within the North Pennines Area of Outstanding Natural Beauty, with precious reserves of periglacial plants, such as the unique Teesdale violet and the spring gentian. Here in the 1960s, in the magnificent desolation of this utterly quiet and uninhabited region of beauty, the drama of the conflicting demands of environment and economy was played out once again.

As we emerged from the tangled streets of Middlesbrough, the Cleveland Hills loomed over us to the south. Turning east, we passed through a string of places built on the iron ore found in those hills; together, they turned Teesside into the steel capital of the world. Eston, Dormanstown, Redcar, Saltburn-by-the-Sea, Skinningrove, Loftus – the steel that built Sydney Harbour Bridge was produced here. But the bonanza collapsed almost as quickly as it had begun, and although the overall impression of industry on Teesside today is of a dystopian wasteland, it is actually in the throes of the difficult transition to a less environmentally damaging economy. Hovering on today's horizon are the 27 turbines of the Teesside Wind Farm, the harbinger of a future based on green industries such as hydrogen and turbine production, life sciences, digital and creative, energy and renewables. And there is talk too of making Teesside a freeport to turbocharge this reinvention of itself, backed up by the applied research of Teesside University.

Leaving the dystopian landscape behind, we climbed to the heather-clad moors and wide skies of the Cleveland Hills. The whole of the coast from Skinningrove to Robin Hood's Bay and beyond follows the eastern margin of the North York Moors National Park, and it is a most glorious route to drive along. There was a time when, every August, Joan and I used to drive over the Cleveland Hills to Whitby for the annual Folk Week. There, we would dance ourselves to exhaustion and then wander along the quayside and eat fish, chips and mushy peas to satiety. If we had any energy left, we'd cross the River Esk by the swing bridge and climb the 199 steps to Whitby Abbey to pay homage to Hild. Then, on the way back, we'd mingle with Dracula devotees, buy rings or pendants made of jet, see the house where Captain Cook lived, and eat interesting food at the Shepherd's Purse.

Now, however, we bypassed Whitby, crossing the Esk by the high bridge, snatching a wistful glance at the bustling, picture-postcard harbour down below us. We were heading for a hotel at Wykeham, a small village five miles inland from Scarborough. But first, we had to charge the car. Our battery was low, and the only available charge point was on the northern edge of Scarborough, at Lidl. It was a Pod Point charger; as we already had a domestic Pod Point, we assumed it would be a straightforward process. It wasn't.

It was six o'clock when we got to Lidl. The car park was filled with end-of-working-day shoppers grabbing a quick meal for tired parents and ravenous kids. The CHAdeMO cable was free but the touch-screen informed us that we needed an app, which we didn't have. I called Pod Point, gave our details and set about downloading the app. The signal was not good, however, and no sooner had the app started to download than it froze and remained stubbornly immobile. I had another go, but the same thing happened. It was time to call the helpline.

'Yeah,' came the detached reply. 'It happens. Frequently. It's just a poor signal. 'Fraid there's nothing much I can do.'

Another attempt and another failure. I had still not got the hose inserted, it was getting dark and we were hungry and tired. Nearing exasperation, I had one more go. At that moment another electric car slid into the adjacent bay. It was a middle-aged couple. She, in the passenger seat, looked as fed up with life as I was feeling. He was all smiles and amiability. She opened the window on her side, two feet away from where I was standing, and her husband leaned across her to speak.

'I see it's free. OK if I charge?'

'I'm sorry,' I said, 'I know I'm not hooked up yet, but it's not free. I'm still trying to connect. Didn't realise we needed an app. Just downloading it. Then I'll need to charge.'

She was about to pounce. Lips were pursed even more tightly, eyes narrowed more fiercely, a white-knuckled hand grasped the door through the open window. She was in no mood for waiting. She had home comforts she wanted to get back to. You could see what she wanted to say written all over her face: 'What d'you mean it's not free? Of course it's free. You're not charging and you're not plugged in. We're here and we want to charge. Move over and let us get on with it.'

But amiable hubby saw the storm on the horizon and forestalled it, an expert at neutralising bad magic.

'Going far?'

'Hull, first thing tomorrow morning. There're no charge stations that we can see between here and there.'

'Right-ho,' he said. 'Go ahead. We're not in a hurry, are we dear? We can sit here. No problem.'

'Thanks mate.'

It took 45 minutes to charge and all the time I was conscious of him sitting patiently beside his fuming wife.

'D'you think we should cut short the charge, Joanie?' I said. 'Just do enough to get to Hull and then find a charge point there? It's awfully good of them to wait.'

'Definitely not,' she said. 'They're local and haven't far to go. We're not and do, and there're no charge points on the way. Don't even think of it.'

We went inside the Lidl store to see if we could get a 'coffee to go'. But it wasn't a store for lingering; the charge point was there for customers who have something to do while their car was charging. We weren't customers and just had to hang around. They were still there when it was done, she now calmer, he patient as ever. We thanked them, and they smiled in acknowledgment – both of them.

It was dark when we arrived at Wykeham, but in the morning it was possible to see the lie of the land. It was a small village nestling at the foot of the Moors, overlooking the Vale of Pickering. Four miles wide and 25 miles long, this low, remarkably flat expanse of agricultural land lies between the North York Moors and the Yorkshire Wolds, and running through its heart is the River Derwent.

The unusual thing about this river is that it flows the wrong way. Rising in the North York Moors, just a few miles from the coast, it used to flow the short distance east into the North Sea. It no longer does this, however, for it has reversed its direction of flow. We can blame this on the ice sheet that once filled the North Sea and which, as it retreated, dumped a line of glacial muck along what is now the east coast. In so doing, it created a huge dam that completely blocked eastward-flowing rivers. The waters of the Derwent, with nowhere else to go, formed a large lake behind this dam, known as Lake Pickering. Unable to contain itself, the waters of this lake overflowed at their western end, turning the former eastward-flowing river into a westward-flowing river, away from the sea. In its quest for a new outlet, the new river turned south, joined the Ouse and disgorged itself into the North Sea via the Humber.

After Lake Pickering had drained away, its former bed became the rather lovely Vale of Pickering. In the course of time, settlements grew up on the north and south edges of the former lake, so that today there are two parallel rows of villages facing each other from opposite sides of the vale. Wykeham is just one of many of these villages. Today, the Vale of Pickering is a delightfully pastoral area of lowland, prone to flooding, it is true, but contrasting with the hard beauty of the hills on either side.

And so we crossed this vale, picked up the A64 and turned east towards Filey and then south to Flamborough Head. This is where the chalk of the Yorkshire Wolds falls dramatically into the North Sea. On any map of England, Flamborough Head stands out as one of the most conspicuous points on the east coast. It is a flamboyant edge, and it is where the huge swathe of chalk that sweeps diagonally across England from Dorset to the Yorkshire Wolds comes to an abrupt stop. This is the northern limit of chalk country, and it marks that limit with a flourish. The cliffs here are spectacular, as are the stacks and arches at their foot.

There are two lighthouses on Flamborough Head, the first built in the seventeenth century and the second at the beginning of the nineteenth. Both are still there, and have been standing for more than 200 years. This is not trivia. It is significant, because south of here, recently built houses are falling into the sea, and local authorities are fighting a losing battle to hold back the remorseless logic of geology.

12

ANOTHER HEMISPHERE

FROM THE STUNNING HEIGHTS of Flamborough Head, we dropped quickly to the coastal plain surrounding Bridlington Bay. We kept to the B1242, an easy road that follows the coast most of the way. From here to Spurn Head, 50 miles to the south, this area is known as Holderness. It is rich agricultural land that at one time used to be marsh. Its edge, however, is exposed to the merciless excesses of the North Sea. Because of this, it has one of the fastest eroding coastlines in Europe.

From Bridlington to Skipsea, Hornsea, Mappleton, Tunstall, Easington and Kilnsea, land and houses are being gobbled up at the rate of about two metres a year. Over the past thousand years, a strip of land 35 miles long and two-thirds of a mile wide has been lost to the sea, carried away by powerful currents sweeping south.[44]

The paradox about this erosion of the land is that England only recently acquired it. It comprises the same material that dammed the River Derwent and created Lake Pickering just a few miles to the north: loose, glacial debris. All along this stretch of coast, houses and roads were built on this debris and gardens were cultivated on its soils, yielding excellent produce. But it's not solid rock, like the chalk of Flamborough; it's easily erodible loose aggregate, and 'no part of the British coast is being destroyed more rapidly'.[45] As the Bible has it, the wise man builds his house upon the rock.

Although it is not much consolation to those people whose houses are being washed away, they might take heart from the fact that the land which used to belong to them is not entirely lost; it is simply being reconstituted further south for other people to build on. When the swiftly moving waters of the North Sea collide with the slower waters of the Humber, they are forced to slow down and, in so doing, to drop their load. This process has created the five-kilometre-long Spurn Spit, shaped like a curlew's beak curving into the Humber Estuary and terminating at Spurn Point. The result is one of England's most spectacular spits.

Round the corner, in the Humber Estuary, people are living on new land that has been recently created from the washed-away detritus of the homes and gardens of people living a few miles to the north. Sunk Island was a mere sandbank in

---

44   Oliver Rackham, *The History of the Countryside*, Phoenix, 2000, p377.
45   A E Trueman, *Geology and Scenery in England and Wales*, Penguin Books, 1967, p132..

the seventeenth century but today it is part of the mainland. Nearby Hedon, on the eastern outskirts of Hull, was once a thriving port but is now two miles from the coast. Nature creates and nature destroys.

Kilnsea is on the extreme end of Spurn Point; it's as far as you can go without falling into the sea. It has about 30 dwellings, and the Blue Bell Café provides all the essential services for outdoor types wanting to spend the day walking or photographing birds in the Wetlands Nature Reserve. For residents of the nice bungalows, Hull is only 25 miles away. We parked up, ate our sandwiches and watched an army of ornithologists clambering out of cars, much encumbered with their cameras, telephoto lenses and tripods.

The solidity of bricks and mortar can be misleading. Most of Kilnsea, including the original parish church of St Helen's, its cemetery and its corpses, disappeared into the sea in the 1820s. A new church was optimistically built some 30 years later, but despite this calamitous process of change, the people of Kilnsea seem to be confident they can keep things as they always were. In almost every garden, signs proclaimed 'YWT says NO to Visitor Centre' and 'Keep Spurn Wild'. The Yorkshire Wildlife Trust wanted to keep the Blue Bell Café just as it is. They had no desire to see the development of a proposed smart new centre, which might attract more visitors but, in the process, disturb the bird life and ruin everything.

But things are going to change, my friends, they certainly are going to change. Just remember the old village of Kilnsea, which is now under the sea, and remember the 22 other villages along the Holderness coast that have also disappeared. The process, I'm afraid to say, is remorseless. In the end, geology and ocean currents will have their say. Harsh and difficult planning decisions are going to have to be made.

One problem of touring in rural areas is that you never know just when you might need to respond to a call of nature. An example occurred at Easington, a small village three miles to the north of Kilnsea and a third of a mile from the sea. Looking around in a state of considerable agitation, I espied the community hall, fortunately with its door slightly ajar.

As we stepped inside, a gentle murmur of voices and the soft click of carpet bowls wafted over us. While Joan, who isn't afflicted with the same problem, poked her head through the door of the hall to announce our presence, I hunted around in the lobby area for means of relief.

In a more composed state of mind, I joined Joan, who by this time was at the centre of a small gathering of wrinklies eager to share any news we might be able to give them of the outside world. So important was this visitation from the great outside that they had even stopped the game they were playing. The hall, we gathered, had been funded by Langeled Partners, a consortium of companies bringing gas to England's north-east coast, where six gas terminals, including one at Easington, have been built.

We had parked the car alongside a terrace of three houses; as we returned, a young woman, looking harassed and old beyond her years, was sweeping the doorstep of the middle property. The last shop in Easington had closed the previous September, she told us.

'It's three miles to the shops at Patrington,' she said. 'I go there on my bike. But I can't get all I need in one go. I've got three kids, so I have to go most days. Sometimes my boyfriend takes me to Hull to shop. I get lonely. I keep talking to myself. I'd love to have a house in Patrington near the shops. That's all I want. Just a house in Patrington.'

'Can't you sell up and move there?'

'It's a council house. The others are private.'

Unlike the fortunate residents of Kilnsea, Withernsea would dearly like to see change. Rarely have we felt so dismayed as when we entered this sad little town, 10 miles to the north. It felt like the fag-end of the world. There must have been a sign over the entrance saying *Abandon Hope All Ye Who Enter Here*. Even the young people, whose hearts should have been bursting with pride and energy and optimism, looked as if they had already given up, beaten on the very threshold of life.

Queen Street, the town's central road, where some signs of life might have been expected, looked as if it was struggling. It boasted such shops as Gate Way Charity, Lions Club, Chipmunks Children's Society, Tofs Original Factory Shop, Karmichael's Bargains Galore, Matts Discount Food Store. Tesco's enticed shoppers by offering them £8 off for every £20 spent in the Withernsea branch.

Withernsea, it seems, has always had to struggle. A walk along the promenade led us to a plaque that told us that, approximately one mile offshore, the site of the thirteenth-century church of St Mary the Virgin now lies at the bottom of the North Sea. Slightly to its north, another church, St Peter's, together with the village of Owthorne, are its underwater neighbours. To add to Withernsea's woes, the magnificent pier, which was built in 1877, was also a casualty of the North Sea's voracious appetite; its castellated brick-built gateway, optimistically modelled on the entrance to Conway Castle, is all that remains.

When the Hull-to-Withernsea Railway was built in the mid-nineteenth century, day trippers from Hull poured into Withernsea in their thousands, paid one penny to walk the 1,200 feet to the end of the pier and back, and sat on one of its many seats to look and wonder. The pier gave to Withernsea a fleeting moment of prosperity, but ship after ship slammed into it, unable to withstand the fierce storms that played with them like toys.

The coup de grâce, however, was delivered by Dr Beeching in the 1960s. He told the government that we didn't need branch routes that took people to insignificant, off-the-beaten-track little places like Withernsea. Concentrate, he advised, on trunk routes through the heart of the country – the future lay in the connections between important places. Hey, Beeching was a physicist and engineer, so he knew about these things.

It's odd how snippets from one's youth pop into your mind when considering such details. I was reminded of a puzzling saying by Jesus that now sound like words of pure wisdom: 'For to those who have, more will be given, and they will have an abundance; but from those who have nothing, even what they have will be taken away'.

Places like Withernsea certainly lost out when He allowed

the life-giving railway line to be taken away. So, trunk routes it was; the core of the country was what mattered, and the edges could be ignored.

The prime meridian passes through England just to the west of Withernsea, leaving its residents in the eastern hemisphere and most of the rest of the UK in the western hemisphere. But there seemed to be another invisible line separating the included from the excluded, and Withernsea was on the wrong side of it.

According to a report by the IPPR think-tank, the UK is one of the most divided countries in the developed world. The authors blame this on the excessive centralisation of the British economy.[46] Places like Withernsea are not only in a different hemisphere; they are in a different world, too, remote from the centre to matter. Forgotten.

We drove into Hull along the Anlaby Road to Nissan Trenton to charge the car. The charge point was in use when we drew up: another Leaf. In a corner of the large showroom was a lounge area where light refreshments were available. There we met Paradzai, a surgeon at the hospital.

'I won't be long,' he said. 'Another twenty minutes or so. Join me in a coffee.'

Someone called Eleanor was in the coffee corner, too.

'Are you waiting here long?' she asked.

'Just until the car's charged.'

'What, an electric one?'

'Yes. It'll take about forty-five minutes.'

'Does it cost you?'

'Not here. It's free.'

---

46   IPPR (Institute for Public Policy Research), 2019, *State of the North.*

'Oh, that's good. How far can you go?'

'Depends how you drive. If carefully, about a hundred and forty miles. On the motorways at sixty mph plus, maybe a bit less. But we need to recharge long before that. The Leaf isn't a distance car.'

'Oh, that'd scare me. Everywhere I go, I see petrol stations advertised. That makes me feel safe. I drive long distances each day.'

'I'm jealous. In the seven hundred miles we've done so far, we've only seen one charge point advertised. That was at Tebay. We have to search for every charge point, and even that can sometimes take half an hour.'

'That's why electric cars scare me.'

'What's your line of business?'

'Events catering. I couldn't be doing with all that hanging around and uncertainty. I have to be on the go all the time. Couldn't afford to take the risk. I have deadlines to meet. Can't you carry a spare battery with you?'

'They're a bit heavy,' said Paradzai. 'Three hundred kilograms each. It's no problem for us, we charge at night on the Economy 7. It's the best car I've driven, my Leaf. It's going to happen, you know. There's no reason why we can't all drive EVs. Every garage should have a charge point. I drove a Tesla once. I floored it. Nearly took off.'

'My partner's a carpet fitter and has his own business,' Eleanor said. 'We're both self-employed. No pension. We couldn't afford to take that sort of risk. We've got to have reliable cars and a good range. We drive long distances every day.'

It was a depressing drive along the Anlaby Road to the centre of Hull and our hotel. Rundown, boarded-up shops and houses, cut-price stores and betting shops lined both sides of the street. The people looked dejected.

'I'm distraught.' Joan said. 'It's horrible to see this in such a great city. It's not the Hull I remember.'

13

LADIES OUT!

As the years pass, you notice that your social life filters down to regular meetings with a diminishing circle of friends, especially when you gather to give yet another one a good send-off to their final destination. Conversations are different from those of the happy-go-lucky days of the youth that was wasted on you because you were too young to appreciate it. They tend to involve a game of one-up-manship, based on who can tell the best yarn about failing health.

I was at such an event recently when Ken came along and greeted a small group of us who knew one another from the drama society. As we waited to say farewell to one of our friends, Ken opened the topic of the day.

'Morning all,' he said. 'How're you doing?'

'Yeah, we're great, Ken. How're you?'

'Not so great, to tell you the truth. It's this catheter. It's uncomfortable. Keep having to make lots of adjustments. Keeps me awake at night, too. Doesn't make Margaret very happy.'

'Oh dear,' we all commiserated.

'Yeah. To put it bluntly, I'm pissed-off.'

'Know what you mean,' said Alex enthusiastically. 'I'm having problems with my ball.'

'Which one?' Duncan asked.

'The one in my hip. Waiting to get a new one, a steel one.'

'Ah, steel,' said Duncan. 'Good conductor of electricity. Get it done as soon as you can. It'll be good for you.'

'How so?'

'Well,' interjected Fran, Duncan's wife. 'He'd been fiddling around with something electrical when I heard this scream. I rushed through to find him dangling on the end of a wire, hands and legs shooting out all over the place as if he was electrocuted.'

'I was electrocuted,' Duncan said.

'Anyway, since then he's never been so fit,' Fran said.

'Yeah,' said Duncan. 'I used to have an irregular heartbeat, atrial fibrillation, but now it's gone. Heartbeat's perfectly regular. Problem solved.'

'Do you think I should try electrocuting myself?' I said to Joan afterwards. 'Might save all those tablets.'

'Could go wrong, though,' she said.

I thought of all of this when Joan and I arrived at the Whittington and Cat in Hull. It had this name because the guy who walked all the way to London with not a penny to his name and just a cat for company is reputed to have stayed there. We could see no other reason for it to have a four-star rating. We could see how a young chap like Dick Whittington, having walked all day, would have been happy with anything reasonably flat to lie down on. But we weren't young and we'd got fussy in our old age. Our priorities had changed. One of our priorities was comfort at night, and when a hotel has been given a four-star rating, we expect the service to match the offer.

To give the management its due, the establishment we'd landed up at did have a 'Hotel' sign over one of the doors, but it was in the least conspicuous place imaginable, on the side of the building and hanging somewhat apologetically over what looked like the neglected back door of a building that was about to be abandoned. We tried turning the handle of what purported to be the hotel door. We tried pushing it. In fact, we tried every possible way of manipulating that door handle to get into what called itself a hotel. We looked through the letter box onto a disheartening scene that might have discouraged even Dick Whittington from seeking a night's rest there. What should have been a hallway looked more like a building merchant's storeroom: an arrangement of buckets, ladders, brushes, carpentry equipment and boxes of floor tiles.

'I think we must've come to the wrong place. Maybe we've been ripped off and it isn't a hotel at all. Did we pay in advance?'

'I don't think so,' Joan said. 'In fact, it all looked rather good on the internet.'

'That just goes to show how you can Photoshop any dreary scene to make it look delectable.'

We lugged our suitcases to the other side of the building

and through an open door marked 'Public Bar'. Here we found ourselves in the company of half a dozen seriously old men, hunched over jugs of beer and staring wearily at a black-and-white episode of *Ironside*. One of them looked up as we entered, but seeing nothing of interest, he returned to examining his half-empty beer jug. There was no one behind the bar, so I poked my head through a door that opened onto the other end of the builder's corridor.

'Hello-oh. Anyone the-ere?'

We heard the soft shuffle of slippered feet on bare boards, and a flustered woman appeared.

'Sorry,' she said. 'I was sorting out the beer barrels at the back. What can I get you?'

'I think we must've come to the wrong place. We thought this was a hotel?'

'It is.'

'But where?'

'The rooms are upstairs. Let's just get this paperwork sorted out, then I'll show you your room.'

She led us through the cluttered corridor and up two flights of gloomy stairs, thirty-seven in all, and into a darkened room that was totally black, except for a few white cushions scattered meaningfully over the bed. We were honoured. It was the 'Black and White Room'. Black curtains, black bed, black lamp, black door, black everything, except white cushions and white bed linen.

To be fair, it was a magnificent example of a red-brick Victorian hostelry, a lone island of nostalgia squeezed between the crude modernity of a retail park and a noisy roundabout. Although it did not look like a hotel, the management were doing their best to make it one.

One of the disadvantages of having lived a long and healthy life is that your body no longer allows you to behave in a youthful kind of way, even though your mind may want it to. We were definitely not Dick Whittingtons; we required more than just a place to lie down. We had reached the stage in our lives where you expect certain basic comforts to ease your passage into sleep. An absolute priority is a bedside table where you can put all the tablets you need to keep you ticking over for a few more years, a glass of water with which to wash them down, some reading material and a pair of spectacles to take your mind off the trials and tribulations of the day. And to enable you to deal with all of these things, you need a bedside lamp with an easily accessible switch.

Without these essentials, sleep becomes well-nigh impossible, and this four-star hotel had none of them. It is true that there was a lamp, but it was on the other side of the room, plugged into the only power socket in the room and on a short flex that made it impossible to transport it to the bedside. There was also a light hanging from the ceiling, but the switch for this was out of reach from the bed. My wife and I may represent an abnormal evolutionary off-shoot of the human race, but I am sure we are not alone in regarding a bedside reading lamp as pretty basic in a four-star hotel.

An additional disqualification for four-star status was that there were no shelves or towel rails in the cupboard that pretended to be an en suite, nowhere to put a shaving brush, razor or toothbrush other than on the floor. To be scrupulously fair, the management had thoughtfully provided a smart row of hooks for hanging our clothes on, but as this was immediately above the only mirror in the room, we had a choice of either hanging our clothes on these hooks and blocking the mirror, or using the mirror and leaving our clothes on the floor.

'Joan, are you sure this place really does have four stars?'

'Definitely.'

There's another cruel trick that nature plays on you if you are male and no longer a youth. Your body develops the irritating habit of waking you up several times throughout the night, compelling you to get up and attend to its demands. Under those circumstances, the last thing you want in an unfamiliar room is to have to search for a light-switch on the other side of the room to light your way to the bathroom before nature takes precipitate action.

We'd just settled into bed when I had a Eureka moment.

'I think I've got the solution.'

'Solution to what?'

'The problem of lighting. We forgot the extension lead.'

I got dressed, found my way down the dimly-lit stairs, negotiated the builder's paraphernalia, crossed the car park, rummaged through the car and retrieved the extension lead. Back in the room, I shifted the small table and lamp from the far side of the room and plugged in the extension lead. Triumphantly, I switched the lamp on. I was forgetting however, the demands of the décor, which decreed that the lamp shade should be pitch black. This meant that it blocked out 99 per cent of the light, making it impossible to read. When the inevitable call of nature came I got up, tripped over the cable, knocked the tumbler of water onto the floor, brought the light crashing down, plunged the room into total darkness, woke the wife, and ended up fumbling for the light switch on the far wall.

'You could've settled for that option in the first place,' mumbled a disgruntled voice.

All became clear in the morning when we discovered that we'd inadvertently found ourselves in a 'destination pub'. Apparently, it was on the 'real ale trail'. This meant you could rate your drink and even become part of a national beer scoring system. It was clearly a connoisseurs' pub, probably a four-star one.

Nevertheless, Joan wanted to go to another pub. She was very specific about this.

'I want to go to Ye Olde White Harte. I've got a score to settle there.'

'Do you know where it is, this White Harte?'

'Somewhere on Silver Street, I think.'

We found it in the centre of the old city, which thrived in the good old days when Hull was a member of the Hanseatic League, a kind of North European Common Market. Then, Hull's position on the eastern edge of England had served it well, and our trading relationship with Europe across the North Sea was a good one. The Hanseatic League brought prosperity to the eastern edges of our country. Since then, however, the Cod War and the container revolution have dealt lethal blows to Hull's fishing and shipping industries, so that, by 2009, Hull was at the bottom of the economic prosperity index.

Only 40 years earlier, Hull had been the fourth port of the UK. It took just 20 years to recover from the blistering damage of World War ll, restore its core industries and to recover its port trade. But in another four decades, that was all undone, leaving it with yet another of the country's impoverished coastal communities. In 2003, the *Idler* magazine named Hull Britain's 'Most Crap Town'.

Today, Hull and the greater Humberside region are basing their hopes on becoming the manufacturing hub for turbines to feed the giant wind farms being built in the North Sea. There is even talk of Hull becoming the leading centre for the production of hydrogen from natural gas. Because hydrogen produced in this way can be almost carbon-free, it's possible that hydrogen-powered cars could even supplant electric cars as the non-carbon solution to motoring. In fact, as we shall soon see, a few days later we would meet a garage proprietor with some mighty powerful arguments in favour of this option.

In some quarters, therefore, we found optimism running high on Humberside, but not high enough to quell the bolshiness of the electorate, who felt so strongly about the way they'd been treated that they decided to give the Government a kick in the teeth when they voted by two to one in favour of leaving the EU.

It was in the same revolutionary spirit that Joan's year group had challenged the ancient traditions of Ye Olde White Harte. That is why she was so insistent on revisiting it. Reputed to be the oldest public house in Hull, it was strictly for men only in Joan's day. One Saturday evening, when all the lads had forsaken their girlfriends in the interests of the end-of-week White Harte booze-up, the women rebelled. They invaded the pub and attempted to push their way through the raucous, tankard-waving men, who were singing songs that made the women blush. Horrified by this sacrilegious invasion of male territory, the chorus went up: 'Out, out! Ladies out!' Undeterred, a few courageous sisters – Joan among them – managed to fight their way to the bar.

'A glass of white wine,' demanded Joan.

'We don't serve women here,' came the reply.

Two generations later, Joan was back to see if the service had improved.

'Go and find a seat and leave this to me,' were my instructions, which I duly obeyed.

Approaching the bar, she was surprised when the men there moved aside to let her approach, and she almost fell over in astonishment when the barman asked her what she would like.

'I'd like to see if the service has improved since I was last here,' she said.

'I'm sorry to hear that. What happened?' he asked.

'I was refused service on account of my sex.'

'My God,' he said. 'The service isn't that bad, is it?'

'Well, admittedly it was a little while ago, but I would rather like it if you'd give me the glass of white wine I tried to order then but was refused.'

'Good gracious, that must have been in the bad old days, perhaps just a bit before my time?'

'Well, yes, I can't really blame you or the current management,' Joan said. 'But it has taken me fifty-seven years to get this drink.'

In keeping with their spirit of bolshiness, it was here in this pub that Hullensians hatched the plot that kick-started the English Civil War. A plaque on the wall informed us that the struggle to assert the paramountcy of Parliament began here, in this very pub, in this very room, on St George's Day in 1642. 'Within this Ancient Establishment in Ye Plotting Parlour ... the first blow was struck for, and gained by, The Parliament and thus commenced the Civil War which ended in the defeat and death of Charles.' The other outcome was that, from then on, the powers of the monarch would be seriously limited. The lesson – don't mess with Parliament.

'There you are, madam,' said the barman.

With that score settled, Joan took me the next day to find Thwaite Hall, her old hall of residence. I could feel her agitation as we approached. We parked the car on the gravelled drive and walked round to the front of what used to be a country mansion. For the start of a new academic year, it seemed eerily deserted. We rang the bell. The sound reverberated through an empty silence. There was a scrunch of wheels as a white van drew up, and a young man stepped out.

'Is anyone here?'

'I don't know. I'm just making a delivery. I think it's up for sale.'

Round the side of the building, we found the wing where Joan lived. Ivy was climbing over the windowpanes, eating into the door frames. Hedges were untrimmed, roses had not been dead-headed, lawns were overgrown. We looked through the windows into what had been a student bedsit, someone's home. The mattress was leaning against the wall, chairs on the desktop, the wardrobe open and empty, rugs lifted and piled in a corner.

'I'm choked, Clive,' Joan said. 'It's all so lifeless. It's horrible. It's like the death of an era, the door closing, the shutters finally being pulled down on that part of my life. There's no way back.'

She was tearful now. 'I did so many things wrong, made so many bad choices, so many mistakes. If I were here now, I'd do things so differently.'

'But we opened a new chapter didn't we, when we got together? We had the opportunity to start afresh. A lot of people don't get that and stay stuck with the mistakes and bad choices they made.'

Back at the main university building, we spoke to a student. It was week one of the autumn semester. She was there to study history and politics.

'Do you two work here?' she asked. 'Are you lecturers?'

'No, no, just taking a trip down memory lane,' Joan said. 'I was a student here sixty years ago. We're going to see the Philip Larkin exhibition. He was the librarian when I was a student here.'

'Wow, was he really? What was he like?'

'Tall, domed forehead, black-rimmed glasses, never smiled and always looked melancholy. It was only long after I'd left university that I realised what an amazing poet he was. At the time, I couldn't imagine he had any creative thoughts, because he never seemed to engage with any of the students at all. He seemed to be a loner. I didn't think anything was going on in that great domed forehead of his. But now I've got the utmost admiration for him as a brilliant poet.'

We found the statue of Larkin at the Paragon railway station, all seven feet of him striding off into the distance with a manuscript under his right arm. There, too, we came across Georgina and Catherine, doing their stint at the Culture Stand. Hull had just become the City of Culture, and at the warmest time of the year, in mid-June, more than 3,000 men and women from around the world stripped naked, painted their bodies various shades of blue and filled the streets and squares of Hull to recreate its lost waterways. This was all part of the SKIN exhibition, one of the centrepieces for the Year of Culture.

'We've been running a little land train to show people round during the Year of Culture,' Georgina said.

'So what will happen when it's over?'

'It's been so successful they've asked us if we'd like to continue as guides. I went to university here. It was a sad, depressed place at one time, but now, with the City of Culture, people are smiling. I voted for Brexit. We're on the edge here. We're the forgotten ones. We're better off out.'

'Most people here were for out,' Catherine said. 'My son lives in London. He was horrified when I told him I'd voted for out.'

14

ANOTHER COUNTRY

It was the Civil War that took us to Beverley. Although it is a mere nine miles from Hull, a bigger contrast between the two towns it would be difficult to imagine. Beverley's population of 30,000 is a tenth of that of Hull; it's an inland town, compared with Kingston-upon-Hull's status as a coastal port; and compared with Hull, Beverley is a smart, up-market, wealthy town. More intriguingly, in the Civil War, Beverley was staunchly Royalist. When he was shut out of Hull, Charles I sought – and was given – refuge in Beverley; when Charles II came to the throne, the people of Beverley were jubilant and hung his coat of arms in the Minster, where it remains to this day. The people of Beverley were definitely cavaliers, and Hullensians were definitely roundheads. Curious about what kind of place Beverley was, we decided to have breakfast there, and that was why we ended up in Carluccio's on Toll Gavel in the heart of this minster town.

According to the geographer, Nicholas Crane, the name Beverley means 'beaver lodge', which suggests that, at one time, Yorkshire's abundant woods and streams were teeming with beavers.[47] But the town really took off when a monk called John established a monastery there in the eighth century. John rose up the ecclesiastical hierarchy and became a bishop, first of Hexham and then of York. When he died, his remains were laid in the monastery. The monastery survived the great Dissolution by turning itself into a parish church, which eventually became Beverley Minster. Even then, John didn't let death stop his rise to fame, for he went on to perform several miracles, which resulted in his canonisation, 300 years after his death. In his new persona of St John of Beverley, he attracted a steady flow of pilgrims. Dominican Blackfriars built a friary there, which subsequently became a youth hostel. Not to be outdone, the Greyfriars built a Franciscan monastery. The Knights Hospitallers set up hospitals, and a grammar school followed. Religious tourism, together with the wool industry, boosted prosperity so much that, at one time, Beverley was the tenth largest town in England, and one of the richest. It has, of course, long since lost both its woollen industry and its elite position in the urban hierarchy, but it retains its ecclesiastical status as a minster town. It also helped consolidate Beverley's religious credentials that it was royalist, thus cementing the two pillars of the English establishment: Church and State.

---

47   Nicholas Crane, *The Making of the British Landscape*, Weidenfeld & Nicholson, paperback edition, 2017, p302.

Everything about Beverley's town centre struck us as prosperous and upmarket. Even the vaping shop opposite us had been made to look like an exclusive boutique, 'The Vaping Experts', with ultra-violet lighting and subtle, seductive shades of light and dark. It was all a world apart from Withernsea and Easington, reeking of ecclesiastical history and establishment solidity and prosperity.

We sat in the window of Carluccio's and ordered porridge with summer fruits followed by apricot croissant. And we sat and watched. There were no boarded-up shops on Toll Gavel. It was full of well-to-do, mostly elderly people – all fit, smartly dressed and walking purposefully. We watched them go with their shopping bags and, for those planning a heavier load, their brightly coloured shopping trolleys with neat lids; 30 minutes later, we watched them come back, their bags and trolleys full, their faces smiling and ruddy with good health. Some met friends and chatted for a few minutes, others popped into Carluccio's to join us for an early morning coffee. A few had gleaming bikes, with front baskets and rear panniers full of goodies. Some were grannies, taking their grandchildren with them while both parents in a two-income family spent the day at work. They were slim, upright, well-to-do, chirpy.

As I write, I've just been reminded by the BBC that the UK is the most unequal country in Europe. That is what we saw, travelling first to Withernsea and then to Beverley. The contrast is striking and depressing. As with so many other coastal towns, it was the railway that brought temporary prosperity to Withernsea, which was destroyed when it was closed. But it wasn't the railway that made Beverley; it was the ecclesiastical establishment. Railways come and go, but the Establishment remains. You can close a railway line, especially if the people affected have no clout and are in an out-of-the-way location like Withernsea, but who would dare to close a minster or a cathedral? Religion may be losing its significance in our social lives today and in our personal belief systems, but it is still big business – it still pulls in the tourists, religious and secular.

'We can't see any boarded-up shops,' I said to the waitress.

'Every single one that becomes vacant is immediately snapped up,' she said. 'Even Wilkinson's, that's just closed down at the end of the street, hasn't been boarded up. It's been made to look nice. It hasn't gone bust. They've just moved to a better location in the shopping precinct.'

At the next table, an elderly couple sat and chatted.

'It used to be all right when you were working,' she said. 'I could go out on my own.'

'Well, you could now.'

'Oh no, I couldn't. Not without you.'

And then they descended into silence. They ordered sandwiches of roasted red pepper hummus, squashed avocado and feta cheese, with homemade coleslaw and green salad drizzled with balsamic vinegar. Amid scattered copies of *Good Housekeeping* and *Yorkshire Living* magazines, smartly-coiffured women in svelte gilets discussed community matters of moment with animated faces. Two were studying the programme for York's Grand Opera House.

'It's another country here, isn't it?' Joan said. 'I bet Beverley voted to remain.'

We returned to Hull and charged the car at the Holiday

Inn. It was a Polar Instant. I had the app, but I was out of credit. I tried to top up by £20. A message came up: 'Can't top up unless you present your RFID card.' I phoned the Customer Service number. It was Brendan.

'Am I missing something, Brendan? I've got your app, but it keeps asking me for my RFID card. I thought it was an app-only service?'

'I know, I know,' said Brendan wearily. 'It's a mess. Oh dear, oh dear, we can't allow this to continue. OK, I'll get it sorted. Just hold on. I'll start it at my end.'

So he took control and the dials started whizzing. In the time it took us to have a coffee, our battery was full.

15

WINNERS, LOSERS AND ENVIRONMENTAL THEFT

I HAD WALKED ACROSS the Humber Bridge shortly after it opened in 1981. There was a strong wind coming at me from the west. There was air, there was sky and there was water – holding me up between them was the slender gracefulness of this nearly-one-and-a-half miles of extraordinary engineering. Crossing it to the silent whirr of an electric car, four decades later, felt no less inspiring. But it was also alarming. The huge expanse of water below us, into which the rivers of one fifth of Great Britain empty themselves, was like a thick brown soup, laden with the eroded soils of some of our prime agricultural land. Our most precious resource was being washed away, to be deposited elsewhere. Some would end up as sand for holidaymakers to play on.

Turning off the bridge, we headed east towards Immingham, Grimsby and Cleethorpes. You can see how history makes and breaks towns here. In the 1960s, Grimsby's claim was that it was the greatest fishing port in the world, and it achieved this proud status courtesy of the railways. It was the railway companies that built the ports, and the railways that provided the transport infrastructure to distribute the fish throughout the country. Two hundred trawlers were based at Grimsby in those days, and the demand for trawlers fed a vibrant shipping industry. Fishing, railways and shipping coexisted in a symbiotic relationship, and if some of the ships were too big for Grimsby's limited port facilities, they went to the docks at Immingham next door.

But, as with Hull, Grimsby's 200 trawlers had been decimated by two things: the Cod Wars, which cut the port off from Icelandic fishing grounds, and the common fisheries policy, which opened up British coastal waters to our European neighbours. Local fishermen felt strongly about that. The problem seemed to be that the UK had a much larger fishing zone in comparison with continental European countries on account of its island status. As a result, EU fishermen benefited more from access to British waters than the British themselves did.

In the post-Brexit era, however, it rather looks as if Britain may have landed itself in even deeper waters. We may not, after all, be quite so free to make the rules entirely to our own liking and to restrict access to our waters as we might wish. There is, for instance, the knotty matter of historical claims by European fishermen who have fished our waters for generations, and this may not be quite so easy to settle. According to the Institute for Government, international courts have often ruled in favour of historic access rights to fishing waters and against those states wanting to limit access.[48]

On the southern edge of Grimsby is Cleethorpes, a seaside resort. At one end, it has all the gimcrackery that one associates with boisterous seaside fun; at the other is a magnificent pier and beautifully kept gardens for more sedate amusements. It was the end of the season. Everything was on the cusp of closing: Fantasy World, one-arm bandits, boarded-up fish-and-chip shops, Naughty But Nice hot dogs, the Smile Factory selling buckets and spades, Whippy Dippy Donuts, Fabulous Fudge and Humber Pastimes. It was all made cheerful by lovely flower displays on the promenade, a vast expanse of sand exposed by the retreating tide, and the signs of an abundance of happiness at Seaside Fun for Everyone. All this has been made accessible by the railway, which draws holidaymakers and day trippers from Yorkshire and the East Midlands, terminating on the promenade, right in the heart of all the rumbustiousness of an English seaside resort. And here's the thing: this railway still works. It wasn't cut by Beeching, and this, no doubt, accounts for Cleethorpes' continuing popularity.

At the pier was a grand tearoom: Leonie's. Soft music filled the air, floor-to-ceiling windows flooded the space with light, and enticing cabinets were crammed with a proliferation of cakes. Anton showed us to a table that looked back across a short stretch of sea to the beach. Elderly couples or small family groups were quietly chatting, enjoying a beer,

---

48   https://www.instituteforgovernment.org.uk/explainers/common-fisheries-policy

scrumptious afternoon teas and people-watching. Joan ordered sandwiches and tea while I went in search of the facilities. Behind the tearoom, I was engulfed by enough tables and chairs to seat 500 diners. At the far end of the room, below a wide stage, was a long table at which were seated an agglomeration of British Gas reps in blue shirts, emblazoned with the logo, *Serving the local community*. Above and behind them on the stage was a John Broadwood grand piano.

Back at our table, looking at the beach, we watched a group of children in high visibility jackets excitedly scurrying back and forth, busy and purposeful.

'I wonder what they're doing.'

'Let's find out when we're finished here.'

Anton came with our tea.

'So, when's your busiest time, Anton?'

'It's pretty hectic all the time, especially during that very hot spell earlier.'

'Is this the end of the season for you here?'

'Not really. We're busy all year. Even in the winter, and in the snow, people still come.'

As piers go, this one seemed to have withstood the ravages of time. Seaside piers don't have a good track record. Fire, rough seas or bankruptcy seem to claim a large number of them. This one had probably survived because the railway kept the customers coming and also because it was short and stubby, rather than long and thin, and therefore had less chance of being swept away by furious currents or crashed into by passing ships. It had been purchased by Papa's Fish and Chip chain in 2016, who got it ready in super-fast time for the start of the 2017 season, establishing what it claimed to be the largest fish and chip restaurant in the country. It immediately set about entering the Best UK Fish and Chip Shop competition. (It didn't win, by the way, but it did receive a marketing and innovation award.)

The children, we discovered, were taking part in a sandcastle competition covering a 100-metre stretch of shore. They were from Welholme Academy and it was an inter-house competition. There were three houses at the school – the Roald Dahl House, representing literature; the Stephen Hawking House, for science; and the Ada Lovelace House, for mathematics. 'Did you know,' said one of the teachers, 'that Ada Lovelace was a mathematician, a writer and Britain's first computer programmer?' I didn't know that, but I was impressed that the sandcastles those kids were building were part of a study topic about estuaries and rivers. Before we know it, they'll want to know why all that water in the Humber is brown – and perhaps go on to find some solutions?

Cleethorpes is opposite Spurn Head, and those muddy brown waters fill the gap between them. Those children have a lot to learn about, for a lot is happening on their coast, all the way down to Skegness. Lincolnshire thrusts a bold rounded edge into the North Sea, creating one of the most popular holidaying coasts in the country. Between Grimsby to the north and Gibraltar Point on the tip of the Wash, there is an unbroken 50-mile expanse of sandy beaches to which, for decades, British seaside-loving holidaymakers have flocked for their yearly fix of sand, sea and fun. They relax in their static caravans, sit in their beach huts, play crazy golf or sail their model boats on pretty lakes, in a multi-coloured linear sprawl of happiness.

This happiness is most apparent in the north, between Cleethorpes and Mablethorpe, where the sands are particularly wide. Unfortunately, this is because the coast here is thriving from other people's misery. Much of the abundant sand here has been reluctantly gifted by the people who have the misfortune to live on the coast of Holderness to the north. This part of the coast's wide beach is the happy beneficiary of sandy material stolen by nature from Holderness. The southern half of Lincolnshire's coast, however, between Mablethorpe and Skegness, has been in retreat for several thousand years, as a result of which the sandy beaches are somewhat narrower than their sand-abundant northern neighbours.

And so, 26 miles along the coast road, we came to Mablethorpe, the dividing line between sand-accreting and sand-depleting edges, between growing and diminishing beaches. It was a pretty, genteel kind of seaside town, with colourful murals, sponsored by the Mablethorpe Art Group. It all looked bright and cheerful and thriving, with gardens of tiered flower beds, thoughtfully arranged benches, funfairs and amusements nicely contained in an entertainment hub. It was well-planned and orderly, clean, tidy and lively. There was something for everyone here, of all ages and tastes. A few hundred yards further on, our eyes alighted upon a multi-coloured daisy-chain of beach huts in varying shades of pinks and blues, greens and yellows. I recalled the days when, as a kid, I sat freezing on south-coast beaches on Sunday-school outings, my skin a rash of goose-pimples. I was madly envious of those lucky people who could afford to hire a beach hut. Oh, what bliss it must have been. As we sauntered along the promenade at Mablethorpe, I still felt a pang of envy for those delightful huts stretching out along the promenade, looking over the North Sea where, on the horizon, the arms of the Lincs Wind Farm, five miles away, waved back at them. There were rows of much larger upmarket chalets too, looking like upturned boats. They sat on little hillocks, surrounded by neat lawns and gardens, in as peaceful a setting as one could imagine at a seaside. Together with its Blue Flag beach, Mablethorpe had everything that lovers of seaside holidays could possibly want.

Two miles further on, we were entranced by Sutton-on-Sea. It prides itself on being an 'amusement-and-arcade-free' resort. If we ever wanted a pottering kind of seaside holiday, we could think of no more delightful venue for it. Overlooking a model boating pool, a miniature railway, a play area, crazy golf, bowling green, tennis courts and cafés was an arc of beach chalets in pastel shades. To cap it all, there were miles of coastal walks.

'I wonder how much the chalets are,' said Joan.

'There's your answer,' I said, pointing to one that was for sale for £15,595.

There was a strong sea breeze and the sun was high. I wore my cap with the large peak and Joan her wide-brimmed sunhat, and together we strode off, setting ourselves a brisk pace to get the blood circulating and the lungs breathing.

'Thirty minutes each way?'

'Let's go.'

The first few hundred yards took us past the line of beach huts. At each door, couples sat cosily, soaking up the warmth, reading newspapers or just sitting and smiling. It was early afternoon and the sun had shifted just sufficiently behind them to give some welcome shade from the heat.

'Going far?' called one man.

'There and back. Just there and back.'

'My, what it is to be young and energetic,' he replied.

'D'you hear that? They must be mega old if they think we're young!'

There was a good footpath along the top of the dunes and the walking was energising. It was part of the 2,795 miles (4,500 kilometre) All England Coast Path, the longest managed and fully waymarked walking route in the world, giving access to the whole of England's coasts and shores. The sand dunes were anchored by marram grass and spindly tamarisk hedges. It was such a glorious day that we would have preferred to walk to Skegness rather than drive. We felt we could walk for ever.

This was the tail end of the phenomenally hot summer of 2018, and it had followed on the heels of an abnormally wet spring. It had therefore been a difficult year for farmers, but although yields were depressed and they were going through a tough time, when we passed this way, we could only be delighted by the acre upon rolling acre of golden wheat and barley and the occasional splash of yellow oilseed rape, all ready for harvesting. Almost entirely flat, this rich agricultural land rises imperceptibly inland to the chalk ridge of the Lincolnshire Wolds, some 20 miles away. It made a charming picture – a scintillating blue sea on our left, a patchwork of golds and greens and yellows on our right and a clear blue sky above. All that was missing were the hedgerows.

For those who find the overbearing heat of a Mediterranean summer too much and who love English seaside holidays, it is perfectly obvious why the Lincolnshire coast is still a popular attraction. There's something special about the variability and unpredictability of English weather. On beautifully warm days like this, you can just sit and soak up the sun and not feel as if you are being roasted alive, and if it turns cloudy and a little cooler, you can put your walking boots on and stride out and feel on top of the world, or retreat to your beach hut. What's not to like! Billy Butlin knew this when he opened his first holiday camp on the northern fringes of Skegness in 1936. Even though the mass exodus to the Costa del Sol had not yet started, his intuition was a shrewd one. We passed the site of his original camp as we approached Skegness and the end of our day's driving.

Since Hull, we had done 91 miles, using just two-thirds of the battery. That was pretty good going. Lettie told us we had about 45 miles to spare. I banked on that for the next day's driving. It was to prove to be an unfortunate error of judgement.

16

HYDROGEN OR ELECTRIC?

SKEGNESS IS IMMORTALISED for me by the image of a very round and cheerful fisherman with outstretched arms, dressed in a navy-blue tunic and scarlet necktie, prancing along yellow sand, against the background of a perennially blue sky and breaking waves, and about to tread on a starfish. 'Skegness is SO bracing', the posters declared. At one time, posters like this could be seen in every train compartment and in the railway waiting rooms of every station in the country.

Today's Skegness is well past its prime. Geographically on the edge and off the beaten track, its bracing weather, golden sands, smart pier, faded promenade and once-grand hotels no longer attract British holidaymakers. Just five years ago, the Office for National Statistics identified Skegness as the most deprived seaside area in England.

We attempted to settle into the Grand Hotel, which no doubt was very grand in the Edwardian era when it was built, but which has faced the usual problems of trying to turn such a building into a twenty-first-century hotel. The en suite was squeezed into what used to be a corner of the bedroom, with Heath Robinson plumbing and insufficient room to wield even a facecloth, let alone a towel. We had nowhere to store cases and had to walk sideways like crabs to get to the bed.

There was a definite paucity of charge points in Lincolnshire. Zap-Map told us there was a slow type-2 charger at the Skegness Best Western, a couple of miles away on the other side of town, but that was just for residents. There was also a slow charger on an industrial estate somewhere on the periphery of the town, but it would mean leaving the car there all night, walking two miles back when we were already tired and hungry, and then walking two miles again in the morning to retrieve it. Added to which, there was the problem of leaving the car unattended in some godforsaken place overnight, inviting who-knows-what kind of unwelcome attention.

'I'm getting too old for this, Joanie. Sod it. I don't want to walk another step. In the morning let's go for the nearest rapid charger in Lincoln. It's only forty-two miles, and we've got at least forty-five miles on the battery.'

'Plenty of leeway, then.'

'Don't be cynical. I've got 150 out of her sometimes. You must admit I'm quite good at that.'

'You are. Let's hope you can do it tomorrow.'

We opted for an Italian meal at Tarantino's, on Drummond Road. It was quiet and cosy. Inside, the only noise was the murmur of gentle chat and the distant clatter of pans in the kitchen. It was perfect. I wrote up my notes while Joan inspected the menu and sipped a glass of wine. She chose scampi ravioli with pesto cream; I, rigatoni siciliana.

It was dark when we strolled back to the hotel. The day visitors had gone, but you could still buy candy floss or Skegness rock from neon-lit stores. As we passed the amusement arcade, a slot machine disgorged a cascade of coins, a cacophony of video games tumbled out onto the street, and a few youngsters hovered outside, wondering if they had enough cash to try their luck.

In the morning I switched on the engine and keyed 'Lincoln' into the satnav, only to be shouted at by a rather concerned-sounding Lettie: 'You may not be able to reach your destination.'

'Of course we will,' I muttered.

But I knew it was going to be a difficult day, and I regretted not using the industrial estate charge point. If the worst happened, we could always call Nissan. They'd take us to the nearest charge station within a 30-mile radius. But I wanted to avoid that humiliation.

I get the best out of our car battery on level, gently winding roads when the general flow of traffic is about 35-45mph. However, this road, the A158, was the main road linking Skegness with Lincoln. It was fast and busy. I'd have to feather the accelerator, avoid using the brake pedal except in an emergency, pull away excruciatingly slowly, and let the engine slow us down as we approached roundabouts and traffic lights. All this, I knew, would infuriate drivers behind us.

According to Lettie, our range was now 49 miles and our destination just 43, fractionally more optimistic than my rough calculations.

'There you are; loads of margin.'

'Wow! Six miles. No problem then.'

After I had driven for 10 minutes, Joan said, 'Do you realise you're driving in D mode?'

Damn, how could I make such a stupid mistake! All that regenerative power lost, all that precious range wasted. I switched to eco drive.

'To remember it in future, think of D for dumbo.'

'No time for abuse now, Joanie. Look at that long tailback behind us.'

'Ignore them. They don't have our problem. They'll just have to get used to it.'

At Hagworthingham, a short downhill stretch put a miserable one per cent back into the battery. This trifling amount, perhaps an extra mile on our range, gave me a ridiculous surge of euphoria. Round the next bend, we hit a 'Road Works' warning sign. 'Remember,' I told myself. 'Slow down on the engine. Don't use the brake. Don't waste kinetic energy.'

In no time at all, the battery was down to 14 per cent, with only a 20-mile range left and with 28 miles to go. I began to feel desperate. Then, at Horncastle, I spotted a petrol station.

'Let's pull in there. See if we can use one of their 13-amp sockets. Nothing to lose. They can only say no.'

At the forecourt of The Laurels Service Station, I made for

the check-out desk.

'Haven't come for petrol. We're after some of your electricity.'

'Oh, really?'

'Can we use one of your 13-amp sockets to charge our electric car? We need to get to Lincoln. Our battery is almost flat.'

'You'll have to ask my boss. He's just in there,' she said, pointing to a door at the back of the shop. There we met Guy.

'Come in, come in,' he said. 'This is a subject very close to my heart. Go and see Ben in the workshop. Get him to fix you up and then come back here. I'll make some coffee. I want to talk to you.'

Ben was underneath a hoisted-up car. He poked his head up as I explained the problem.

'Bring the car over here,' he said, as he slid out from below the car and pointed to a bank of power points in the corner.

We'd never used a 13-amp socket to charge the car, so it would be the first opportunity to try out the special cable that we have kept in the boot for this very purpose. It goes by the grand title of EVSE (Electric Vehicle Supply Equipment), and can take anything up to 12 hours using this method. Back in the office, Guy organised coffee.

''Fraid we allowed ourselves to get short,' I said. 'We rely on rapid chargers on long journeys, and there aren't any in Skegness.'

'No, you won't see them here. Anyway, electric's not the way I see it going. Nationally, we'd need 22,000 charge points. The infrastructure for electric just isn't there. Can't see it happening. In any case, petrol and electric don't mix. And who's going to pay me to put a charge point here?'

'You wouldn't have to pay to install one, would you?'

'Yes. Although we've been selling Shell for fifty-five years, we're not a Shell-owned company. This is a family-owned business. We'd have to pay to install them. We won the Best Shell Garage competition in 2015. Can't afford to damage that reputation.'

'But it'll happen, won't it? I mean the government is phasing out petrol and diesel. They're putting all their eggs in the electric basket.'

'Nah, the future's hydrogen. That's where my money is. Lots of money's been made available for hydrogen in Germany, and Shell already has five or six hydrogen sites.'

'Have you driven a hydrogen car?'

'No, but I've seen one and I'm interested in driving one. Shell are putting money into it. Milton Keynes has an experiment in hydrogen cars for police.'

He showed us some YouTube footage of a Shell hydrogen refuelling station on the M40 at Beaconsfield, which opened in March 2018. The first one, he told us, was opened on the M25 at Cobham in Surrey in February 2017.

'Hydrogen cars can refuel in minutes,' continued Guy, 'and they can go hundreds of miles before needing to refuel. You couldn't put a rep in an electric car, could you? Turn him into a lazy so-and-so, spending half an hour every few miles recharging while he sits and does nothing. It won't work. Give a rep a hydrogen car and it'll work – but not electric.'

'But Teslas can go 300 miles, and the new Leaf can do up to 215.'

'No one around here can afford a Tesla. In any case, they

catch fire, you know.' With that he found a YouTube film of a Tesla self-igniting. 'They hush all this up. Anyway, who in Skegness can afford a Tesla? There are just three in this area. Skegness is the working man's coast. It's kiss-me-quick and have a bit of fun. People go there for a weekend or a day out, all year round. It never really stops. They're not electric car drivers here. Wouldn't have the patience to hang around for an hour to charge it. But hydrogen's a different matter. It can be produced on site, you know. All that's needed is an electrolyser, water and electricity, so no massive deliveries would be needed, like the tankers that deliver our petrol. It's a changing world. It's going to happen, you'll see. I mean, Primark came along and is killing M&S, and hydrogen, possibly electric, will eventually kill off petrol and diesel. I'll put electric in when we're ready, but I'm not convinced yet.'

We went back to the workshop to see how Ben was getting on.

'OK if we leave it for another hour or so while we walk into town and have a spot of lunch?'

'Sure,' he said. 'It's only half an hour's walk. It'll be OK here with us.'

At Myers Café, we ordered a sandwich and a pot of tea.

'Haven't seen you around here before,' said our waitress. 'Staying here?'

'No, just passing through. Got ourselves into a spot of bother with our electric car. Battery nearly ran out. We stopped at a garage back there to get some electricity. Not many charge points around here.'

'Oh, you mean The Laurels?'

'That's the one.'

'Welcome to Lincolnshire. We don't even have a motorway, let alone charge points. Lincolnshire's a bit basic.'

We returned to the garage. I switched the car on. The charge had taken us back to 26 per cent and, according to Lettie, we had 23 miles to go to the Holiday Inn. An hour and a half of charging and we'd added just 12 per cent. I could have wept. On a busy road with impatient traffic and getting hillier, it was going to be a nail-biting time.

'Thanks Ben, thanks Guy. You've been great.'

On the winding road, another long tail-back accumulated behind us. As it straightened, a stream of angry drivers shot past us with much hooting and shaking of fists. One desperate driver overtook on a chevronned area, horn blazing, two fingers raised, face contorted with anger, yelling some obscenity. More inclines and the battery dropped to 15 per cent.

'Lettie will start blowing her top soon,' I said, 'when we drop to 13 per cent.'

And then she did it. All the usual systems closed down. She refused to give us the range, flashed a yellow warning light at us, and issued a strobe-like message: 'The battery level is very low. Search for nearest charge point?'

'Of course, you stupid woman,' Joan yelled, as she pressed the 'yes' button.

Lettie searched her database. Back came the answer: 'Doesn't exist for this location.'

'Is she saying there's no charge point in Lincoln? Check with Zap-Map. Surely to God, I can't have got this wrong.'

Back came the confirmation from Zap-Map: there definitely was a rapid charger at Holiday Inn.

'Ooh, look, there's a lovely view of the cathedral,' said Joan.

'For heaven's sake, Joanie. I can't afford to take my eyes off the road. I'm trying to get us there without tortoising, and you're admiring the scenery.'

'It's all too terrifying. My hands are sweaty. We'll either get there or we won't. Why pile on the agony? It calms my nerves just a little bit to look at beautiful things. You don't begrudge me that, do you?'

'Of course not, my darling. It's just that I'm a bit stressed too.'

'Anyway, one thing's for sure.'

'What's that?'

'You're going to take me to the cathedral some other day if we don't get to see it today.'

A short downward stretch made us ludicrously optimistic, as two green dots appeared on the console, giving us an extra dribble of electricity.

'In 200 yards, there is a speed camera,' Lettie warned.

'Oh well, I'd better slow down then.'

'One point two miles to go,' Joan said.

'One mile.'

'Nearly there. Zero point seven.'

The tension was unbearable. At the worst possible place for conserving power, there were traffic lights. Halfway up the Lincoln Cliff, I was forced to stop the car. It would take a huge surge of energy to get us going again up that incline. Then, still climbing, we had to turn right. I made the futile gesture of turning the indicator off to save electricity.

'That'll give us another couple of yards.'

'Seven hundred and fifty yards,' Joan said, with mounting

excitement. 'We're going to do it, Clivo.'

I turned the corner and the steep hill continued. The white dots shot up: four, five, six. We were golloping electricity. But it was impossible to ease back on the power on account of the tailgaters pushing up behind me. After a couple of hundred yards the road levelled, and I almost began to breathe properly.

'Two hundred yards, and there's a massive roundabout ahead,' Joan said.

'Oh God, please let us not stop here.'

We were halfway round when Joan shouted. 'I can see it. Over there,' and she pointed to 11 o'clock, the fifth exit. Never have I been so relieved to see that beautiful Holiday Inn sign.

'You must charge now', screamed Lettie.

'We know, we know,' we yelled back hysterically.

We were euphoric now and utterly devoid of caring.

'In the far corner. We made it!' Joan shrieked as we turned into the car park.

I felt her relax into her seat. Her shoulders eased back, she dropped the notebook onto the floor, wiped the sweat off her hands, smiled, kissed me, and mumbled something about coffee.

And then I saw it too, the gorgeous white box. No other car was there. It was free for us to use, a Polar Instant UltraCharge.

'Stay here,' I said to Joan as I pulled into the bay, 'and don't let anyone else come and use that CHAdeMO while I OK it with Reception. Have your hand on it if necessary.'

Inside, I spoke to Lorna.

'Is it OK to charge our car here?'

'Of course. Just register your car, then go ahead. Get some tea or coffee, and here's a card for a 25 per cent discount on whatever you buy.'

We bought papers, drank coffee and wallowed in the bliss of de-stressing.

'I don't think we're going to make it to the cathedral, are we?' Joan said.

'Well, we've got sixty miles to go to King's Lynn. Couldn't do it justice today.'

'However, I'll let you at least treat me to a proper English afternoon tea. I've been reading about a place called Bunty's, halfway up Steep Hill. It's the fourth steepest street in England, so it'll remind us – you especially – of the pilgrims who laboured their way to the cathedral above and were given penances for remission of their sins.'

'Ouch!'

They did things properly at Bunty's Tea Room: Lincolnshire Plum Bread served with butter in a porcelain dish; loose-leaf tea made in a bone china teapot, kept nice and hot under a tea cosy and poured through a strainer into Queen Anne china cups; soft background music – 'We'll Meet Again', 'A Nightingale Sang in Berkley Square', 'Don't Sit Under the Apple Tree'. On the walls, a Bovril advert showed a robust Edwardian woman in a red jacket, green-tweedy-calf-length skirt, golf club over her left shoulder, having just confidently despatched the ball to the horizon. *You too can do this*, the poster promised, *if you take Bovril – For Health, Strength and Beauty*. A carpet beater on the wall brought back memories of Saturday morning jobs at home. A poster told us that a balanced diet consisted of a cake in each hand. In a browsing area on the mezzanine floor was an occasional table with copies of the 1940s girls' comic *Bunty* scattered around.

'If I promise to bring you back for a long weekend specially to see the cathedral, as soon as you've finished with the panto, will I have paid back all the brownie points I owe you?' I asked.

'Quite a few of them. But I'll think of one or two ways of paying the rest back.'

SOUTH-EAST COAST

SKEGNESS
IS SO BRACING

Skegness
Hunstanton
A17
Kings Lynn
Blakeney
A149
Cromer
Happisburgh
Eccles-on-Sea
A140
Norwich
A115
A146
Snape
Aldeburgh
A12
Ipswich
Sudbury
Chelmsford
A12
Coastal Erosion
Thurrock
LONDON
M2
Canterbury
Sandwich
M25
A2
Dover
Reigate
M20
M23
Hythe
Dungeness
Burgess Hill
A27
Battle
A27
Alfriston
Hastings
Brighton
and Hove
Eastbourne

Boating at Snape

Romney, Hythe and Dymchurch
Railway

17

CRUMBLING EDGES

ALMOST UNIQUE IN BRITISH topography, the huge area of flatland known as the Fens rarely rises more than 50 feet above sea level. The Fens represent some of the newest land in the country, land that has been painstakingly reclaimed from marsh and fen by succeeding generations for 2,000 years.

It was begun by the Romans, continued by the Anglo-Saxons, and more actively carried on from the seventeenth century. Following the Dutch model, south Lincolnshire acquired numerous windmills, which sucked water out of the land and, in so doing, shrank it to below sea level. Appropriately, the area was named New Holland, known today as the district of South Holland. The aim was to convert wetland to arable land,[49] and in the process, those who had

---

49   Nicholas Crane, *The Making of the British Landscape*, Weidenfeld & Nicholson, paperback edition, 2017, p369..

used these wetlands on a seasonal basis for generations lost their livelihoods, while the land improvers grew rich on their new cornfields and orchards.

On the coasts of the Wash, new land is being added as material eroded further north is deposited there. Because of this, you can track the way the land has changed and new land created, simply by studying the names of places surrounding the Wash: Bicker Haven, Fleet Haven, Moulton Seas End, Surfleet Seas End. All of these places, once on the coast, are now up to 10 miles inland.[50]

South Holland today is the horticultural capital of the UK.[51] This is the land of agro-industrial factories. It is a landscape of parallel roads and drainage ditches, which produces 22 per cent of our horticultural crops, 28 per cent of our vegetables and 40 per cent of our bulbs and flowers. It was the flattest land we had come across – a perfect plain, brimming to the horizon with cloches, poly-tunnels, potatoes, sugar beet, flowers and enough cabbages to throw away at the world cabbage hurling championships – which, by the way, are held at Holbeach, another name that betrays its former coastal location.

Such heavy dependence on one major industry is not without its problems, however. Looking for wider horizons and more diverse choices, many young people leave the area. This has created a labour shortfall that traditionally has been filled by seasonal workers from eastern Europe. The social

---

50   W G Hoskins classic book, *The Making of the English Landscape*, Book Club Associates, 1981.
51   Mike Leeder and Joy Lawlor, *GeoBritannica: Geological Landscapes and the British Peoples*, Dunedin, 2017, p83.

discontent that this sometimes causes was one of the factors accounting for the massive 'Leave' vote in the EU referendum. On a 75 per cent turnout, South Holland voted 73.5 per cent to leave the EU, only marginally lower than Boston's 75.6 per cent.

Rounding the Wash, we entered the land of the Anglo-Saxons. East Anglia, once the most densely populated area of England, is reputed to have more medieval churches than any other region of the country. This is because it developed a lucrative wool industry in the medieval period and many of the wealthy merchants, as they got closer to their Maker, developed guilty consciences, perhaps realising that they could have treated their workers more generously and taken a bit less for themselves. They therefore invested their surplus wealth in the building of churches. This secured them local popularity, gave us some of our classic village landscapes and provided them with clean consciences and, they hoped, a place in heaven.

We chose King's Lynn to stay overnight on account of its rapid charger. Unfortunately, this was two miles away from our hotel, and that was a bore. Hotels are incurring an enormous opportunity cost through their lack of charge points – it doesn't make sense to have to spend an hour or so charging your car in often bleak and inhospitable conditions when, with a bit of forethought, hoteliers could invest in charge points and so attract more custom. Some are beginning to do this, but not enough. The majority of hotel managers we spoke to hadn't even thought of it.

'Oh, I see what you mean,' comes the reply. 'I'll take it to the next board meeting.'

At the end of a long day, the site, at the rear end of a multi-storey car park, was depressing. It was all concrete and bricks and ugliness. The shops were closed, there was no traffic, the area felt dead, hollow, abandoned. Somehow, we had to find a way of spending an hour in this lifeless place.

There were two Charge Your Car charging cabinets, each one with two connecting hoses – a CHAdeMO and a CCS. On most charging cabinets, both connecting hoses can be used concurrently. At the first cabinet, the CHAdeMO hose was being used by a gleaming black taxi, and so was unavailable to us. At the other cabinet, however, a black BMW was using the CCS connector.

'Brilliant!' I said to Joan. 'The CHAdeMO is free. We'll be done in a jiffy.'

I flipped open the charge point lid, leapt out of the car, pushed the nozzle home, registered the RFID card, and waited. Nothing happened. Not a click, not a movement of any dials. I tried again, but there was no response. It was dead.

'You won't be able to use it as long as that guy's there,' the taxi driver said.

'Why on earth not?'

'They only do one at a time.'

'But they're made for two cars to charge simultaneously,' I said.

'They are, but not here,' he said. 'And you won't have much luck with that BMW. He won't come back. It's been there for hours.'

'So as long as he's there, I'm not going to be able to use it?'

'Correct.'

'Thoughtless prat,' I said. 'Why do people behave like this?'

'Beats me. Going far?' he asked.

We told him our story.

'You've done well,' he said. 'I love electric. This taxi is brand new. Got it just a few weeks ago. All electric. Take a look.'

It was a magnificent beast. Black and shiny, and a superb electronic version of the familiar London taxi cab.

'I had a diesel cab until a few months ago. Sold it and bought this. Love it. It easily pays for itself. Look, I'll unplug now. Don't need to top up fully. I can come back later. You have this one.'

'Very kind of you. Thanks.'

Our objective that morning was Hunstanton. We wanted to see the striped cliffs. The route took us through the Sandringham estate, past houses of beautiful small red bricks with the occasional fleur-de-lys set in a wall, ornate chimneys with intricate brickwork and manicured grounds, giving an air of solid wealth and a deeply ordered way of life. It was easy driving; we covered 16 miles using just 10 per cent of battery. Extrapolated, that would have given us a range of 160 miles. If only!

Parking on the cliff top, we donned our walking boots, followed the track down to the shore and walked along to where a group of students were working. The cliff face was magnificent, like a multi-coloured slice of cake with a brilliant layer of white chalk at the top, followed by a layer of brilliant red chalk below and, at the base, a layer of orange sandstone.

A psychedelic cliff. The red chalk – the first time I had seen such a thing – derives its dazzling colouration from limonite, a red oxide of iron. It is called the Hunstanton Formation.

The students on the beach were a group of Year 11 geographers from John Ferneley College, Melton Mowbray. They were counting and measuring randomly identified samples of shoreline particles, researching long-shore drift, the process that carries beach material along the coast, washing land away from one area and depositing it in another, creating coasts of erosion and coasts of deposition, coasts of creation and coasts of destruction. Norfolk has both.

The north coast of Norfolk, from Hunstanton to Cromer, is mostly a coast of deposition – it is being built up by long-shore drift. A good example is Scolt Head Island, which is slowly elongating westwards on account of longshore drift. A few miles east is Blakeney Point, another spit created by longshore drift and also extending itself westwards. And of course, the Wash itself is gradually filling up as new material is deposited and new land created.

This matter of longshore drift is of considerable importance to the inhabitants of coastal East Anglia; while parts of their coast are being built up and have become places of Special Scientific Interest and Areas of Outstanding Natural Beauty, much of their coastline is also disappearing and their houses falling into the sea.

It was gratifying to see that fieldwork of this kind is taken so seriously at an 11-16 secondary academy. I went to a grammar school in Surrey and specialised in geography. Although it was situated on the Lower Greensand ridge that runs parallel to the North Downs, in the heart of the

Weald, in one of the most iconic landscapes in the country, never once were we taken out of the classroom to the natural laboratory on our doorstep. The students of John Ferneley College, however, had travelled 98 miles to see this glorious geological spectacle and to do their research into one of the most important coastal processes in this part of the country.

The road along the top of Norfolk was superb for driving an EV. The A149 hugs the coast the whole way, twisting and turning through little seaside towns, scarcely wide enough in places to allow a car and a lorry to pass each other. It squeezes itself between houses with front doors that open onto almost non-existent pavements. There was an abundance of road signs, no doubt telling us to slow down, to halt, to give way, or to warn of danger or a road junction, but we had no idea what they said because they were illegible, hidden behind the prolific foliage that made the road such a delight to drive along. We passed lovely flint churches at Brancaster and Burnham and a cluster of fine old flint buildings at Holkham. All of this added up to a leisurely and relaxed drive that was very economical on the battery. And it seemed, somehow, very English, or at least the kind of Englishness I grew up with.

On the shoulder of Norfolk at Cromer, the road turned southeast and onto one of the most vulnerable stretches of coast in the country. The independent Committee on Climate Change reported in 2018 that many of the small communities along this 90-mile length of coast were not worth saving from the ravages of the sea on account of climate change, and that they should be left to fall into the sea. There are 'tough choices' ahead, it warned.[52]

52   *The Daily Telegraph*, Friday 26 October 2018.

Threading our way through a dense network of unclassified roads, we managed to keep close to the coast as far as Happisburgh (pronounced Haze-bruh by the locals), where we saw the fragility of the shoreline for ourselves. Houses here had already lost half their gardens to the sea, fences had long since become driftwood, back doors were within metres of doing the same, roads terminated at the precipice, and caravans were so dangerously close to the edge that they would soon have to be moved. But caravanners are the lucky ones in England's fast-disappearing village: they can take their homes with them, while Happisburgh is going the same way as the village of Whimpwell, which long ago disappeared into the sea.

Just off the coast lies Dogger Bank, the remains of Doggerland, which once made us geographically part of the European mainland. Doggerland, however, was swept away almost overnight about 10,000 years ago, when a tsunami originating off the coastal shelf of Norway raced down the North Sea, sweeping Doggerland away and turning us into the island we have become. But the work of that tsunami is not done. Climate change, rising sea levels and longshore drift are continuing the process.

At Eccles-on-Sea, where a bungalow was about to fall into the sea, we turned inland towards Norwich. Joan navigated us through a labyrinth of narrow tracks wide enough only for a tractor. As we eased ourselves cautiously round a sharp bend just out of Happisburgh Common, the familiar bonnet of another Leaf hove into view. It pulled into a passing place by a farm gate as we drew level. We stopped opposite each other and simultaneously opened our windows.

'How's it going then?'

'Great! Best car I've ever had.'

'Going far?'

'Following the coast to Sussex.'

'Where from?'

'Northumberland.'

'You've done well.'

Another car appeared, and we had to move on all too quickly, but that brief encounter was surprisingly heart-warming. The recognition was enough. We were cutting-edge motorists, not freaks, and belonged to an exclusive club, membership of which brought instant camaraderie.

Best Western seems to have a policy of installing charge points at most of its hotels, and the list is growing. That was why we chose Annesley House, in Norwich. The going had been easy all the way from King's Lynn; the lie of the land was gently undulating and the roads sinuous. This kept our speed down without us feeling we were enraging motorists behind us, so we had maintained an average range of 148 miles on a full battery. We drew up at the hotel with a comfortable 37 miles in reserve and plugged into the slow charger. This gave us time to walk into the city, explore one of its two cathedrals, enjoy an excellent meal back at the hotel and wake up to a full battery the next morning, which was ample to get us to Aldeburgh, and our next charge point at Ipswich.

18

ANGLO-SAXON COUNTRY

IF THERE'S ONE KIND OF MUSIC that I grew up detesting, it's opera. I can never hear the word without immediately being taken back to a mental image of my father slumped in an armchair, smoking his evil-smelling pipe, eyes closed, radio blaring with people singing in a foreign language, as he told us all to be quiet so he could fantasise about his glorious days in the Italian campaign.

When he and his fighting colleagues drove their triumphal way through the full length of Italy, from the Calabrian toe to the Lombardy Plain, they were fêted as liberators by euphoric crowds. In Milan, he visited La Scala opera house and immersed himself in Italian opera. After all this heady stuff, he found civvy street was not at all to his taste, so he would retreat into his inner world by sinking into his favourite armchair by the fire, lighting his pipe and looking dreamily out of the window. He would then switch on the Third Programme and turn it up full blast to fill the house with Mendelssohn's *Italian Symphony*, Verdi's *La Traviata*, Mozart's *Don Giovanni* or Wagner's *Tannhäuser*, in the process giving us all a life-long loathing of opera.

As a result, I approached Aldeburgh that day with very mixed feelings. The very name Aldeburgh spoke to me of seriously high-brow music, whereas I'm definitely low-brow. Operettas such as *The Pirates of Penzance* and *HMS Pinafore*, which many regard as light-hearted trivia, are more my style. But in Aldeburgh, I was entering the heart of England's musical establishment, and at its core was the English Opera Group. You can't get more high-brow than that.

The contrast between this place and Skegness was unsettling. It was as if we had passed into a different country. There was an air of hushed gentility about the town. There were no boarded-up shop fronts, and it was permeated by a feeling of prosperity. We found a car park at the end of High Street and called in for a coffee at the East Coast restaurant. Almost before we could get in, an over-eager young man approached.

'How can I help you?'

'We'd just like a coffee, please.'

'Oh yes, sit this side please, the side where the sugar is.'

'Well, we won't be wanting that,' Joan said. 'So we'll sit the other side.'

Visibly shocked, he blurted out, 'Oh no, you can't do that. We like to keep *this* side for coffee. The *other* side's for wine.'

It was buzzing on the wine side, with people who spoke with

what my father would have regarded as correct BBC English. They wore designer-casual clothes, were studiedly laid back and were engaged in hushed, meaningful conversation. A middle-aged man sat immediately opposite. What little hair he had was outrageously curly and spiralled upwards. His black-framed glasses were perched where his hairline used to be, and he wore a black jacket over a white T-shirt.

'We have a strange relationship,' he was saying to a younger woman, with designer-grunge jeans and a blue linen shirt.

'Well, there's a few things we need to get clear,' she was saying.

Alas, we never did learn what it was they had to get clear, as the hiss of the machine making our coffee made eavesdropping their conversation impossible.

Outside, in a narrow passageway on the other side of our window, an elderly couple sat at a vintage picnic table, sunglasses perched high on matching grey hair, up-turned shirt and blouse collars under designer gilets, one aubergine, the other racing green. As they spoke, they twiddled with champagne flutes, which they periodically refilled from a bottle in an ice bucket.

Joan finished her coffee and went to find the loo. I studied the road map, my half-full cup of coffee in front of me. The young man came back, saw Joan had left the table and promptly whisked both cups away.

'Thanks very much,' he said.

'Er, no, I'm not finished yet.'

'So very sorry,' he said, and as quickly replaced it.

Outside, we turned onto Crag Path and headed for the Moot Hall, the sea on our right, a row of brightly coloured

Edwardian terraced houses on our left. Rarely have I seen such immaculately kept dwelling places. All were smartly painted – yellow, pink, blue, grey – some with beautifully pointed bare brickwork, some with bay windows and balconies facing the sea. Rounding a corner, we met Mr Keith Batt.

He was in his wheelchair, against a brick wall, tucked into a corner, in a perfect spot to catch the warmth of the sun as he read his daily paper.

'Hello,' I said, 'that looks a cosy corner.'

'Yes,' he said, 'It's my favourite, on sunny days.'

'You've chosen well. We're looking for the Tourist Information Centre.'

'The remnants of it are in the foyer of the cinema. You can't miss it. It's a mock Tudor building. It's what's left of the proper T.I.C. Are you staying here?'

'Alas, no. We're just passing through today. We're driving down the east coast in our electric car.'

'Is it like mine or a bit bigger?'

'Just a bit. It's a Nissan Leaf, but yours looks just as comfortable.'

'We don't have a coast road here, which means we don't get the crowds. On the south coast, the roads all follow the coast and you get the whole world and his wife. But it does mean we're a bit backward.'

'It's like where we live,' said Joan. 'Few roads. Sparsely populated.'

'Where're you from then?'

'Near the Scottish border.'

'Near Alnwick?'

'That's a bit further south.'

'I was stationed at Catterick and used to go into Northumberland. And of course, you've got the best beaches in the world. I'm the Publicity Officer for the Aldeburgh Festival. We've just had the 76th show. Name's Batt, Keith Batt.'

Just ahead of us we saw a sign on a black wooden shack on the edge of the beach. 'We Smoke Fish', it announced. As we drew up to the makeshift counter, a middle-aged man emerged, coughing and spluttering from the smoke at the business-end of the shack. Any misgivings we might have had about hygiene were overridden by the tempting array of dishes before us. It was a good place for lunch and we each chose smoked trout and spinach filo.

'Lunch for two for £5.60. That's not bad,' Joan said, as he handed back the change. 'Have you been doing this long?'

'I'm kind of in-between, waiting for my product design business to take off. Meanwhile I'm doing this for what I hope will be no more than 18 months.'

Just then his supplier arrived, and the two of them discussed how much he might need to meet likely demand for the afternoon. It was decided on 10 kilos of mixed seafoods.

'Where're you going?' he asked.

'Coastal drive, by electric car.'

'I knew someone who had an electric car. She was a life coach. Absolutely useless. There was a mate of mine who'd been promoted beyond his level of competence and needed advice on how to go about his new position, get skills with people, etc. He paid this woman, his life coach, £800 to tell him how to organise his life, and she couldn't organise her own. Threw a wobbly because her car ran out of charge; she hadn't planned her journey and didn't know how to get it charged.'

'Yes, we've met a life coach like that,' Joan said.

'Yeah, it's like if you're no good at anything else, do some life-coaching and tell people how to do theirs.'

In the mock Tudor building, we found the cinema-cum-Information Centre, as Mr Batt had predicted, and here we picked up information about the flora and fauna of the Area of Outstanding Natural Beauty that covers almost the whole of this fragile coast of Suffolk. A few paces further on was the Moot Hall, a seriously genuine Tudor building, 400 years old. It was almost on the beach. But of course, it hadn't always been there. As befits a town hall, its original position was in the centre of the medieval town of Aldeburgh, which was well inland. But it was the land that had moved and not the building. As the town hall, it would have been the focal point for the community, the place where all the great and the good met to deal with the management of the town and the administration of justice; hence the term 'Moot Hall' – the gathering place where knotty problems, moot points, would have been discussed. It had been lovingly and beautifully preserved as the town's museum, more or less in its original Tudor condition, and it realistically conveyed the purpose it had served more than 400 years earlier. But now it looked absurdly out of place, way off-centre and the tide almost lapping at its doors.

As well as documenting the history of the town, it also

told the story, common to most of East Anglia's coastal settlements, of the town's ongoing struggle with the erosive power of the sea. This continuing pounding, together with the subsidence of the land in post-glacial times, explains the character of the East Anglian coast. The subsidence caused some of the region's river valleys to be flooded and subsequent erosion has given this, and the whole of East Anglia, its particularly smooth coastline. This is nowhere better illustrated than here, at Aldeburgh.

About 1,200 years ago, the mouth of the River Alde was where it belonged, at Aldeburgh. Now, however, the continuing erosion of the East Anglian coast to the north and the deposition of pebbles and other coarse material further south – our old friend, longshore drift – has built up what has to be the most impressive spit in the country, known as Orford Ness. This shifted the mouth of the river southwards, so that 400 years later it was at Orford. That is why Orfordonians claimed the river for themselves and named it the River Ore. Now the mouth of the Alde is at Shingle Street, a dozen miles to the south of Aldeburgh, only now it's the mouth of the River Ore.

On our way back along Crag Path, we saw two partially sighted women whose assistance dogs were being troubled by a yapping, long-haired creature that seemed to be running amok at the end of a long lead. At the other end was the owner of the yapper, an elderly lady, smartly dressed in town clothes, out for her afternoon promenade. She was, clearly, proud of what she perceived to be her beloved's friendly behaviour, unaware of the havoc and distress it was causing. It was disorienting the assistance dogs, and the women who depended on them for guidance were clearly confused and frightened. Understandably, they tried to shoo the dog away.

'Come on, Georgie, let's go,' said the town woman petulantly. 'You're obviously not appreciated here.'

As we neared the car park, we saw a couple of portly men leaning over a stone wall, looking out to sea and chatting. I followed their gaze to a patch of water that was lighter than the rest. Further south was the scarcely perceptible outline of an offshore wind farm. I was curious about what they were looking at, and I went to join them, while Joan off-loaded our backpacks into the car.

'Is that a sandbar over there?' one of them said as I, too, leaned over the wall.

'Could be,' I said. 'The North Sea's very shallow. Good location for all those offshore wind farms. Are you locals?'

'No, we're from Northampton – the furthest you can get from the sea. Hunstanton is our nearest coast.'

'Ah, where the multi-coloured cliffs are. Here for long?'

'Only a few days, then we're moving further north where there are lots of traditional seaside resorts. Not like this. It's a bit exclusive here, isn't it?'

'Yeah, I suppose so. A bit upmarket. We were in Skegness a few days ago. Someone we met described it as kiss-me-quick-and-have-a good-time working class.'

'You can do that here if you like,' said the other one.

'Oh, I've got my wife with me,' I said. 'I'm a happy man.'

I left them and walked across the road to the car park to dump my daypack. Joan went to find sunscreen and I rejoined the men.

'We've got our wives now,' they grinned as I approached.

'We like coming here,' said one of them. 'It's nice and quiet.'

'Yeah,' said one of the husbands. 'It's real Anglo-Saxon country.'

'Ooh, I don't think we're allowed to say that,' said the other.

'Well it is,' said the first man. 'Proper Anglo-Saxon. They've kept out all the foreigners. No immigrants.'

'But those Anglo-Saxons are immigrants. Came from Europe, from Germany in fact. Pushed the Brits to Wales and took over our country.'

'Oh, really?'

The River Alde is only 33 miles long, but it flows through some of the most biologically diverse wetlands in the country. It meanders through mudflats that are drowned twice a day with the incoming tide, giving rise to a mixture of saltmarshes, grasslands and reed beds that provide excellent habitats for internationally important populations of breeding and over-wintering birds.

The red brick buildings of the Snape Maltings gradually revealed themselves through the abundance of this botanical miracle. We turned through some gates into a drive and scrunched over a gravelled car park. Some, like us, were just arriving; others were leaving. It was the tail-end of the day and we only had an hour or two at the most, but that was enough to feel that this place was special.

It seemed to me to be another 'Thin Place', where you find yourself transported into an alternative dimension. It was different here. The rush and hurriedness of life had been calmed. The transition from brewery to internationally-renowned music and arts centre had been achieved unobtrusively during the half century of its existence, with total respect both for the buildings which housed it and the biodiversity which surrounded it. A reverential hush, a contemplative stillness, a respectful silence, permeated the whole complex. People spoke in a manner that was mindful of others, unobtrusively, considerately. From a window we looked out over the reed beds and watched a yacht sailing over of a bed of deep greenery. On a wall was an extract from Don Marquis's book, *The Almost Perfect State*:

> *'The purpose of the universe is play. The artists know that, and they know that play and art and creation are different names for the same thing.'*[53]

A clock ticked on a far wall, muffled sounds from a kitchen reached us. We followed them and were soon sipping tea and eating fruit cake in as tranquil a setting as we had ever known.

'I suppose we ought to get going,' Joan said. 'We've got a hotel and a charge point to find.'

---

53   In *Incisive Letterwork*, by Annet Stirling and Brenda Berman.

19

NO ONE EVER USES THAT POINT

THERE ARE TWO BASIC RULES for the positioning of EV charging stations. Rule number one: you must be able to park legally. Rule number two: the connecting cable must be able to reach the car's charge port. The Polar Ultra-Charge Point at the Novotel Hotel, Ipswich, met neither of these criteria.

The charge station was just a few yards from the hotel entrance. As we approached, it was clear something was wrong. If, because of the way your car is made, you need to park nose first to get charged, but the bay layout tells you to park sideways, then that's going to be an issue. So, following normal procedure, I ignored the orientation of the designated parking bay and drove up to the charging point nose first.

'There's just one problem with that,' Joan said. 'Not only is half the car outside the parking bay, but we're also blocking that car, which, by the way, is parked perfectly legally. He's not going to be able to get out.'

'Ah well,' I said, 'I'd better do as instructed.'

So I parked sideways on, fitting the car snugly into the parking bay. The result, as expected, was that the nozzle couldn't reach the charge port in the nose of the car. So I eased the car back about a metre, to bring it within reach of the nozzle.

Joan got out.

'You're now straddling a yellow-striped area. We're blocking access for emergency services.'

'Ok, let's overlap at the other end then.'

I turned the car round, brought it back and parked it the other way round, this time overlapping the other end of the bay.

'Let's see if that'll do it.'

'Well, it's a nice bit of parking,' Joan said. 'There's just one problem.'

'What now?'

'The back of the car is now completely blocking the exit from that private car park.'

I could hardly be blamed for missing it. It was on the other side of a pretty hedge. It was a nice bit of landscape gardening though, and one could understand the designer's wish to hide the unpretty car park from view.

'Ok, I've had enough. Let's go to Reception and find out what we're supposed to do.'

The hotel was part of the Ipswich Centre. We entered a frenetic world of busyness, of smartly besuited young men and women deftly tapping messages into their mobile phones, standing in groups engaged in urgent conversations or huddled around low tables and bent over laptops. Others strode confidently to and fro, clutching important-looking documents, in and out of the swishing automatic doors. Everything, it seemed, was up-to-date in Ipswich city. Except that it wasn't. They just didn't get it as far as EVs were concerned.

The automatic glass doors opened into a smart atrium, making us feel bedraggled in our touring clothes. A solitary young man stood at a computer console at the far end of a long, curved desk, a neat pile of A4 paper beside him that he was methodically working through. The young man welcomed us cheerfully, and we explained our predicament.

'Oh,' he exclaimed. 'No one ever uses that point. We don't do electric cars here. The future is in hydrogen-powered cars. That's what we're planning on. In all my time here, I've never known anyone to use that charge point.'

'Well,' I said. 'That's nice of you to explain your policy, but meanwhile we do not have a hydrogen car. We have an electric car and, as you've had the foresight to install an EV charge point rather than a hydrogen unit, we'd quite like to use it.'

'That's fine, sir. Go straight ahead.'

'Problem is we can't charge it without parking illegally. We have the choice of blocking that car over there, or the exit to that private car park, or access to the emergency services. What do you suggest?'

'Oh, I don't think you should block those other cars in. It's a busy car park, you know. No, no, can't do that. You'd better pull back and block the emergency services access. If anyone has a heart attack, or anything like that, I'll call you.'

'Are you serious?'

'Yes, go ahead. I'll call you if there's an emergency.'

'OK, so what do we do when we've finished charging? Where shall we park?'

'Just fit yourself neatly into the EV parking bay where you'll disturb no one and you can stay there all night.'

'But what if someone else comes along and needs to charge their car?'

'They won't. I tell you, it's never used. No one will want to use it. We do hydrogen here.'

'So you're not going to get me up in the middle of the night to move my car.'

'It won't happen, I promise you.'

As it happens, it didn't. The car was nicely charged in the morning, no one had had a heart attack, no traffic warden had seen the arrangement, and no one else had wanted to charge.

'Joan,' I said, over my scrambled egg the next morning, 'I'd like to divert to Sudbury. My friend Keith – you know, from Africa days – he lives there.'

'How big a detour is it?'

'Not much; just 21 miles. I've never been to Sudbury, and I'll probably never go there again, but it's important for me to see Keith now, before it's too late.'

'Was he the one who was head of the school where you taught?'

'Yes. A Methodist minister. We both worked at that mission school in Rhodesia I told you about. Right out in the bush. We went there in January 1966, just a couple of months after Ian Smith had declared UDI.[54] Keith was a good headmaster. He's a few years older than me and I gather he's rather frail. We could be there about ten and we'd still have plenty of time to get to Canterbury.'

Keith's home was in a cul-de-sac. I parked the car under the fading racemes of a buddleia. It was a fraction before 10 o'clock.

Keith's carer opened the door to his little apartment. He was coming down the stairs on his chairlift as we entered. It seemed me to be so wrong. Here was a man who had given the whole of his working life to the service of underprivileged Africans in a country ravaged first by civil war and then by the murderous incompetence of Mugabe. And now here he was, alone and struggling. I remembered him as a dynamic, active man, striding along the dirt roads and pathways that criss-crossed our forested campus, and now he here he was, frail and dependent, but still radiating his trademark smile of welcome.

'He's such a very nice gentleman,' Joan said afterwards.

And that's exactly what he was: unfailingly courteous, and always kind, even when things were strained and difficult. His was the steadying hand that steered our little pioneering ship through the turbulent early years of UDI.

'*Mangwanani* Keith.'

'*Mangwanani* Clive.'

'*Marara here*?'

'*Tarara kana mararawo.*'

54　Unilateral Declaration of Independence.

'*Tarara.*'[55]

'So you still remember a bit of Shona,' he said.

'Oh, just a fraction. That's all I remember now.'

We squeezed against the front door to give him space to negotiate his way out of the stairlift and into his walking frame. Then, painfully slowly, he led us into a small lounge-cum-diner where a table was set overlooking the circle of the cul-de-sac. His carer helped him to make the transfer from walking frame to chair and then retreated to the kitchenette to get him his breakfast and make us a cup of tea.

'Talk,' he said. 'Talk to me while I have my porridge. Tell me how you've come here and what you're doing.'

It was the same voice, the same business-like manner and we both felt at ease.

'Are you still in contact with anyone from Zimbabwe?' I asked.

'Not much,' he said. 'But I read the papers and keep up with what's going on there. I'm sorry that one or two of the lads we taught are now working for that nasty regime. What about you?'

'The last time I was in Zimbabwe was when I stayed with you. You were working in Harare. 1988, I think it was. I couldn't resist seeing the old school again. When I found myself driving along a smooth, wide tarmac road, I couldn't believe I was going to the same place. A bit different from the dirt tracks of our pioneering days, eh!'

We spent an hour reminiscing, and then he was tired, and it was time for us to leave.

---

55   'Good morning. Have you slept well?' 'I slept well if you did also.' 'I have slept well.'

'*Endai zvenyu,*' Keith said.

'*Sarai zvenyu.*'[56]

Although I'd never been to Sudbury before, and never expected to go there again, I was to revisit it in a curious kind of way at our next port of call.

It was 84 miles to Canterbury, an easily managed distance, but first we'd need to find the charge point Zap-Map told us was at Thurrock.

20

RAGE

AT THURROCK, WE COLLIDED with bedlam. It was a land of angry fists and blaring horns. Frantic drivers were quite happy to risk arriving thirty years early in the next world rather than three minutes late in this one. It was a manic mass-addiction to Russian roulette. But we needed to be there, to charge the car.

We were in deepest Essex, home to authentic England, the land, according to popular mythology, of brash, culturally barren, money-worshipping individualism, typified by Harry Enfield's *Loadsamoney* – white, right wing, vulgar. It's a stereotype, of course, but a tenacious one. The truth is more mundane, for this is also Windrush territory, where the ship carrying 500 migrants from the Caribbean docked in Tilbury in 1948, marking the beginning of the rise of multicultural Britain.

We had hoped to avoid using the M25, but the Dartford Crossing was the only realistic way of crossing the Thames, so a short stretch was inevitable. According to Zap-Map, somewhere between junctions 30 and 31, at Moto services, there was a rapid charge point. Lettie interpreted this as a lorry park, from which there was only one way out, and that was back onto the motorway. So we exited, went round a five-pronged roundabout and, by ignoring the satnav, found our way to the car park.

'There it is,' Joan said. 'In that corner.'

As we pulled up at the white box, a big bruiser of a uniformed man headed towards us.

'This is only for electric cars, you know,' he said.

'Well, yes. That's why we're here – to charge our car.'

'Didn't know electric cars were so big. Always thought they were little things, like buggies – you know, like old folk use. Never seen one before.'

'Well, when we get old, perhaps we'll get a buggy. Now you know what an electric car looks like, perhaps you can tell the chaps who run this place. And then tell them we've been all over trying to find this charge point.'

'Well, it's only been open a couple of months.'

'That's no excuse. Everywhere we go it's the same – no signage whatsoever.'

'Well,' he said, 'it's up to the government or the local authority. They've got to put the signs up.'

'Come off it. All motorway service centres have enormous signs and arrows in the road telling cars where to go for petrol. Never seen one for EV charge points, though.'

'See what you mean,' he said.

His buddy, a short, slim man, approached. He had a red earring and tattoos obliterating his right arm.

'Can't you just put some petrol in it?' Mr Earring said. 'It's a hybrid, isn't it?'

'No. We're all electric. No petrol at all in this car.'

'You should have solar panels on the roof. Might save you a lot of bother.'

'So what happens when it's snowing or raining, or just cloudy?'

'Put some little wind turbines on your wing mirrors?'

'Brilliant idea,' I said. 'Now, are you going to let us charge our car?'

'You mean you really want to use this thing then?' said the bruiser.

'Sure do,' I said. 'It's taken long enough to find it. Is there a problem?'

'No, it's just that we've never seen it used before.'

'You're joking. You mean we're the first to use it?'

'Yes. We thought it was a waste of time.'

Mr Earring perked up. 'How does it work then?' he asked.

I went through the procedure with them and waited for the blue lights to flash.

'Hear that click? See those blue lights flashing? That shows it's all working.'

'Blimey. It's a bit complicated, isn't it?' said the Bruiser. 'Never seen that before. How long's it going to take?'

'About forty-five minutes. Just enough time to get a coffee and a bite to eat. Don't forget to tell the management to put some signs up.'

'Will do.'

'I know I'm on home ground when I hear those guys talk,' I said to Joan. 'Just like I used to when I was a lad. I find myself slipping into it. Wonderful.'

As we entered the cafeteria, some guy grinned at us. 'You got in then,' he said, 'but you'll be lucky to get back out in under an hour. D'you know, this place has just been voted the worst motorway services in England?'

'Thanks for the warning.'

We did get out, eventually, and drove hesitantly up the slip road and onto the approach to the Dartford Crossing. We were then sucked into a roaring line of thousands of drivers hunched over their steering wheels in manic-eyed concentration, crawling at 10mph, desperately on the alert for any opportunity to switch lanes in the hope of getting past the car in front and gaining a few extra precious seconds.

The M25 morphs into the A282 to cross the Thames at the Dartford Crossing, a four-lane bridge if you're travelling south, tunnels if you're going north. The official speed limit is 50mph, but it never got above 10mph for us. The bridge carries an average of about 160,000 vehicles a day, but it must be empty most of the time because all 160,000 of them seemed to be crossing it at the precise moment we were using it.

'I think everyone here must be on the edge of a nervous breakdown,' Joan said.

'Well, it *is* a bit stressful. Never known anything like it. It's madness.'

L'hôte Boutique Hotel is situated on the Old Dover Road, diagonally opposite the St Lawrence Cricket Ground, the home of Kent County Cricket Club. It's Norman Tebbit country. More than 500 first-class matches of this most English of games have been played on the edge of this most English of cities in this very English county, which used to be known as the Garden of England.

We were in Canterbury, on the far edges of the Home Counties, and we wanted to park our car for a few days and walk and forget about looking for charge points. Despite the manic driving from Thurrock, we'd done pretty well, 43 miles on 35 per cent of the battery, an average of 141 miles to the charge. Not bad.

L'hôte Boutique Hotel was a smart, new hotel and this was its opening week.

'Sorry,' Monsieur le Patron told us, 'there's only on-street parking and it's limited to four hours. You're OK for the weekend, but after that you'll have to use the Park and Ride. It's just a couple of miles away.'

'So if we park for four hours in the morning, we can just take it round the corner for another four hours in the afternoon, yes?'

'No. No daytime parking for more than four hours is allowed anywhere in this postal district. No moving around from one street to another. They're sharp here; if you're caught, you'll get a ticket. Sorry.'

'What about this nice little space here?' I suggested, pointing to a gravelled area in what was obviously at one time a fair-sized garden. 'Couldn't you open this up for parking?

'Oh no, we're keeping that for al fresco dining – we've already ordered the space heaters.'

So you can see why people are so screamingly angry here

in the Home Counties. They love their cars, but are not allowed to park them. Looking out of the window, Monsieur le Patron pointed to a gap over the road.

'Park there,' he said. 'Grab it while you can. It'll be good for the weekend.'

It took more than one attempt to reverse-park into the gap. I pulled out once more to rearrange my rearwards trajectory. This was a very unsatisfactory state of affairs for the driver of the Range Rover that drew up behind us. We were holding him up and he had an important meeting to attend. Time, after all, is money. He put one hand on his horn and kept it there while with the other he opened the window, shook his fist and screamed. His face, contorted with rage, went a deep shade of crimson. I thought this was a bit excessive for what I considered to be an innocent attempt to comply with the local parking laws. Suspecting that the poor man was going to have a nervous breakdown or perhaps burst a blood vessel, I said, 'I think you're going to die. Don't you think you ought to calm down?'

This wasn't the right thing to say, apparently, for he blew another gasket. It was all too much for Joan. She went up to the man, who was still screaming at us through his open window.

'We're only parking our car, you stupid man. What's the matter with you?'

When we'd settled down to coffee and biscuits in our room, Joan said, 'Well, at least you kept your cool.'

'Just about managed to hold it in. That kind of behaviour makes me see red.'

'Talking of which, what's the matter with your eye?'

'Which one?'

'The left.'

'You tell me. What *is* the matter with it?'

'It's all red.'

'Is this a joke?'

'No, I'm serious. It's turned red. Go and look in the mirror.'

I did, and was surprised to see I had a spectacularly red eye. No white to be seen anywhere.

The minor injuries unit at the East Kent Hospital was just twenty minutes' walk away. The triaging was done by Christine, who took my blood pressure.

'I thought there was an ophthalmology unit here,' I said.

'Oh, there used to be,' she said, 'but we've just been downgraded to a minor injuries and emergency hospital only. All our specialist staff have gone to the upgraded unit at Ashford. No specialists here at all now. Hello, your pulse dropped to 45 and then to 29. That's very low. I'm going to do an ECG. I think you ought to be on a pacemaker.'

As we sat and waited, three boys from Canterbury Rugby Football Club came in with shoulder, knee and leg injuries between them. A group of four young people – two couples – sat and looked at their telephone screens. An older man came back from the consulting room.

'She says I'm perfect,' he said to his missis.

'Huh,' she grunted. 'She obviously doesn't know you.'

'Just so there's no misunderstanding,' said Christine, 'I said that his blood pressure was perfect.'

'Huh,' said the missis.

And then it was my turn to see the doctor.

'It's a subconjunctival haemorrhage,' he said. 'Have you

been under any stress recently?'

'The Dartford Crossing was a bit difficult,' I said. 'Not used to that kind of driving. And then we had an altercation with a local motorist who objected to my parking technique. He was in a bit of a hurry.'

'Here, everyone is,' he said. 'Well, whatever it was you were holding in, it's caused a small blood vessel in your eye to burst. It'll clear up in a few days. But the nurse seemed more concerned about your pulse rate. It's probably all connected, you know. Stress can do that kind of thing.'

'So all this stressful driving has given me a burst blood vessel and a palpitating heart. Do they all drive like that here?'

'It can be pretty bad,' he said, 'but we learn to take it in our stride.'

21

ANOTHER THIN PLACE

It was a warm Sunday, and Canterbury was full of bright young things, mostly students going up to university for the start of the new academic year. Along St Margaret's Street, groups of them spilled out onto the pavement at eating places, coffee bars, bistros. They popped into Alberrys, No. 35, the Urban Wok Box. We wove our way through them, their excited chatter lightening our hearts, bringing back memories. On High Street, we made for the Visitor Information Centre, where we explained our parking problem to the young lady at the desk.

'The problem is,' I said, 'we want to be able to park for the day and walk, but we can't find a way round the four-hour limit. It ruins our day.'

'The best thing would be to use Park and Ride,' she said. 'Where are you staying?'

'On the Old Dover Road.'

'Ah, right, so there's a Park and Ride at the junction of Old Dover Road and New Dover Road. You can park there for £3.50 a day and it has an electric vehicle charge point.'

'What kind?'

'Polar Instant.'

'Brilliant. Thanks.'

Ahead of us, at the end of Mercery Lane, was the dramatic entrance to the cathedral precinct, the Christ Church Gate. We felt the sudden shift in historical perspective. From dealing with a very twenty-first-century problem, we were transported back 1,500 years, to an age where none of that could have even been imagined. It was like stepping through a gateway into a different world, a walled medieval religious settlement embedded within a twenty-first-century city. Alongside was the cobbled area of the Buttermarket, bustling with activity: milling tourists, drinkers outside the Shakespeare pub, Nicholson's Pie House customers eating al fresco.

In the cathedral, the cantor was singing: 'O Lord, open Thou my lips,' and the response came, 'And our mouth shall show forth Thy praise.' And suddenly, although I have few specific religious beliefs these days, I felt deeply moved to praise whatever it was that had made it possible for us to be there, in that place, at that particular time, amid all that beauty. 'Praise ye the Lord,' sang the cantor. 'The Lord's Name be praised' came the response.

Just outside the cathedral, on the other side of Broad

Street, we chanced upon Lady Wootton's Green and a story about the beginnings of Anglo-Saxon Christianity in this busy corner of England. Its position on the edge of the country and so close to the European mainland has always guaranteed a brisk exchange of people and ideas across the Channel from the very earliest of times. On a monument in this quiet garden, we found the story of two people's comings and goings, a story of love, marriage, religion and politics.

Bertha, it seems, was married to King Æthelberht of Kent, who was the first Anglo-Saxon ruler to convert to Christianity. She was a Frankish (Germanic) princess and a practising Christian. Æthelberht's roots seem to have been Scandinavian, his forbears probably coming from Jutland. He did, however, also have Frankish connections. All this explains why a Frankish Christian princess ended up marrying a Kentish pagan king living on the other side of the Channel. As part of the marriage settlement, Bertha insisted that she be allowed to continue practising her Christian faith. Æthelberht, for reasons of love, politics or both, therefore, gave her a church at Durovernum, later to be known as Cantwara-burh (which means the Stronghold of the Kentish people).[57]

A couple of decades later, Pope Gregory sent a group of missionary monks to Kent, headed by Augustine, tasked with converting the British from their paganism and setting up an archbishopric in London, the old Roman capital. Æthelberht, it seems, was impressed by their teaching, and it was not long before he, together with several thousand others, were

<hr/>

57 Additional material from Marc Morris, *The Anglo-Saxons: A History of the Beginnings of England*, Hutchinson, 2021, pp56-60.

converted. However, as Augustine was entirely dependent on Æthelberht's authority, it seemed politic to establish the archbishop's throne in Canterbury, not London, and this is why the ecclesiastical province of Canterbury still reflects the area of Æthelberht's ancient jurisdiction.

We see Canterbury as the heart of Christian England, epitomising Englishness. It is, after all, the headquarters of the Church of England, and the cathedral is often referred to as England in stone. But Augustine, its first archbishop, was Italian, not English, and the cathedral itself, which we see as quintessentially English, was completely rebuilt by the Normans, after they colonised us in 1066, as part of their strategy of extinguishing as much of Anglo-Saxon England as possible. Canterbury Cathedral became French!

Henry II was the first Plantagenet king, and it was at his instigation that Thomas à Becket was murdered in the cathedral. The Plantagenet dynasty lasted for 240 years, coming to an end only when Henry VIII nationalised the Church of England and we officially became Protestant and religion in this island state became English rather than Italian. So, during Plantagenet times, Latin, not English, was the language of religion, and French was the language of our conquerors and courtiers, the language of law, of the aristocracy and of the high-ups.

Chaucer, however, wrote in English, the language of everyday folk. In this, he followed in the footsteps of King Alfred, who, to promote unity among the warring kingdoms of what would later become England, insisted that the *Anglo-Saxon Chronicle* be written in the language that people spoke in their everyday lives. Chaucer's *Canterbury Tales* were in that tradition. His often bawdy, sometimes humorous, occasionally romantic, but always light-hearted and frank tales told by a bunch of ill-assorted strangers on a pilgrimage to Canterbury marked the beginnings of English literature for ordinary English people, for whom the usual Latin and French texts were out of reach.

Chaucerian English, however, was deemed too common for Henry II. Although he was, by all accounts, a highly educated man who spoke Latin and French fluently, he wasn't inclined to learn the language of the people over whom he ruled.

The Cathedral and Metropolitan Church of Christ Canterbury, to give it its full name, struck me as being another thin place, like Lindisfarne, one where you can feel yourself stepping through an invisible curtain into another universe, 'a rip in the mysterious membrane separating the world of mortals from the realm of the gods'.[58] I felt it most strongly when I put my head into the Sudbury Tomb. Here I was again, back at Sudbury.

This curious monument marks the resting place of the man known to history as Simon of Sudbury. He was Bishop of London for fourteen years before being promoted to the Archbishopric of Canterbury. While holding that post, he was also appointed Lord Chancellor, which turned out to be an unfortunate step in his entanglement with the affairs of state that was to cost him his life.

It was a dangerous time in England. Following the Black Death there was an acute shortage of labour; landowners tried to keep down wages; the poor were expected to keep their

58   Francesca Stavrakopoulou, *God: An Anatomy*, Picador, 2021, p368.

place; and Parliament made yet a third attempt to impose a poll tax on everyone. The peasants were having none of it, and in the great Peasants' Revolt that ensued, Simon of Sudbury was regarded as the villain of the piece and was dragged to Tower Hill, where he was beheaded. His head was stuck on a pole on London Bridge and eventually ended up in St Gregory's Church, Sudbury, where it remains to this day. His body was taken to Canterbury, where, ignominiously, it has a cannonball in place of his head. The story has it that on the anniversary of his death, the cathedral asks St Gregory's if they can have his head back. St Gregory's says no, but could they please have his body back. Each Christmas, however, the Mayor of Canterbury places a wreath of red roses on Simon of Sudbury's tomb in gratitude for all that he did for the city.

There's a vaulted canopy over Simon of Sudbury's tomb in the cathedral, below which is a series of niches that were designed to be individual spaces for private prayer. You are invited to:

> *Kneel down and lean your head into the space, then talk in a normal voice. Those outside cannot hear what you are saying. You cannot hear others speaking either. Outside noise becomes a gentle murmur.*

My lack of religious beliefs does not prevent me from feeling deeply moved when I enter some places of worship, be they Christian, Buddhist, Hindu, or a woodland glade with sacred trees. I don't know if that is caused by nostalgia, beauty, stillness, or simply a reminder of humankind's unending angst-laden search for meaning in an indifferent universe.

The Cantor sings, 'He hath shewed strength with his arm; he hath scattered the proud in the imagination of their hearts.'

And the response comes, 'He hath put down the mighty from their seat; and hath exalted the humble and meek.'

Cantor: 'He hath filled the hungry with good things, and the rich he hath sent empty away.[59]

Coming out of Guildhall Street and back onto High Street, we spotted an elderly-looking man sitting on a well-used sleeping bag on the opposite side of the road, an affectionate dog by his side.

'Hello. What're you doing here?'

His dog clambered over me as I squatted beside him.

'Marriage broke up,' he said.

'When?'

'Seven years ago.'

'Did you lose your house?'

'Yes.'

'Did you have a job?'

'Yes. I was a painter and decorator. But who wants to employ someone who is smelling because they can't keep clean and who can't give them an address?'

'Where will you go tonight?'

'Behind the library.'

'On your own?'

'No, there's a group of us. We keep together for safety and to keep warm. In warm weather like this, we can stay on the

---

59   From the Magnificat, Order of Sung Evensong, Book of Common Prayer, based on Luke 1:46-55.

street, but in the cold we huddle up behind the library.'

'How long have you been homeless?'

'Seven years.'

He wasn't elderly. He just looked it.

'So what the cantor sang isn't true, is it?' I said to Joan. 'He doesn't always fill the hungry with good things and send the rich empty away. It's a lottery who gets to eat and who doesn't.'

Not far away is Thanington Without, an inner suburb of Canterbury outside the city's medieval walls. Here, it is possible for a father and mother in the same household both to have paying jobs but still not have enough to pay for rent and food. Here too, on the edge of this most prosperous-looking city, is an area that counts as one of the most deprived in the country, where people just about manage by relying on food banks.

According to Patrick Cockburn, a journalist for the *Independent* newspaper, there is here a pervasive sense of institutional neglect, which generous funding from the EU some twenty years earlier had never been enough to dispel. No doubt, suggests Cockburn, it was this persistent feeling of abandonment that persuaded the majority of the population to vote 'Leave' in the 2016 EU referendum. On our way back along the Old Dover Road, just a few hundred metres from the city centre, we saw a scattering of homeless people settling down for the night.

Further on, we came across two women, one at the cashpoint, the other doing some exercises in the middle of the pavement. She was smartly dressed, with a warm, light blue gilet, smart jeans, white hair.

'Looks as if you're enjoying a spot of yoga,' I said.

'Just stretching, while I wait for my friend to get some cash.'

'Isn't it nice,' Joan said, 'not to have to worry about what people think?'

'Oh, it's so freeing.'

'Where're you from?'

'California.'

'Some years ago, we drove from Seattle to see Crater Lake.'

'Oh yes, that's near California. I've come to England three or four times, and I used to drive, but I've lost my nerve now, with all this traffic congestion.'

'It's shaken us too. We come from the north of England, and we just don't see traffic like this up there.'

Monday morning, and time to vacate our parking place. A couple of miles along the Old Dover Road, we found the Park and Ride interchange. The plan was to charge the car and leave it there for the day, leaving us free to explore Canterbury on foot.

It was a large and full car park, but we found the charge point on the far side, near the bus terminal and next to the attendant's office. We had a Polar Instant app and drove into the parking bay. I opened the port lid, inserted the hose, got out the app and pressed the buttons. A message came up telling me to swipe my RFID card, but as it was supposed to be an app-only service, we didn't have one. I phoned the contact number, but the line was dead. Joan looked around and found the attendant.

'Oh, you can't park here without a permit,' he said. 'You just need to apply to the local authority for a card. It's very easy. Just fill in this form and you'll get it in a few days.'

'But we need to charge now.'

'They'll be as quick as they can.'

Just then a young, flustered woman with a diesel car drew up and pulled into the adjacent bay.

'Are you going to charge your car?' Joan asked.

'No, but I have a child with me and can't find anywhere else to park. This is the only space there is. I have a bus to catch to get him to nursery and I've got business to do in town. It's all right. I'll be back this afternoon.'

'But it's reserved for electric cars.'

'Well, this used to be a parent-and-child parking place and now they've taken it for an electric car. There are loads of charge points all over the city. So it's not a problem for me to park here.'

'The nearest rapid charge point is at the Holiday Inn,' I said to Joan. 'Let's go.'

It was a few miles out of Canterbury. A Tesla was parked at the charging cabinet, but the second bay was vacant. Teslas have their own dedicated charge points and aren't supposed to be able to use CHAdeMO connectors, the type we needed. But that is exactly what this Tesla was doing.

'I'll go to Reception. See if I can find out whose car that is. Whoever it is, it won't be long. It's already charged 98 per cent.'

Just then, a tall, lanky, bespectacled fellow, with scholarly demeanour and a mop of grey hair, came out. I guess he was in his early fifties.

'It's OK,' he said, 'it's mine.'

'How do you manage to use CHAdeMO?' I asked.

'I've got an adaptor.'

'Didn't know you could get them. How much?'

'Four hundred pounds. I'm just topping up. On my way to my girlfriend's place.'

'What's your range?'

'About two hundred and fifty miles in this weather. I've come from Portsmouth, going to Margate. Do this trip often. Where're you from?'

'Scottish borders. We've driven seven hundred miles to get here.'

'Crikey. What's your range then?'

'In this weather, about a hundred and forty. But realistically, we need to charge every eighty to a hundred.'

'It's OK, isn't it? I mean, you still need to stop for a pee. Tell me, who drives for more than a hundred miles and doesn't stop for a cup of coffee or a pee? It's a mindset. It's all about changing your attitude. It'll happen. It'll come. You'll see.'

'Well, we like the camaraderie among EV users. It's nice.'

'Yeah, but it won't last. You wait till everyone has an EV. Then it'll be back to everyone for themselves.'

Back in Canterbury, we were served afternoon tea at the Café St Pierre by a French lass from Clermont-Ferrand.

'Ah, the Puy de Dôme,' Joan said.

'You know it?'

'Yes, I used to teach French and know the country well.'

'And I passed through Clermont on the train many years

ago. It's different, the Massif Central. A land of extinct volcanoes and lentils.'

'You know about Puy lentils?'

'Of course we do. They're famous in our family. We use them a lot.'

'I'm amazed. I usually tell people I'm from Lille, because no one knows where Clermont-Ferrand is, but you know everything about it.'

We were sitting in what would otherwise have been a delightful walled garden, giving us some shade and relief from the intense heat. Unfortunately, the walls also had the effect of ensuring that the smoke from two nicotine addicts was unable to escape. This ridiculous law forbidding smoking inside restaurants and pubs but not in their gardens has driven smokers outside in the summer, stealing all the nicest places. So we made our way to the deep inside of the Shakespeare pub, by the Buttermarket, where there was a pleasant medieval gloominess and a complete absence of smoke.

The summer of 2018 was the hottest summer since that other great sizzler of 1976. This had had profound implications for chips. 1976 is still talked about in potato circles because of its effect on the size of potatoes, and in the realm of professional potatoism, size matters. Now with this long hot summer of 2018, it looked as if history was repeating itself. While I was gulping down my Carlsberg Zero and Joan was sipping her Pinot Grigio, the landlord told us about the potato problem.

'I can normally buy a twenty-five kilo sack of potatoes for five pounds' he said, 'but now I'm having to pay eight or nine pounds. It's happening all over Europe. You'd never believe it, but the potatoes that are used for the mass production of frozen chips are usually about the size of house bricks. That's how you get those nice big chips. Now, however, they're coming out of the ground not much bigger than eggs, which means everyone's going to have to put up with much smaller chips. They're not gonna like that.'

Outside, in Angel Courtyard, we found some scattered benches and tables with awnings and redundant space heaters. It was a good place to finish our drinks, until it filled up with smokers, whereupon we made our farewells to the landlord and moved next door to Nicholson's Speciality Pie House for our evening meal.

The following morning, before breakfast, I crossed the road to Sainsbury's to get some sandwiches for the day. It was strategically placed next to the opening to the Kent Cricket Ground. This was clearly a special day. From all directions, hordes of men were streaming into the ground. They'd come for the Kent v Glamorgan four-day match. There were thousands of them. With the advantage of prior knowledge, some had managed to park their cars at the Park and Ride interchange and then walk to the ground. Most of the enthusiasts, though, arrived in a convoy of coaches. In one long continuous stream, they stepped out and filed through the gates. They were nearly all men, young men in their 30s and 40s, dressed smart casual, with neatly pressed slacks and chinos, trim jackets, man-bags with their packed lunches over their shoulders. It seemed as if the whole male population of Kent was out for the day. There were older, more portly men, too, in shorts and summer shirts, carrying nothing but a thin coat. They were the ones who poured into Sainsbury's to buy their food and drink for the day. It was a lengthy business, relishing their independence, indulging their appetites. They had been let off the leash and they were going to make the most of it. I took my place in the queue and we edged our way forward, the air alive with the buzz of anticipation and excited chatter. Among the hundreds of men, I counted about a dozen women.

'My, you're brave. There must be ten thousand men pouring in here, and only about a dozen women.'

'Well, they'll have the queues at the toilets then, won't they? That'll make a change. It'll be nice to have the boot on the other foot.'

Back in the hotel I joined Joan at breakfast as Monsieur le patron came in.

'Morning,' I said. 'Cricket match, I see. Lots of people milling around.'

'Yeah, we're overcrowded. That's the problem. Got to stop everyone coming here.'

'We're from a part of the north where it's pretty empty. It didn't seem crowded till we came here. Anyhow, it's only for a few days, isn't it?'

'I suppose so, but the trouble is, this is where everyone arrives. It's basic geography, isn't it?'

'Yes,' Joan said. 'The thing is, you pay a price for being in a prime geographical location. That's why you can easily nip over to the continent for your summer holidays. Must be nice. We often wish we could do that.'

'Where're you off to now? he asked.'

'Dover, and tomorrow the Romney Hythe and Dymchurch Railway.'

'Danny Martin runs that railway; he's a fanatic.'

'Dungeness is now becoming quite trendy,' said his wife as she joined us. 'You'll like it.'

22

MERRIE ENGLAND

THE COMIC OPERA *Merrie England* has everything in it that we associate with being English.[60] Apart from singing the praises of the reign of Queen Elizabeth I, it also marks such well-loved English heroes of Tudor England as Walter Raleigh, the Earl of Essex, the royal foresters Long Tom and Big Ben, and the tinker, tailor, soldier, sailor of every town in the realm. Above all, it's a paean of praise to the yeomen of England, the small landowners, holding their heads high somewhere between the gentry and the labourers, in homesteads and cottages throughout the realm, and forming the backbone of England.

And it is England we're talking about here, not Britain, and not even the whole of England. It's an idealistic, stereotypical fantasy of life in pastoral, lowland England. That is exactly

---

60　By Edward German and Basil Hood.

where we were now, in the Home Counties, where this romantic vision of Englishness is set. 'The heart of medieval England,' Dan Jackson reminds us, 'was always London and the wide and fertile southern plain.'[61] This is the setting for *Merrie England*. But it's a myth, of course. London-centric Englishness is a distortion of our national identity.

I was reminded of all of this as we drove through the Kentish countryside on our way from Canterbury to Sandwich. We had taken a bit of a detour to see some hop fields on the southern fringe of Canterbury. In the days when I used to cycle in the Wealden countryside, hops were everywhere. They reached 15 feet into the sky on giant trellises, and scattered among them were red brick oast houses, with their trademark conical roofs, where the hops were dried before sending them off to the breweries.

Hop fields were an essential part of this corner of England, but now we had to seek them out. The hop poles were a product of the sweet chestnut coppices that used to be characteristic of the High Weald. Nowadays, both chestnut coppices and hop poles are a rarity, and something about the English countryside has been lost. But never mind, we are now importing hops from our neighbour across the Big Pond, so that's all right then.

With the longest continuous row of Tudor buildings in the country, Sandwich is the most complete medieval town in England. The medieval Guildhall has its own copies of the *Magna Carta* and its very own *Charter of the Forest*, which restored to freemen the rights for access to the royal forests

61   Dan Jackson, *The Northumbrians: North-East England and Its People, A New History*, Hurst & Company, London, 2019, p13.

that had been taken away by William the Conqueror and his heirs and successors. It was here, too, in the year 43 CE, that the Romans landed on our beaches and took over our country. Being right on the edge of England and close to the continental mainland, this was an obvious place from which to launch their invasion. We soon forgave them for this and now proudly display their legacy as an essential part of our Englishness.

It was also reputedly here that King Canute, as well as demonstrating that not even he had the power to resist the ineluctable forces of nature, gave permission for the Christchurch monks to build a ferry over the River Stour. It was at Sandwich, one of England's principal ports, that Edward the Confessor gathered his ships to see off repeated threats of invasion from Scandinavia, and Harold II gathered together here 'greater naval and land armies than any king in this country had ever gathered before'[62] to face the imminent threat from Normandy, which was eventually to be the undoing of Anglo-Saxon England.

Several hundred years later, John Montagu, the fourth Earl of Sandwich, decided to put a sliver of meat between two slices of bread so that he could eat his meal while continuing to play the tables without interruption. Everyone thought this was a good idea, and the sandwich was invented. And then there's that gullible, impetuous, 'weak as water' English hero, Mr Polly, who had his home here in Sandwich, except that in the book, *The History of Mr Polly*, HG Wells tried to disguise Sandwich as Fishbourne.

---

62 Marc Morris, *The Norman Conquest*, Windmill Books, London, 2012, p148.

Sandwich is as English as you can get. Except that it isn't. As Jeremy Paxman points out, when you dig into it, 'the first thing you discover about the English is that they are not English – in the sense of coming from England – at all. They had arrived from Jutland, Anglen (sic)[63] and Lower Saxony. The "English race", if such a thing exists, is German.'[64]

But there is more. The English, it seems, are not even British. The story has it that, in the middle of the fifth century, King Vortigern invited some Saxon mercenaries to help the Britons defend themselves against their enemies, the Scots and the Picts. The mercenaries liked what they saw when they landed on the Kent coast and so invited some of their compatriots back home to come and join them. This opened the floodgates to a stream of Jutes, Angles and Saxons from modern Denmark and north-west Germany.

But having come here to assist the Britons, these newcomers turned against the Brits and effected a coup d'état. They pushed the Celtic British to the western edges of our island, and we became an Anglo-Saxon land, which eventually morphed into what we now know as England. So if you're looking for the true Brits, you have to go west.

All of this is part of the story that we now tell ourselves about how we became a nation. But what we normally mean by that is how *England* became a nation. *Britain* is not a *nation* in the strict meaning of the word; it comprises three nations: English, Scots and Welsh. If you want to include Northern Ireland, then it's the United Kingdom of Great Britain and

---

63   This should be Angeln.
64   Jeremy Paxman, *The English: A Portrait of a People*, Penguin Books, London, p54.

Northern Ireland. But we never say someone is UK-ish in the same way in which we say they are British, English, Scottish, Welsh or Irish. The UK, in short, is not a *nation*; it's a *state*, and within it, four *nations*.

Perhaps Englishness is about inconsequential things such as coffee, or perhaps tea. The waft of coffee drew Joan and me into the No Name Shop in No Name Street, and it felt delightfully English. As we climbed the narrow wooden stairs and entered a low-ceilinged room with wooden beams, wooden tables, wooden seats and a creaking wooden floor, it gave me a reassuring feel of at-homeness.

Joan was at the counter placing our order when a woman behind her complained, 'Isn't this wind terrible?'

'D'you think so?' Joan said. 'I quite like it.'

To those of us who live in the north-east of England, constantly battling icy blasts and the frequent chill of North Sea frets, this sounded a bit pathetic. The prolonged warm, dry weather was heaven for us, and the delightful breeze that silkily wrapped itself round us was more than perfect.

'Pampered southerners,' Joan muttered as she sat down.

'Don't be too hard on them,' I said. 'They have to endure the horrors of the daily commute.'

Mind you, in my day they commuted in style. Twice a day, the Brighton Belle whizzed along the top of the railway embankment at the bottom of our garden. It was the world's only all-electric, all-Pullman train service and I always thought its purpose was to take posh people to high-powered jobs in London. The umber and yellow first-class coaches were given girls' names – Hazel and Doris, Gwen and Mona, Audrey and Vera. The train oozed luxury. Sometimes, when it was forced to slow down, I could see all these important people sitting at tables, each with its own individual lamp with tasselled shades, framed by windows with neatly tied-back curtains. It seemed to me to be a rather glorious way of commuting, all these eminent people, discussing the business of the day over breakfast on their way to work and relaxing over afternoon tea on their way home. These, and all the other people who travelled into London every day from north, south, east and west, lived somewhere in one of the counties surrounding the great metropolis. They all left their homes, did a day's work and returned to their homes. And their homes were in the Home Counties.

They still make this daily journey into London. Only today it's not so luxurious. Four million people cram into rattling, diesel-belching sardine tins. The lucky few get seats, the rest stand, and because they are squeezed and pushed and jostled, they hide behind newspapers and smartphones and pretend everyone else is not there.[65] They come from even further afield now – from Bedfordshire, Hampshire, Oxfordshire and Cambridgeshire, and these have now been added to the Home Counties list. The rest of us live in 'the Provinces', where it's not Home Counties, and therefore not really England.

These wretched commuters endure the daily misery of the train or the drive over the Dartford Crossing, and at weekends they retreat to England, the real England of rolling downs, country lanes and neatly trimmed hedgerows, the England of oast houses and the occasional windmill, of pubs

---

65   This, of course, was in BC, the era Before Covid-19, when we learned the new skill of social distancing.

overlooking the village green – and, of course, the England of cricket.

'So, welcome to the Home Counties, Joanie.'

'Why's it called the Home Counties?'

'The superficial answer is that they all share the same beating heart – London – to which they all commute from the surrounding counties. The more serious members of this class really do think that this is what England's all about – that the values and way of life here in this little corner of our United Kingdom actually define English values, just as they did in medieval England. Or even define British values. The rest of us are "provincial".'

'Yes, and that's the problem. Those so-called leaders of ours who go to Eton, Harrow or Radley and then to Oxford or Cambridge, think this little bit of England is how the whole country is. But like Roger in that tourist office said, they don't really know a thing about the rest of the country. England to them is the Larkins in the *Darling Buds of May*: rosy-cheeked country farmers, retired colonels running country pubs and comfortable bank managers chairing parish councils. In the North, they did all the mucky jobs, dug the coal, extracted the iron ore, built the ships, made the iron and steel, made themselves ill and dirty and died prematurely, while all the money found its way here, to the South, where the owners of the coal mines and factories lived in their fine houses, and this was the real England. It wasn't and it isn't.'

'Didn't know you felt so strongly about it.'

'Well, it's true, isn't it? I grew up in Yorkshire, where we knew what real work was. You grew up in cushy, leafy Surrey.'

'Steady on, we weren't at all cushy. We were dirt-poor and

lived in a council house in a rough corner of posh Surrey, on the edge of a working class railway town, Redhill. I've no desire to return. Couldn't bear the overcrowding, manic roads and noise. But there will always be a part of me that belongs here. We got the Danes and Vikings up North; they got the Angles and Saxons down here. So our origins are Scandinavian, theirs Germanic. Still English, though.'

23

VULNERABILITY

'IS THAT A HOBBY OF YOURS?' a voice behind me asked.

Turning round, I saw a smartly dressed couple out for a stroll.

'Not really,' I said. 'I'm just interested in why many of the boats look so sorry for themselves.'

It was Deal, and I was jotting down the names of some of the boats drawn up on the beach while Joan was doing a recce for an early lunch. Many boats looked abandoned, and I was wondering if some of them represented what remained of the fishing industry. A few months earlier, the local MP, Craig Mackinlay, had joined Kent fisherman protesting about the government's failure to secure an EU deal that would protect their industry. He, along with a dozen or so other MPs, was threatening to vote against the imminent Brexit transitional arrangements. The fishermen wanted full control of British waters.

Spread out before me was what looked like the detritus of an industry in its death throes. Scattered over the pebbles were rusty old winches, tatty bits of rope, neglected lobster pots and dilapidated signs that made promises that seemed impossible to keep: 'GaryAnne Boat Trips', 'You can buy Deal Herring on Friday', 'Skate for sale', 'Fresh fish caught locally'. Some boats were unnamed, but a few brightly coloured ones appeared to be still in use: the Sally Joy, Denise, Morning Haze, Amora, Polar Bear.

'I'm Chris,' she said, 'and this is my husband.'

'Archie,' he said as we shook hands, 'Archie Houston. I'm secretary of the Deal branch of the Royal Marines Association. What makes you so interested in places like this?'

'We're touring the east coast in our electric car,' Joan told them. 'It's all new to me, but Clive knows this part of the world.'

'I used to live next door, in Surrey, but never really got to know this part of the Kent coast.'

'Did you know,' said Archie, 'that Deal has been the spiritual home of the Royal Marines since 1869? This coming Saturday, 22nd of September, is the anniversary of the Deal Bombing in 1989. It happened at 8:22 am. The IRA placed a bomb under the culvert of the recreation room of the Royal Marines. Eleven men were killed, and several others were seriously injured. They'd obviously been observing our movements and knew how to inflict maximum damage. Every year we commemorate it.'

'I didn't know that.'

'Well,' Chris said, 'here's something else you may not know.

That hotel over there, the Royal Hotel, is where Lord Nelson and Lady Hamilton used to have their assignations, and that's where we're going for coffee. Nice to meet you. Bye.'

'And we,' said Joan, when they'd gone, 'are going to have lunch at Love Drinks on the High Street. It looks just the kind of place where we can get a good sandwich.'

It couldn't have been a better choice, although I didn't think so when I first set eyes on the sandwich collection.

'I know this chap the Earl of Sandwich got the whole sandwich idea going, but isn't it time we realised there are other things you can put in them besides cheese or meat?'

'They look a friendly lot,' Joan said. 'Let's see if they're up for suggestions.'

So I spoke to Lucie, who was behind the counter. 'Do you have any sandwiches that don't have cheese or meat in them?'

'No,' she said with a smile. 'Sorry.'

'What kind of thing do you have in mind?' interjected her sister Candy.

'Roasted vegetables, hummus, egg, salad, tuna and red onion?'

'We can do tuna I think,' said Candy. 'I'll go and find out.'

Then Samantha came over. 'This card has our wi-fi code on it,' she said. 'Next time you come, let us know and we'll make sure we have something you like.'

'There won't be a next time,' Joan said.

'Oh dear, why not? Where're you from?'

'Scottish borders, by electric car.'

'Wow! Father's got an electric car. Loves it. Your nearest charge point from here is at Lidl, just outside Dover. How d'you charge your car back home?'

'In the garage. We have a charge point.'

'Where're you going next?'

'South coast, Eastbourne, maybe Brighton,' I said. 'As a kid, I used to cycle to Brighton from Redhill.'

'My brother's done the London to Brighton cycle race,' said Samantha, 'and my father. We're all sisters here, you know. It's a family business.'

It was a short walk from the car park to the rear entrance of the Dover Best Western Hotel. Approaching the door, we passed a young woman rummaging through a rubbish skip. She tried to hide as we passed, crouching low behind its harsh metal. She was scarcely tall enough to reach into it, for whatever scraps she was hoping to find.

'It's just chance that makes you fall on one side or the other of the great divide, isn't it?' Joan said.

I am bombarded with the usual flood of guilt about the unfairness of it all, of wanting to help, but feeling impotent. We passed her by, and the glass-fronted rear door of the hotel swished open, welcoming us into a world that she could only dream of. Reception issued us with our parking permit and we ordered our evening meal, blanking out the desperate young woman outside, seeking nourishment from what we threw away.

There was time for a quick walk along the England Coast Path to the top of Dover Cliffs, from where it was possible to make out the French coast. Below us, 120 metres (nearly 400 feet) down, a constant stream of shipping was arriving and departing, a few were at anchor, waiting for clearance.

'You do get the feeling here,' Joan said, 'of the vulnerability to invaders of this corner of England.'

All the way along this coast, you can see the defences. The castles at Dover, Deal and Walmer, the Roman Fort at Richborough, Dover's Western Heights at Drop Redoubt – they all stand testimony to Britain's spirit of resistance to invasion. Dover has always been Britain's first line of defence. During the war, it was known as Hell's Corner and was bombarded by more than 2,000 German shells. The history of Dover is one of almost constant readiness. Even in Victorian times, fortifications were built to defend against possible invasion by France.

Nicholas Crane says that the South East was always Britain's 'default development zone'.[66] It was this region that was settled when the Romans disembarked at Sandwich. But even before then, from the very earliest times, this southeast corner had been the first to be developed, when people from what is now Germany walked across Doggerland to reach what are now our shores. It was the chalk that attracted these newcomers. 'Chalk,' writes Crane, 'was laid like a path all the way from the continent to Britain.' The settlers were familiar with chalk landscapes, for the chalk does not end at the iconic White Cliffs of Dover. It reaches across what is now the English Channel to northern France, and it continues to the lowlands of the Seine and the Somme, the Scheldt and the Rhine, and it underlies the now-drowned Doggerland. When these earliest migrants walked across Doggerland to Britain, they were following an ancient geological pathway.

66   Nicholas Crane, *The Making of the British Landscape*, Weidenfeld & Nicholson, paperback edition, 2017, p198.

The South East also hosted the Anglo-Saxon and Norman invasions. When settlers, invaders and missionaries came from Europe, the southeast coast was their first landfall. Today, however, says Patrick Cockburn, Dover's coastal defences consist of high-tech craft patrolling the Channel, hoping to deter would-be immigrants and presenting a 'defiant image of Britain repelling an external threat'.[67]

Dover is Britain's closest point of contact with the European mainland, just 21 miles away. Geography is a great determinant of outcomes; in this small corner of England, the edge that Britain presents to the world has always been critically important, and Dover has the sharpest edge. Each year, Dover sees 12 million passengers, three million lorries, two million cars and £122 billion-worth of imports and exports pass through its port. Dover is, says Patrick Cockburn, 'a money-generating machine'. Yet little of that wealth touches the majority of the people who live in Dover. The town, he tells us, feels a sense of 'marginalisation', of having been 'left behind', 'left out', of being on the edge of society. The high Brexit 'Leave' vote of 2016 reflected a feeling of impotent rage; under such circumstances, it is all too easy to look for scapegoats.

While there, at the top of those cliffs, we spoke to a gentleman who'd returned from Canada five years previously.

'I spent fifty years in Canada,' he said, 'but then had to come back. There's a house here that has been in the family for a hundred and twenty years.'

'So is that why you came back? For the house?'

---

67 Patrick Cockburn, *Choke Point*, London Review of Books, Vol. 41 No. 21, 7 November 2019.

'That was part of it. I'd retired and needed to come back. This place drew me. It gets into your skin. I spend three or four days a week up here, looking, breathing the air, doing a crossword, reading. It's magic.'

The east of the US had been taking a battering from Tropical Storm Florence, which had been inflicting catastrophic damage on the Carolinas. We in this part of England, however, were basking in a wonderful Indian summer, with temperatures in the mid-20s, as warm, sub-tropical air was drawn north on the western edges of a high-pressure system. All this time we'd been travelling in bright sunshine against a backdrop of azure skies and silver seas. By comparison, when we had arrived at Dover the previous day, the White Cliffs looked distinctly grey. The next day, however, against a grey sky, they appeared brilliantly white. It was a sign that the beautiful weather was coming to an end. I just wanted it to remain for one more day. I'd been waiting for tomorrow for more than 60 years.

24

SHINGLE

JOAN WAS NOT IMPRESSED with the idea of being shaken to pieces, squeezed into a miniature railway carriage, clattering across England's only desert and the largest area of shingle in Europe, whose only buildings of note were a couple of nuclear power plants and a few wooden shacks. This day, however, had been on my bucket list since long before I knew what a bucket list was.

Sometime in 1958, I'd been sitting in the school library writing up my geography notes when I happened to turn the pages of the *Geographical Magazine* and come across an article about the Romney, Hythe & Dymchurch Railway (RH&DR), a miniature train crossing one of England's most intriguing landscapes, a small triangle of land that had only recently, in geological time, attached itself to the Kent coast. My excitement now, more than 60 years later, was totally lost on my long-suffering wife.

Entering the railway station at Hythe was like stepping back into the 1950s, a world of lovingly tended machinery, of huffing and puffing engines immaculately cared-for, beautifully kempt station gardens, signal boxes, litter-free platforms, smart station officials and a proper clock with hands that reassuringly ticked. The smart café was humming with life and busyness, and I assumed this was just a summer high.

'No,' said the young woman who served us coffee. 'I work here permanently. It's all go, summer and winter. Never stops.'

The RH&DR is a major tourist attraction, and it is holidaymakers who keep the railway going financially. Even though it is a miniature railway, with a gauge of just 15 inches (381 mm), and with a maximum speed of 25mph, it has also performed serious civic duties. In the Second World War, it served as a military line to carry troops and armaments. Children go to school on it, and locals use it for shopping trips. It was in the 1930s, though, when the idea of having a week's holiday was becoming mainstream, that the railway started to deliver holidaymakers to the string of holiday camps that had begun to spring up along the route.

The train is pulled by a magnificent engine, the *Northern Chief*, livery a subdued racing green, the coaches a cheerful blue. We strolled along the platform, head and shoulders above the carriages, looking for our seats: coach A, seats 7 and 8.

'It's like Alice in Wonderland,' Joan said, as I squeezed myself in beside her, my head within an inch of the roof. Huddled together, we occupied the full width of the compartment.

Romney Marsh, together with the Walland Marsh to the west, forms an area of perfectly flat land on what used to be open sea. There was once a bay here, the former coastline of which is marked today by the old cliff line that is now several miles inland. It is marked also by the Saxon Shore Way, which follows the ancient coastline round this corner of England, as it was in Saxon times. The Royal Military Canal also follows the foot of these cliffs; it was built at the beginning of the nineteenth century as part of the defensive works against expected invasion by Napoleon.

Human effort combined with longshore drift have reclaimed the former bay, turning it into what are now these two great marsh areas. The whole is overlain by a lattice-work of drainage ditches, known as sewers: Brenzett Sewer, Wallsfoot Sewer, Abbatridge Sewer – enduring monuments to humankind's determination to take control of natural forces; latter-day King Canutes, keeping the sea at bay.

The process isn't over, however, for longshore drift continues to push England's edge outwards here by a metre or two each year. Ancient towns, such as Old Romney, Tenterden and Lydd, that used to be right on the coast and formed part of the Cinque Port confederation, now find themselves stranded inland.

This triangle of land jutting into the Channel is one of England's newest edges, an attractive haunt for quirky houses and nuclear power plants. And it is along the eastern edge of this inhospitable land that the Romney, Hythe & Dymchurch Railway chugs its daily way.

With a hoot, at 10.30 sharp, the *Northern Chief* pulled

away. Tatak-tatak, tatak-tatak, soon we were tearing along at 20mph. We clattered past the ends of gardens, fences just an arm's stretch away. A little girl playing on her lawn put her hands to her ears as we hooted past. Another waved and we waved back. A woman in blue slacks, white sleeveless top and yellow rubber gloves was depositing garden cuttings on her compost heap. Llamas grazed on a field of maize stubble.

At Dymchurch, we put down and picked up passengers. The station was in the middle of a residential area, a land of glasshouses, garden sheds, lawns, patios, garden toys, plastic paddling pools and sun loungers. Buddleia was still in bloom here, in this long Indian summer, and helianthus too; ours at home had long since started to fade. It was this that brought out the nostalgia in me, the boyhood memory of long, balmy summer days lingering well towards the end of September. The far North East has many things to offer that make it worthwhile living there, but its short summers and chilly evenings are not among them.

We waited for 30 minutes at the next halt, New Romney Station, to take on 330 gallons of water.

'Most of it is used in one run,' the driver said.

A little boy sat on his grandmother's knee, his hands on the ledge of the wide-open window. He leaned forward to feel the breeze on his face, smiling blissfully. The engine whistled and he turned to look into his grandma's eyes, his face screwed up with laughter. She joined him in the merriment of the moment. At Romney Sands Holiday Park, the St George's flag flew from one of the chalets, and as we gathered speed again, the little boy laughed with glee and so did Grandma. Then followed a short tunnel, prompting him to put his head to the window and squeal with delight.

Two swans sat in a field of cabbages, and a group of people in high-vis vests were guiding a line of yet more llamas for a walk through a field of maize that had not yet been harvested. We clattered through a narrow defile lined with nettles and convolvulus, elder and beech, a tangle of hawthorn, sycamore and ash tumbling over a chestnut paling fence. A sign in gold and yellow lettering attached to a garden fence bade us 'Welcome'.

And then Dungeness Power Station loomed into view. At the same time, so did a cluster of small wooden houses, of all shapes, sizes and colours – black, grey, white, green, blue. Many of them were transformed railway carriages.

'It looks desolate,' said Joan. 'What makes people want to live here, I wonder?'

'Probably fear of running out of electricity. Or maybe you can get a cheap house for the price of an old, full-sized, railway carriage.'

There is something compelling about brutal landscapes. I like being enclosed by elemental things, the raw force of nature pushing up against you. In harsh landscapes like this, you know who is the boss, and this is somehow consoling. Even when we drew near to Dungeness and the nuclear power stations, it was strangely compelling. If ever there was a settlement on the edge, it is this: on the tip of a wedge of shingle, on the edge of ecological viability, and on the edge of mainstream life, culture and everyday facilities.

Given that we all want electricity to power our toothbrushes, carving knives and smartphones, these monstrosities are considered necessary, or at least they were at the time, before we discovered that renewables could produce quite a lot of our energy at much lower cost. Deciding where to locate a nuclear power plant has always been a major problem. You don't want to put it where there might be an earthquake or volcano or, as we now know after the Fukushima disaster, a tsunami. But you do want it to be near water – Dungeness B, for example, uses 100 million litres an hour to cool its turbines – and near locations where any unwanted or leaked radioactivity can be dispersed. For many reasons, therefore, a coastal location seems a good idea.

There's always the tricky issue of public acceptance. However illogical it may seem, and however much we are told that Advanced Gas-cooled Reactors (AGR), such as Dungeness B, are considered safe to live near, most of us do not want a nuclear power plant in our back yard. And you particularly do not want to build them in areas that are generally agreed to be scientifically and scenically special, like Romney Marsh. It therefore seemed odd that so many people had chosen to live here among the shingles, in this near-desert environment. Maybe they wanted the challenge of a harsh landscape, to get away from the fripperies of modern life, to embrace the solitude and the specialness of this unique triangle of land, or simply to be near the sea, on the edge.

That they had embraced the area and lovingly made it their home, there could be no doubt. They had given their dwellings names – Sea Breeze, Mossy Cot, Caithness, Quiet Moorings and, of course, Prospect Cottage – Derek Jarman's black house with yellow windows. Jarman had gone there determined to make a garden against all the odds on a shingle beach in the harshest, most impossible gardening environment imaginable. He created what he called 'a garden paradise'. Now that's what I call a success story.

The Royal Military Canal forms a 28-mile arc from Cliff End near Hastings to Seabrook near Hythe. It was built, in the early nineteenth century, to cut Romney Marsh off from the rest of the country in the days of the Napoleonic threat. It was feared that this wide expanse of flat land would be an open invitation for Napoleon's troops. So, with the Royal Navy's patrol ships in the Channel and the long line of round Martello Towers along the southeast coast, the Royal Military Canal was the third line of defence. The canal had the added advantage of being backed by those ancient sea cliffs.

Nothing seemed to stop Napoleon. After his disastrous invasion of Russia in 1812, his expulsion from Spain and Portugal in the Peninsula War, and his defeat by a coalition of European states in the Battle of Leipzig, he was forced to abdicate and was exiled to Elba. Escaping from there, this war lord marched on Paris and then Belgium, where, against another coalition, this time of Dutch, Belgian and German troops, as well as the British led by Wellington, he finally met his Waterloo, ending once and for all the threat to our security from this serial offender.

Now at this point, and at this time, most other countries would have executed the man who had caused such mayhem throughout Europe and so much defensive anxiety in Britain. But we didn't hang him. Instead, we did the gentlemanly and very English thing of sending him off to do some gardening.

We picked a secluded tropical island, St Helena, that needed some attention and told him to spend the rest of his life thinking about his sins, which were many, and sorting out the garden, which was a mess. Admittedly, he did quite a bit of work on the garden, but it may not have been quite so straightforward as it seems, for there are suggestions that Napoleon may have been murdered on his island retreat.

The cruise company that Joan used to work for at one point entered into a contract with another cruise company to purchase one of its ships, and everything in it. This new ship was about to sail round the world on its final voyage before being handed over to its new owner. Joan's job was to accompany this ship and to see to it that its new owners received it in the same condition as when they first inspected it. This meant that she had to count all the duvets, cutlery and lifeboats to make sure that nothing had been secreted ashore and that the numbers tallied with the records of the head office in Folkestone.

When she was most of the way up the Amazon River at Manaus, and seeking a diversion from this onerous work, she sent me a letter asking if I'd consider marrying her. She didn't get my reply until she had picked up her mail at St Helena. As it turns out, that decision has been one of the best I've ever made, so it was quite agreeable, as we ambled along the side of the Royal Military Canal, to be reminded of all of this.

Now that we were away from the clatter of the railway, it was delightfully tranquil walking along the banks of the canal, the water still, the vegetation lush, the air soft and breezy and humming gently with insect life. The leaves of the trees that lined the canal flipped from dark green to silver, back and forth, back and forth, with each gentle gust of the breeze, like a mild strobe effect.

'I wonder what those trees are. Let's look it up when we get back to the car.'

'Yes,' Joan said, 'but first tea. A nice prolonged tea, with all the trimmings.'

The Truly Scrumptious Tearoom was set back from Hythe High Street, in a tree-shaded corner of a small cul-de-sac. Inside, it was as English as you can get, with Union Jack cushion covers, Victoria sponge, fruit cake, several types of scone, teacake, tea in a teapot with a woollen tea cosy, fresh-cut red and white roses in cut-glass vases, and in the background, Dame Vera Lynn singing 'Blue Birds Over The White Cliffs Of Dover'. We sat on black leather sofas, facing each other. Joan divvied the cake to the strains of *I know we'll meet again some sunny day.*

We found the charge point at Lidl that the sisters at Deal had told us about. It was a Pod Point and the app worked well. It would take forty minutes; it was a chilly evening and there was no refreshment area, so we bought a cold goat's cheese focaccia, which we didn't want, and ate it in the car, wrapped in blankets and studying the tree book.

'I think they're grey poplars,' Joan said.

Once back at the hotel, we had time for another walk on the cliffs. It was wild and windy up there now, a foretaste of the weather heading our way from the Atlantic. Tangled bushes of gorse, hawthorn and brambles had been sculpted smooth on one side by the prevailing wind, on the other like unruly, windswept fringes. Under them were scatterings of disposable cups. The white horses on the sea suggested a wind of roughly Beaufort force 9. Despite these conditions, there was still an interminable relay of passenger ferries, each carrying several hundred people, to and from the same European continent 21 miles away that a majority of the population had just expressed an eagerness to leave. On our way back, Storm Florence kept stopping us in our tracks, trying to blow us over the cliffs. It would be good to be going home, before it hit us properly. Before our evening meal, we made our plans for the following day, deciding on a hotel at Eastbourne.

'One other thing,' I said, before I put the phone down, 'do you have a charge point for an electric car?'

'Is it a buggy?' the receptionist asked.

'No, we've come seven hundred and fifty miles in it. It's a car, an electric one.'

'One of those scooter things?'

'No, a car. It goes on the road.'

'And you want to charge it?'

'Yes.'

'Hold on, please.'

I did, and she forgot to press the mute button.

'There's this old guy on the phone,' I heard her say. 'Wants to know if we've a charge point. Something about an electric car.'

''Spect he means one of those scooter things old people use.'

'Yeah, sounds a bit confused. He's probably forgotten the word. Y'know what these oldies are. Said he'd driven it on the road. Can you believe it?'

'Poor old chap. Tell him he can charge it in his room.'

Then she came back to me.

'It'll be all right sir,' she said, 'don't worry. You can charge it in your room.'

'Oh, what a relief,' I said. 'That's so very kind of you. Excellent service, I must say.'

2 5

SUNSHINE CAPITAL

THE SOUTH EAST IMPRESSES with its busyness, the close proximity of towns and villages, the dense road network, the incessant hum of traffic. It seemed that we were no sooner out of one place than into another, cars everywhere, never still, never silent, rarely out of a 30mph speed limit, never away from street lights.

By contrast, the 12-mile drive from New Romney to Rye took us across the sparsely populated area of the marshes, an outlier of quietude in the midst of all that hustle and bustle until, towards the western edge of Walland Marsh, we crossed Kent into East Sussex and entered the little town of Rye.

Rye used to be a coastal port, a member of the Confederation of the Cinque Ports, but it is now two miles inland. It sits very prettily at the confluence of four waterways: the rivers Rother, Tillingham and Brede and the Royal Military Canal.

Although it's no longer on the coast, so much water surrounds it that it's almost an island.

There was an air of prosperity about the town centre. It was a middle-England kind of town. A weak sun made its way through a thinly-overcast sky. Prosperous-looking retirees were out enjoying the late summer warmth. A poster invited us to experience the 'Rye Antiques Trail'. We noticed that there seemed to be a great abundance of antiques shops; we counted twenty-two of them.

Inside the Coterie Tea Rooms, the quiet hum of human voices, the subdued clatter of crockery and the absence of background music made for an agreeable lunch. We were served by trainees of the Canterbury Oast Trust, a charity with the purpose of supporting people with learning difficulties. This included training in baking and restaurant skills, horticulture, art, woodwork, ceramics and animal care, all at the Trust's 100-acre Rare Breeds Centre. It was uplifting to see so much goodness.

We calculated we had sufficient battery to get to Battle before seeking a charge point. I particularly wanted to go there because the last time I'd seen it was when I was a teenager. It was wasted on me then. I'd been having a week's holiday at Hastings with my friend David's family. I can't say Battle left a huge impression on me; I was bored by history in those days. The main thing I learned was that the Battle of Hastings was not the battle of Hastings at all but, rather, the battle of Battle.

Returning a lifetime later, I found it sobering, and not a little disturbing, that this famous battle – which marked such a fundamental turning point in our culture and way of life

– was brutally decided by hand-to-hand combat in bloody carnage on a few small acres of sandy soil in East Sussex, six miles to the north of Hastings. It was waged by William, Duke of Normandy, who reckoned he was entitled to the throne of England because he was the first-cousin-once-removed of Edward the Confessor. More to the point, he had been promised the crown by Edward.[68]

What particularly interests me now is the way in which the fortunes of a nation can hang on the quirkiness of superstition. In the infamous year that every schoolchild knows – 1066 – Halley's Comet flew across the sky. According to the *Anglo-Saxon Chronicle*, 'Throughout all England a portent such as men had never seen before was seen in the heavens.' In January of that same year, Harold II had been crowned king of England. This had been organised with 'unseemly haste', because he wasn't really entitled to the crown. It had been promised to the Duke of Normandy, so when everyone, including the new king and his courtiers, saw the comet, it was interpreted – no doubt as a result of guilty consciences – as a 'terrible omen',[69] a clear sign that there was trouble ahead.

William of Normandy and his advisors, however, also saw that same comet and *they* all said that it was a *good* omen. This encouraged the Duke of Normandy to take the necessary steps that would change the history of England for ever. As a result of the strength of that belief, less than a year after Harold II had been crowned king of England, William

68   Marc Morris, *The Anglo-Saxons: A History of the Beginnings of England*, Hutchinson, London, pp381-384.
69   Marc Morris, *The Norman Conquest*, Windmill Books, London, 2012, p146.

the Conqueror became our first Norman king, on Christmas Day in 1066. The Normans swept away the established ruling class and transformed our customs, culture and language. In an act of 'architectural cleansing', they destroyed most of our Anglo-Saxon places of worship, replacing them with Norman-style edifices, and, within a generation of the invasion, filled the landscape with 500 castles.[70]

In short, what happened at Battle in 1066 was a desperate battle for the preservation of Anglo-Saxon England. Anglo-Saxon England lost, and we became Norman-French instead. Harold II was, in fact, the last Anglo-Saxon king of England, and that alleged arrow through the eye was the end of one era and the beginning of another. So significant a role did Halley's Comet play in all of this that it has been preserved for posterity in the Bayeux Tapestry.

You see, it's not so much what is true that influences the twists and turns of history; it is what is believed to be true. Beliefs are always more powerful than facts. Nowhere is that more true today than in Donald Trump's America, and perhaps even in Johnson's Brexit UK. Those two gentlemen sitting on the wall at Aldeburgh who were convinced they were soaking in the atmosphere of the true Anglo-Saxon England were in fact basking in the sunshine of Norman-French England, with substantial bits of Germanic and Latin thrown in.

When thinking about what it is that makes us English, it is certainly not our lords and masters; ever since 1066, there has not been an 'English' dynasty ruling over us. And those

---

70   Nicholas Crane, *The Making of the British Landscape*, Weidenfeld & Nicholson, paperback edition, 2017, p.91.

quintessentially 'English' barons who forced King John to sign Magna Carta in 1215 did not speak 'English'.[71]

After that thought, our minds turned to the more prosaic matter of our nearly-empty battery. Our nearest EV charge point was at St Leonards, on the western edge of Hastings. St Leonards was one of several south-coast seaside resorts familiar from my childhood, in the heyday of the great south-coast seaside bonanza, when railways and motorcars liberated the great British public from their desks, production lines and typing pools to pour out of London at weekends and summer holidays. Worthing, Eastbourne, Bognor Regis, Bournemouth, Hastings – I never knew them when there weren't teeming throngs lounging on beaches, strolling along promenades, licking ice creams, disentangling hair from candyfloss or queueing for tickets at funfairs and slot machines.

Once a year the five of us – four brothers and a sister – joined with thirty or forty other kids from Redhill Baptist Tabernacle, packed our sandwiches, scrambled onto a coach, and made a beeline for a window seat, to be whisked off on the one great treat of the year, the annual Sunday-school outing. Hastings was as far east as we ventured, Bournemouth the furthest west. I remember the yellowy-brownish sandy cliffs of Hastings. I didn't like them; they seemed oppressive and towered over me in an ugly sort of way. When the tide was out, the beach was sandy enough, but in places it was muddy

---

71   Benedict Anderson, *Imagined Communities*, Verso, tenth impression, 2000, pp21, 118.

and unpleasant. I far preferred the pristine white of the chalk between Brighton and Beachy Head, or the wide sands of Bournemouth.

I first saw St Leonards through the eyes of my grandmother. She had spent some time there when she was a young woman, and she spoke of it as a rather elegant place, ideal for gentlefolk. She herself was a softly-spoken woman with impeccable pronunciation, whose station in life, through circumstances beyond her control, had fallen from middle- to lower-middle class. She still hankered after a gentlewomanly lifestyle, and St Leonards seemed to epitomise this for her. With its smart hotels, Regency seafront houses and large public gardens, it was a fashionable seaside destination in the nineteenth century for the distinctly better off, a place for promenading in one's finery, taking dainty afternoon teas and enjoying smart evening dinners.

Since those heady days, things have gone badly wrong. As we passed through Hastings-St Leonards hunting for the charge point we knew to be there, it had the air of a down-trodden, dejected and desolate kind of place. In fact, it has become the most deprived small town in the whole of the south-east of England, a truly left-behind community. Embedded within this gloom are pockets of even greater misery; some parts of the Borough of Hastings are counted among the most deprived one per cent of England's population, all of them in coastal locations, all on the edge.[72] To witness such a colossal change of fortune in one's own lifetime is a sober reminder of the impermanence of what we take so easily for granted.

The sky was a steely grey, and a blustery wind was blowing. The seafront was bleak and unwelcoming. We had to work hard to locate the only EV charge point in town. Somewhere, in the midst of a plethora of signs pointing us to petrol stations, rest areas, picnic spots, refreshments, public toilets, local beauty spots and fish-and-chips emporia, a charge point was to be found, the one item for which no sign was deemed necessary.

We eventually found it in a small car park on the seafront. No one else was there and the electronic wizardry informed us that the job would take forty minutes. The thought of killing that amount of time in a dreary car park in nasty weather was depressing, so we determined to put in some brisk walking along the marina, twenty minutes in each direction. On our return, a young woman was walking agitatedly up and down beside our car.

'You've had your thirty minutes,' she called as we approached.

'Pardon?'

'You're only allowed thirty minutes. You've been charging for forty.'

'Who says?'

'Read the sign.'

I did, and she was right. This stipulation was clearly intended for local people who had nothing better to do than run around town, but thirty minutes of charging would not give us enough fuel for the motoring we had to do the next day, and neither, it seemed, would forty.

'So sorry.'

'I'm going to a party and I'm going to be late.'

'Sorry you're running late,' Joan said. 'We've got a long journey tomorrow. Would you mind if we stay for another five, ten minutes? That's all it'll take.'

'Well, all right,' she said, 'but please be quick.'

'We will, and thank you.'

Several years ago, I came across a map showing the annual average sunshine for all areas of Britain. Areas coloured dark blue had hardly any, pale blue regions had slightly more, pale yellow yet more, and so on up the colour hierarchy to deep orange and red. Red areas were like the Côte d'Azur. There was only one red place on that map, and that was the tiny triangle of land that juts into the English Channel with Beachy Head at the tip and Eastbourne alongside it. Sussex is reputed to be the sunniest county in the country and Eastbourne the sunniest town.

I was hoping that Eastbourne would live up to its reputation the following day. We were looking forward to a walk to the cliffs at Beachy Head, which Joan had never seen, and then along part of the River Cuckmere to see the famous meanders. But the outlook wasn't good. It was miserably cold, the skies were grey, and the wind was still gusting. We drew up on the seafront, opposite the hotel. I dealt with the luggage while Joan went to the reception desk.

'I'm Mrs Wilkinson. I think you have a room for me and my husband.'

'Yes, that's fine, Mrs Wilkinson. It's street parking, so you'll need this permit. Your room is on the third floor. I'm Amanda. Anything you need, just let me know.'

'There's just one thing, Amanda,' said Joan. 'I thought you'd have given us a ground-floor room.'

'Did you request one?'

'No, but when you said we could charge our vehicle in our room, we assumed it would be on the ground floor.'

'Oh, so you're *that* Mrs Wilkinson. So sorry. No worries, we've a lift. Just wheel your husband in and we'll see him safely upstairs. You can plug it in there.'

'Are you quite sure about this? Perhaps you'd better come and have a look at it. It's just across the road.'

With that, she led Amanda across the foyer to the entrance and pointed across the road.

'Just over there.'

'I can only see a white car,' Amanda said.

'That's it. That's the one,' Joan said with a grin.

Amanda turned and looked at Joan. 'You've been having me on, haven't you?' she squealed. 'So it really is a car, not a scooter!'

'Or even a buggy. And here's my husband, who, by the way, is as fit as a fiddle.'

'You didn't believe me,' I said as I approached. 'And I was so looking forward to getting charged up in the bedroom.'

'You've got a right one there, haven't you?' said Amanda to Joan, and they both walked away with linked arms, chatting amiably the way women do, while I went out to get the cases, the way men do.

26

CHALK

THAT NIGHT, OUR WINDOWS were battered by mighty winds. A woman had been killed in County Galway a few days earlier, when the caravan she was staying in was blown off a cliff. No sooner had that storm blown itself out than another one, gusting up to 78mph, arrived on our western shores. The storms that had been giving the east coast of America such a hard time finally reached us. Storm Ali had been succeeded by Storm Bronagh. Floods and fallen trees blocked roads and railway lines in the west of the country.

We were therefore surprised the next morning to see the sun shining brightly. It was a peerlessly blue sky and the sea was silver but agitated. The forecast assured us that we would escape the worst of the weather, but it would be windy. Horrendous storms were on their way. For one more day at least, Eastbourne would live up to its sunny reputation.

I went out before breakfast to find a newspaper and some paracetamol. I was looking forward to a brisk walk in the bright morning air. Just outside the hotel entrance, I walked straight into a group of prematurely aged hotel residents, wrapped up against the elements as if they were in the Arctic and frantically drawing in an early morning fix of nicotine before the coach arrived to take them home. Round the corner, at the back of the hotel, another group of gaspers were getting their furtive fix. It had clearly been a gargantuan effort for these death-wish addicts to drag themselves to their fixing posts, but they'd managed to cough and splutter their way there thanks to walking sticks, Zimmer frames, wheelchairs and sheer desperation.

After breakfast, we drove to the Beachy Head car park, donned our thickest windproof jackets and set off for the top. It was a place I had visited many times in my youth. It never failed to fill me with awe, the lure of excitement tinged with danger. A friend once told me that her brother had thrown himself from the edge. This massive cliff rises 162 metres (531 feet) above the sea in a dramatic wall of pure, gleaming white chalk. If you can overcome your vertigo and peer down, you can see the red-and-white striped lighthouse, battered by foaming waves, as small as a child's toy.

When I first cycled along this stretch of coast as a boy, I was stunned by the brilliance of the line of white cliffs between Seaford and Beachy Head, known as the Seven Sisters. The landscape here is one of exquisite beauty, the dazzling light intensified by the massive dome of the skies, the sparkling intensity of the sea and the extraordinary whiteness of the chalk. I used to feel on top of the world, caught between heaven and earth, with the glittering ribbon of the English Channel on one side, the rolling green of the South Downs on the other, and heaven above. Bliss indeed was it in those days to be alive.

Beachy Head marks the end of the South Downs, the spot where the chalk of the Downs has been cut off by the forces that created the Channel. From here, these hills march back west through Sussex and into Hampshire, loop north towards Basingstoke, then swing east towards Guildford in Surrey, by which time they become the North Downs. They then slice through the middle of Surrey and Kent and finish at the White Cliffs of Dover. This 180-mile loop of chalk hills is shaped like a horseshoe. Cradled inside it are clay vales and sandy ridges, also horseshoe-shaped; right in the centre is a massive block of sandstone known as the High Weald. This land of sandy ridges and clay vales enclosed by the North and South Downs is known as the Weald, the landscape of my boyhood, forging my early understanding of Englishness.

Chalk is geology's stroke of genius. It is also one of our most remarkable rocks. It belongs to the Cretaceous geological period, which lasted for 80 million years, from about 146 to 65 million years ago. All the rocks of the Wealden area – sandstones, clays, mudstones and shales – were laid down during the Cretaceous Period, but it is the chalk that gives the sequence its name, from the Latin for chalk: *creta*. Chalk is the defining rock of the Cretaceous Period, and it is chalk that gives geographical and artistic completion to the Weald.

Chalk owes its existence to a great inundation known as the Cenomanian Transgression, when the British Isles were drowned to a depth of up to 300 metres, which is nearly

1,000 feet. It is worth pausing to think about the coalescence of time and space that are encapsulated in that dry chemical symbol for chalk that I was taught at school: $CaCO_3$. Those four letters and one digit symbolise 35 million years of painstakingly slow work.

Infinitesimally small petrified remains of marine organisms with calcareous shells, such as coccoliths and foraminifera, sank to the bottom of that huge Cenomanian Sea, each no bigger than 15 microns. That's 15 millionths, or 0.000015 of a metre, or 15 thousandths of a millimetre. You would only be able to see one of these tiny creatures with a powerful microscope. It has been calculated that it took a million years for between 20 and 40 metres of chalk to accumulate. That's approximately a one-centimetre-thick layer of chalk for every 500 to 1000 years. In places, chalk is 550 metres thick.

Great swathes of chalk sweep through England, largely in the south-eastern half of the country. It extends from the Yorkshire and Lincolnshire Wolds on the east coast, through East Anglia and Cambridgeshire, on to the Chilterns and the Wealden Downs, the Marlborough Downs, the broad expanses of Salisbury Plain, the Hampshire Downs, and finally on to Dorset and the Isle of Wight. The Needles, made of solid chalk, stand proudly at the westernmost tip of the Isle of Wight as a magnificent symbol of what can be achieved if you wait long enough.

These laboriously slow processes have produced landscapes of grassy downland and smooth rounded curves that sweep across the southeastern half of England, a landscape of short grass and thin soils, home to stately beech trees and

Southdown sheep. These small sheep, originally bred near Lewes about 200 years ago, were exported to New Zealand, where they were used in the breeding of Canterbury lamb. They then came back to England and were served up on our dining table for Sunday roast. As a nation we're still importing Canterbury lamb, but it no longer ends up on my dining table; the madness of bringing it halfway round the world, and our vegetarian proclivities, have put a stop to that.

Light is always abundant up there on the Downs; the colours are delicate, the shades subtle. The hand that created such landscapes did so with a delicacy of feeling and a lightness of touch that is unrivalled elsewhere in England. No wonder the Weald is littered with specially designated areas of great beauty: the Surrey Hills and Kent Downs Areas of Outstanding Natural Beauty, the South Downs National Park – England's newest – and the 100-mile-long Greensand Way, reaching from the coast of Kent to the furthest corners of west Surrey. Such beauty in one tiny corner of England!

It is no wonder that landscape artists have been drawn to this area: Paul Nash's *Wood on the Downs* gets it perfectly, *Cuckmere Haven* by Eric Ravilious captures the majestic meanders of the River Cuckmere in Sussex, and John Constable's *Petworth Park* shows us the smooth curves of the Downs and the massive skies that enfold them.

We stood for some time on the top of Beachy Head, the screaming wind unsteadying us as we ever-so-carefully crept as close to the cliff edge as we dared. It was breathtakingly humbling. You can feel the raw, terrifying power of untamed nature up there. It casts us in our true light, as diminished, vulnerable, creatures of nature.

On our walk back to the car park, we negotiated our way through a swarm of youngsters bent double, some against the wind, others consulting their mobile phones. What is it about humankind that, even here, on one of the most iconic and awe-inspiring landscape features of our country, the virtual world is capable of eclipsing the real world?

Beachy Head has a reputation as a lure for disturbed souls. It was good to see the chaplaincy team up there, their purpose to save the lives of those whose despair is so great that they are tempted to end it. These excellent men and women patrol this area of Beachy Head 24 hours a day. On a bronze plaque were the words of Psalm 93 verse four:

The LORD on high is mightier
Than the noise of many waters,
Yea, than the mighty waves of the sea.

As we sipped our coffee at the Beachy Head Hotel, two ladies at the next table were explaining the Brexit problem to an American friend, who seemed to have difficulty getting his head round the problem of the Irish border.

'What's the difference between a soft border and a hard border?' he asked.

'Oh, it's going to be a massive problem,' came the reply.

And then they got lost in the intricacies of explaining how something that was inherently impossible could be made possible by the wizardry of an as-yet uninvented computerised system and a political determination to get Brexit done at all costs, even if it meant the government had to bend its mind round six impossible truths every day for the rest of its life.

'The thing is,' they said, 'the people have spoken and so we must get Brexit done. That little matter of the border can be sorted out later with a bit of legerdemain from Boris. He's good at that.'

'Ah, I see.'

Below Alfriston, the River Cuckmere famously winds its way to the sea by a series of extravagant meanders, which have been captured by Ravilious in an equally famous painting. Many people, Ravilious among them, have regarded this scenery as quintessentially English. I'm not so sure about that. English landscapes seem to me to be so diverse that it is not possible to say that any one of them typifies England more than any other. But I can understand the Alfristonian mindset in thinking that where they live is more English than anywhere else. They are, after all, surrounded by heartrendingly beautiful scenery.

As for Alfriston itself, you could be forgiven for thinking that this really is the heart of England. Not much seemed to have changed since the days of Alfred, King of Wessex. It has an ancient flint church with a spire, a village green, a lovingly preserved unexploded wartime mine, red-tiled cottages, half-timbered buildings, twisty narrow streets and thatched roofs. It even has an old farmhouse in the middle of High Street and young women riding horses along the riverside.

But the really intriguing thing about Alfriston is its religious squabble.

What is now Alfriston United Reformed Church began life in 1801, when a group of Dissenters broke from the Anglican Church. They built their own chapel on the other side of the green in a little side street known as The Tye.

Thirty years later, a senior trustee of the chapel, Charles Brooker, had a disagreement with the ordained minister, the Reverend George Betts. The problem was that the reverend gentleman was deemed to have deviated from the truth. So profound was Mr Brooker's disagreement with the minister that he arranged for a preacher with the right attitude to the truth to take the pulpit one Sunday, without the courtesy of giving prior notice to the incumbent. So, when the legitimate minister turned up expecting to preach and saw what was happening, he politely took his place in one of the pews and sat through an alternative exposition of the truth.

Meanwhile, a bunch of smugglers were having a drink or two in the local hostelry, and word got to them about what was going on. As it happened, they didn't like the coup's organiser, Mr Brooker, one little bit, so they suddenly became filled with righteous indignation, slammed their tankards down, stormed out of the pub and into the chapel, turfed the pretender out of the pulpit and reinstated the reverend gentleman in his rightful place. You can't get more quintessentially English than that.[73]

It was not far from there to where the Long Man of Wilmington had been carved into the chalk of the South

---

73   Details from a plaque on the wall of the United Reformed Church, Alfriston.

Downs. There's no bigger human figure carved into the landscape in the whole of Europe than this mysterious Long Man. Etched into the north-facing escarpment, it is tilted at a steep angle, as if on an artist's easel, making it visible from many miles away. There is no certainty about its age or its purpose, but the man at the information centre had his own theory. He reckoned that the Wilmington Priory was 'sister' priory to the priory at Battle, and that the Long Man was the abbot holding the emblems of his office, the two big sticks.

We sat and thought about that while we waited for our pot of tea in the gardens of the Giant's Rest in the village of Wilmington. But we couldn't bring our minds to bear on the matter because it was getting cold and drizzly. We therefore moved indoors to the comfort of hot drinks and cake, and this was so enjoyable that we decided it was best to leave the problem of the Long Man's identity as we had found it: a complete mystery. Mysteries are so much more satisfying than explanations.

It was an excellent place to turn inland and head for home. It would have been good to complete the round trip, via the Cornish Peninsula and the Welsh borderlands. But the days were getting shorter and cooler, significantly shortening our already short range, we were tired, and our friends Roger and Val lived just 20 miles to the north. They'd often said to pop in if ever we were in the area, and here we were. So we gave them a call and they said to come and stay. We spent an enjoyable evening recalling the foibles of our youth.

The next morning, we discussed the route home. Some

thoughtful planner had decided to place an EV charge point in the corner of an insignificant car park on the top of Reigate Hill. It would be a perfect place to charge the car. I knew it well. It would be good to drive along old familiar roads I'd only ever known from the saddle of my bike. It was an appropriate spot to end our odyssey before taking the motorway home. Roger warned me, however, that the road layout was not what it used to be.

'Best to take the motorway. Use your satnav. And by the way,' he called, as he and Val waved us off, 'you can get an excellent bacon sandwich at the kiosk on top.'

That short drive, over a landscape I had once known so intimately, saddened me. I lost my bearings as soon as we got onto the motorway system. Nothing was familiar. All sense of topography and distance escaped me. We were caught up in a system in which speed was everything and landscape and place meant nothing. That quiet road, the A23, that I used to cycle along on my way to Brighton, had become the snarling beast of the M23. The M25 now scythed its way across the top of the North Downs, and now these two thunderous conveyor belts meet in an unholy embrace in a monstrous cloverleaf junction on the field where I used to fly my kite, look for frogspawn and gather blackberries. It was heart-breaking.

The North Downs, 750 feet (230 metres) high in places, once formed the margin of my known world. To get to London by road, you had to climb up and over them. There was no avoiding them. Yet, on this day we had arrived at that iconic spot on the top of the North Downs with no awareness at all of having gained height. All sense of place had been totally erased.

A lifetime ago, I had known the little gravelly car park that we turned into as a picnic spot. Cars were a rarity then, but on this day it was filled to capacity with a handful of vehicles. Still little more than a clearing in a wood, and overlooking the Vale of Holmesdale to the south, it was exactly as I had known it, except for the café in the corner and the charge point beside it. It was called Junction 8 Café, after the motorway junction a stone's throw away.

We parked there, plugged in and heard the comforting whirr that told us everything was in order. In fifty-three minutes, the battery would be full. We made for the café to get the sandwich Roger had recommended. Huddled under an awning, sheltering from the cold wind, a group of friends sat with their picnic. We joined them.

'How far can you go in that, then?' asked one of the men.

'We charge every eighty to a hundred miles, have a sandwich and hot drink, and then move on,' I said.

'Going far?'

'Back home. North East, near the Scottish border. We've been driving down the east coast.'

'Bit tough up there, isn't it?' said one of them, with a grin.

'Well, you know, we've got houses, and some even have television.'

'How far've you done?'

'Over a thousand miles.'

'Blimey. You're sorted then.'

'Yep, sorted.'

As the clouds lifted briefly, we were able to see Reigate several hundred feet below. There was enough visibility, too, to make out the line of the North Downs stretching fuzzily into Surrey's western edges. From where we stood, Beachy Head was just forty miles directly south of us.

There's a footpath from the car park leading to a pedestrian bridge that crosses the London road in a single 100-foot span. The path continues to the other side, where it opens onto a well-worn track through a magical world of beech trees, whose round, smooth, metallic-grey trunks form a grand avenue through which to stride, beechnuts crunching beneath your feet. Beyond the trees, you come to open grass and the horizons fling open, taking in the whole of the Weald. I used to be on top of the world there, looking down at the Vale of Holmesdale, a miniaturised Reigate town, and the silent puffs of smoke from the steam trains escorting their passengers to Redhill, Dorking, Guildford. It was utterly silent there, a world away from the busyness of the work-a-day world below. It wrenches my heart that that silent world of beauty has been so wantonly marred by the incessant roar of motorway traffic just a few hundred metres away.

The Pilgrims' Way follows the line of these hills. It is a good place to return to. From there, you can look along the escarpment reaching into Surrey's far west where it curves south towards Winchester, from whence Chaucerian pilgrims had tramped their way to Canterbury. I still imagine I can hear the soft shuffle of their feet trudging these same hills on their way to holiness at the shrine of Thomas à Becket. Perhaps they also discovered that chalk country is the most agreeable to walk over, with its tightly-packed grassy sward, neatly trimmed by generations of sheep.

This section of the Pilgrims' Way was, in those days, incomparable in its unsullied beauty, and I can think of no other landscape that matches it. I didn't feel the need to follow those pilgrims' footsteps. I had found my pearl of great price here, in the quiet beauty of those hills.

As we eased our car out of that little woodland car park and onto the M25 approach road, we readjusted our psychology. After weeks of leisurely driving on costal roads, we were now about to launch ourselves into the feverish business of motorway driving. Our route home would take us 350 miles along the central axis of the country, as far away from England's edges as it was possible to be. It was a shock to the system, like leaving a quiet garden and suddenly finding yourself in the hectic clamour of a concrete and tarmac cityscape.

The purpose of motorways is to speed things up, avoid towns and villages, smooth out the inconveniences of geography and anonymise the landscape – the very opposite of what we'd been doing. Speed does, of course, have a place in our lives, and it was good to be able to get home quickly, but this rushing along on motorways in straight lines, avoiding everything that might give you a sense of place, is an emotionally barren way of driving; we were always relieved to get back onto quiet, meandering roads. These had taken us peacefully around 1,300 miles of England's edges, getting to know the stories of places we'd never seen before or knew only superficially. Every place had a name, a history, an identity: Seaham, Withernsea, Sutton-on-Sea, Alfriston, Bowness-on-Solway, Silloth, Millom. It was a satisfying way to drive, and – apart from wondering where our next charge point would be – totally stress free.

EPILOGUE

THE JOURNEYS DESCRIBED in this book covered 1,936 miles. Most of them – 1,300 – were along coastal or border roads. Of necessity, however, more than 600 were on motorways and other trunk roads, mostly to get us quickly back to base. Taking the whole 1,936-mile journey together, the average cost of charging was 2.6 pence per mile. At the time, in 2018, the average cost of petrol was 115.9 pence per litre, or approximately £5.27 per gallon. A medium-sized car covering the same ground as our route and averaging 50 miles per gallon would have incurred a cost of roughly 10.54 pence per mile – four times as much.

In the four years since our trip, the EV revolution has progressed with astonishing speed. According to our trusty source, Zap-Map, as of January 2022, there are now 18,249 public EV charge points distributed throughout the UK, giving a total of 48,789 connectors. Between 2016 and 2021, the number of public chargers on UK roads increased by 335 per cent. There has also been a huge increase in the provision of on-street slow chargers, for EV drivers without off-street parking.[74] There are now more EV charging stations in the country than petrol pumps. Rapid chargers mostly use CHAdeMO or CCS connector types. We depended on those during our project but now rarely use them. For the most part we are content to charge at home, using a 7kW Type 1 connector, which takes about eight hours to charge, and stick to local trips of no more than about 100 miles.

The kind of range anxiety we experienced, and on which we report in this book, has now been massively reduced by improvements in battery technology and engine efficiency. According to Buyacar in December 2021, the range of the Volkswagen ID.3 was 336 miles, for the Skoda Enyaq it was 329, and the Audi Q4 e-tron did 315.[75] Even when bearing in mind that real road performance is usually 10 to 15 per cent below official ranges, these are still way ahead of what we had, with our paltry 155-mile range. Our Leaf is definitely not a distance car! Even if we'd had the Nissan e+N-TEC, which claims an official range of 239 miles, our experience would have been very different. With these longer ranges, diversions or steep hills would not have had the same catastrophic impact on our anxiety level as that caused by the rugged relief in the Scottish borders.

Not all is perfect, however, as the following recent incidents

74   www.zap-map.com/statistics/ 27 January 2022.
75   www.buyacar.co.uk/cars/economical-cars/electric-cars/862/longest-range-electric-cars

demonstrate. On a visit to Edinburgh, we needed to charge the car at Lauder. We arrived at a Polar Ultra-Charge point only to find that our app had fallen out of date and we had to download a new one. The mobile signal was poor and it took five calls, lasting a total of 48 minutes, before we could download the new app. The whole process, including the actual charge and the installation of the new app, took two-and-a-half hours. And on a visit to Newtown St Boswells a few months ago, getting the car charged took one-and-a-quarter hours. It was a wet, cold day in a small town, with nothing to do but tramp the streets and drink coffee.

Lettie continues to misbehave from time to time. She is still only capable of depositing us in the middle of a postcode area, leaving us to search around without her electronic help for the actual charge point. Usually, we've had to drive around or ask someone where the charge point was. However, sometimes it can be easy, as on a recent visit to Durham City. From the spot in Gilesgate where Lettie informed us we had arrived at our destination, we could see the charge point. We were lucky (although not totally – the first three charge points we looked at on Zap-Map were out of order before we eventually found this one in working condition). The charging process was much simpler, too. There were no apps or RFID cards involved. We simply had to plug in the connector, enter our credit card details, and everything clicked into place. And the weather was kind, too; we were able to go for a pleasant walk in a lovely city while we waited for the charge to complete.

However, inclement weather would have made it a miserable experience. If you are going to have to hang around for an hour or two during the charging, you need access to decent refreshments. Especially on long journeys, charge points need to be strategically located where there are good facilities for relaxation and refreshment. As I write, the Electronic Forecourt at Braintree is not only up-and-running and capable of charging up to 36 cars simultaneously, it also comes replete with refreshment facilities. Such facilities would have made our odyssey a very different experience. You pay a price for being an early adopter. Much to my surprise, however, it also proved to be a great driving holiday.

Meanwhile, England's edges are in a state of flux. Although most of our goods still come to us by sea, today they mostly do so via just a few giant ports capable of receiving mega vessels, such as Felixstowe, Southampton, London and Liverpool. Once entirely dependent on our coasts for international exchanges, now people, culture and ideas jump over borders, seas and oceans aerodynamically and electronically, bypassing many of our coastal ports.

Nevertheless, the electronic and green revolutions are changing the geography of our edges. On the west coast, Barrow, where population numbers were recently described by the Office of National Statistics as being in terminal decline, now looks out on the massive Barrow Offshore Wind Farm. Hull, less than 20 years ago described as Britain's most 'crap town', is now building a reputation as a 'green port' specialising in the manufacture of blades for wind turbines. The wheels of fortune are turning once more, putting the city's geography in a superb position to take advantage of the era's new resource: offshore wind power. The Yorkshire coast is becoming a world leader in renewable energy.

The south-east corner of Northumberland was dependent a century ago on coal for the development of the heavy-engineering industries that once defined the North East; it is now leading the way in the manufacture of batteries for electric cars. As I write, work is about to begin on the Britishvolt 'giga factory' that aims to produce 300,000 lithium-ion EV batteries a year. Blyth and its little neighbour Cambois were once bywords for the dire social and economic consequences of industrial collapse; they are now at the leading edge of the Green Industrial Revolution.[76] Together with the Nissan factory down the road in Sunderland, these developments are a welcome sign of the North East's rejuvenating edges.

There are now approximately 11,000 wind turbines in the UK, with a capacity of 24.4 gigawatts, almost half of them from offshore turbines.[77] Six years earlier, there were 81 wind farms in the North Sea, with a total of 3,589 turbines, according to the EU.[78] Doggerland, once swept away by a tsunami and now submerged as Dogger Bank, is re-emerging as the home of the world's largest offshore wind farm. It is expected that Teesside will produce turbine blades of 107 metres, or 351 feet,[79] almost the length of a soccer field. Wind is the resource of the twenty-first century,

---

76 *The Journal*, 21 January 2022.
77 https://en.wikipedia.org/wiki/Wind_power_in_the_United_Kingdom
78 https://northsearegion.eu/northsee/e-energy/offshore-renewable-energy-developments-offshore-wind/
79 https://doggerbank.com/supply-chain/ge-renewable-energy-blade-manufacturing-plant-for-dogger-bank-wind-turbines-gets-green-light-from-planners/

and the North Sea has abundant supplies. So great is the demand for wind power from countries round the edges of the North Sea that a proposal has been put forward to build an internationally-linked 'multi-country-connected offshore meshed high-voltage direct current (HVDC) grid' to link the UK, Belgium, the Netherlands, Germany and Denmark, the five major players in north-western Europe. This would enable supply to be distributed wherever demand might be at a particular time, and possibly mark the beginnings of a European super-grid.[80]

As we saw at the beginning, the North Sea was once a medieval 'web of communications'; it is now being transformed into a twenty-first century 'industrial wind hub', with an internationally linked power grid. A new industrial revolution sees England's margins rediscovering themselves.

Our edges are beginning to matter once more.

---

80   Heidi Vella, *Electrifying the North Sea: a gamechanger for wind power production*, Engineering and Technology, Friday 17 September 2021.

ACKNOWLEDGEMENTS

I DISCOVERED LONG AGO that one of the best ways of sorting out ideas is to take a long walk. This I have done on many occasions with my brother, Alan. His interest and insight about the scope and style of my book as we've talked and walked together over the Northumberland fells have been invaluable. I have always come away from those treks feeling energised. Thank you, Alan.

And then there are the members of our creative writing group, to whom I am deeply grateful: Graham, Maria, Geoff, Carey, Mags and Tony. Thank you all for your critical observations and keen interest as I read successive chapters each month; you have been hugely supportive and encouraging. A special word of thanks is due to Chrissie for reading early chapters of my manuscript, for her wise comments, and for her excellent maps. Thanks also to Sam

Jordison of The Literary Consultancy, who read an earlier version of my manuscript and whose comments motivated me, if not to go back to the drawing board, at least to reconstruct whole sections, and to murder many darlings.

I'm indebted to Olwyn Hocking, whose meticulous copy editing has been invaluable. As well as the routine cleaning up of the manuscript, she reined in my prolix tendencies, spotted repetitions, clarified ambiguities, and introduced me to the arcane mysteries of ellipses, hyphens and dashes.

Thanks also to the fantastic team at Eye Books – Dan, Simon, Clio and Rosemarie – for delightfully surprising me with their enthusiasm for my book, identifying any remaining sentences and paragraphs that needed sharpening, encouraging me to fill out the details of Simon of Sudbury's extraordinary life, correcting the Latin inscription on one of the maps, meticulously fine-tuning the text in such a helpful and collaborative way, for the excellent cover design, and for being so accessible. What a team! Brilliant to work with. Thank you.

Thank you to all the wonderful people we met on the journey, with whom we had sometimes challenging, but mostly hugely enjoyable conversations.

My most especial thanks go to Joan, my wife and travelling companion, without whose support and enthusiasm this project would not have been completed. Her irrepressible optimism and refusal to be downhearted kept us going when it would have been easier to give up. She took over the navigation when the satnav failed, insisted on treating those wearisome episodes of charge-point failure with light-hearted insouciance, and dragged me on to yet another historical information plaque when all I wanted was to call it a day and put my feet up at the next hotel. Back home, she tolerated, up to a point, the times when I kept her waiting for that promised walk over the hills or that keenly-awaited game of croquet, as I struggled to find the right words to pin down a particularly elusive idea. At times, she insisted, wisely, that I leave it and get out in the garden, when all would become clear; it invariably did. I am the most fortunate of men.

If you have enjoyed *Charging Around*, do please help us spread the word – by putting a review online; by posting something on social media; or in the old-fashioned way by simply telling your friends or family about it.

Book publishing is a very competitive business these days, in a saturated market, and small independent publishers such as ourselves are often crowded out by the big houses. Support from readers like you can make all the difference to a book's success.

Many thanks.

Dan Hiscocks
Publisher
Eye Books